PLAY THERAPY in MIDDLE CHILDHOOD

PLAY THERAPY in MIDDLE CHILDHOOD

Edited by
Athena A. Drewes and Charles E. Schaefer

American Psychological Association • Washington, DC

Published by
American Psychological Association
750 First Street, NE
Washington, DC 20002
www.apa.org

To order
APA Order Department
P.O. Box 92984
Washington, DC 20090-2984
Tel: (800) 374-2721; Direct: (202) 336-5510
Fax: (202) 336-5502; TDD/TTY: (202) 336-6123
Online: www.apa.org/pubs/books
E-mail: order@apa.org

In the U.K., Europe, Africa, and the Middle East, copies may be ordered from
American Psychological Association
3 Henrietta Street
Covent Garden, London
WC2E 8LU England

Typeset in Goudy by Circle Graphics, Inc., Columbia, MD

Printer: Maple Press, York, PA
Cover Designer: Mercury Publishing Services, Inc., Rockville, MD

Library of Congress Cataloging-in-Publication Data

Play therapy in middle childhood / [edited by] Athena A. Drewes and Charles E. Schaefer.
— First Edition.
pages cm
Includes bibliographical references and index.
ISBN 978-1-4338-2083-0 — ISBN 1-4338-2083-8 1. Play therapy. 2. Child psychotherapy.
I. Drewes, Athena A., 1948- editor. II. Schaefer, Charles E., editor.
RJ505.P6P544 2016
618.92'891653—dc23

2015015235

British Library Cataloguing-in-Publication Data

A CIP record is available from the British Library.

Printed in the United States of America
First Edition

http://dx.doi.org/10.1037/14776-000

To the growth and well-being of all children in middle childhood.
—*Athena A. Drewes and Charles E. Schaefer*

CONTENTS

CONTRIBUTORS

Courtney Borsuk, MS, Department of Counseling, University of Texas at San Antonio

Kara Carnes-Holt, PhD, Department of Professional Studies, University of Wyoming, Laramie

Angela M. Cavett, PhD, LP, RPT-S, Beacon Behavioral Health Services and Training Center, West Fargo, ND

Peggy Ceballos, PhD, Counseling Department, University of North Carolina—Charlotte

Laura H. Dinehart, PhD, Florida International University, Cooper City

Athena A. Drewes, PsyD, MA, RPT-S, Astor Services for Children and Families, Middletown, NY

Karla K. Fehr, PhD, Department of Psychology, Southern Illinois University, Carbondale

Jeffrey T. Guterman, PhD, Family Therapy, Nova Southeastern University; Jeffrey Guterman Counseling Services, Fort Lauderdale, FL

Susan Hansen, PhD, LCSW-R, RPT-S, Department of Child and Adolescent Psychiatry, New York University Child Study Center

Michael J. Karcher, EdD, PhD, Department of Counseling, University of Texas at San Antonio

Maureen C. Kenny, PhD, Florida International University, Cooper City
Terry Kottman, PhD, RPT-S, Encouragement Zone, Cedar Falls, IA
Karen Levine, PhD, Harvard Medical School, Lexington, MA
Diana Garza Louis, LPC, LMFT, RPT, Rio Grande Counseling Center, Austin, TX
Clayton V. Martin, MS, Barry University, Talbott Recovery Campus, Atlanta, GA
Kristi McClatchy, MA, NCC, Department of Counseling, University of Texas at San Antonio
Kristin K. Meany-Walen, PhD, LMHC, RPT, University of Northern Iowa, Cedar Falls
Justin R. Misurell, PhD, Child Study Center, New York University Langone Medical Center
David L. Myrow, PhD, RPT-S, Private Practice, West Seneca, NY
Akiko Ohnogi, PsyD, RPT-S, Ohnogi Psychotherapy and Counseling Clinic, Minato-ku, Tokyo, Japan
Sandra W. Russ, PhD, Department of Psychological Sciences, Case Western Reserve University, Cleveland, OH
Charles E. Schaefer, PhD, RPT-S, Fairleigh Dickinson University, Teaneck, NJ
Craig I. Springer, PhD, Metropolitan Regional Diagnostic and Treatment Center, Newark Beth Israel Medical Center, Newark, NJ
Karen Stagnitti, PhD, School of Health and Social Development, Deakin University, Geelong, Victoria, Australia
Charles B. Winick, PsyD, Private Practice, Cooper City, FL

PLAY THERAPY in MIDDLE CHILDHOOD

INTRODUCTION: DEVELOPMENTALLY APPROPRIATE PLAY THERAPY IN MIDDLE CHILDHOOD

ATHENA A. DREWES AND CHARLES E. SCHAEFER

The goal of this book is to enhance the ability of therapists to provide developmentally appropriate play interventions for clients ages 6 to 12 years. Indeed, this is the first book to provide clinicians with information about developmentally sensitive and effective play therapy for children at this age period. In the past, play and play therapy have been associated with early childhood, and much of the literature has focused on the development and application of play therapy for children ages 5 years and younger. Consequently, relatively little attention has been given by therapists and researchers to the play of clients in middle childhood. This period is often known as the "forgotten years" of development because most research has been focused on early childhood development and adolescent growth.

Middle childhood is a very important period in a person's life as essential skills of adult life begin to be forged—namely, a person's ability to engage in productive work, develop competencies, and form friendships. In addition, children this age experience major advances in their sense of self, regulation

http://dx.doi.org/10.1037/14776-001
Play Therapy in Middle Childhood, A. A. Drewes and C. E. Schaefer (Editors)

of emotions, and self-confidence. They become increasingly independent of their parents and seek close connections with their peers. In addition, rule-governed behaviors and personal achievements resulting from sustained efforts are particularly valued and sought out (Collins, 1984). These qualities form the foundation for continued psychological growth in adolescence and adulthood.

In the middle years, the fantasy play so popular with preschoolers declines, and a work orientation emphasizing intellectual mastery and physical competence replaces fantasy play as a compelling interest (Erikson, 1963). Fantasy play is still engaged in by school-age children, but it is gradually supplanted by the desire to play games and sports. As school-age children become increasingly adept at putting internal states into words—fears, worries, anger, and other feelings—they are better able to delay acting on these feelings (Davies, 1999).

The practice of play therapy with middle childhood clients must address a wide range of developmental issues and a high rate of developmental change (Russ, 2004; Vandermaas-Peeler, 2002). Therapists need an understanding of development to formulate all aspects of treatment: diagnosis, treatment goals, treatment approaches, and outcome.

This introduction provides an overview of the main developmental tasks during middle childhood. These different aspects of a child's development are interrelated, so change in one part will have an effect on the others. The chapter contributors to this book will further explain how knowledge of child development assists clinicians in implementing specific play interventions for elementary school children.

CENTRAL DEVELOPMENTAL TASK

According to Erikson (1963), each of the eight stages of life from infancy through adulthood has a central task that is psychosocial in nature. Serious problems occur when a person doesn't accomplish the task of his or her developmental stage. Erikson stated that the key growth task of school-age children is to develop "industry" (sense of productivity) versus "inferiority" (sense of incompetence). Children this age learn to make things, use tools, and acquire the skills to be a worker and a potential provider. They are motivated to succeed and willing to practice to develop skills. For successful personality development in this stage, children need to experience success in performing tasks. Feelings of inferiority arise when this primary task is not accomplished. Inferiority feelings are reflected in the sad pessimism of children who have little confidence in their ability to do things well. Conversely, psychological strength is obtained when this central task is completed, which helps school-age children master the rest of Erikson's stages of life.

Many of the favorite play activities of school-age children involve a sustained effort to be productive; examples include constructing objects with blocks, making figures with clay, telling stories, acting out the role of a superhero, solving puzzles, and throwing balls at targets. Successful completion of these challenging activities boosts a feeling of competence, whereas failure results in a feeling of inadequacy. School-age children compare their achievements with that of their peers to determine how competently they are performing. Children with disabilities or severe developmental delays are particularly at risk to develop inferiority feelings and are likely to need adults to scaffold their play, modify the rules of games, and cultivate a unique talent or interest so they can be successful.

MILESTONES IN CHILDREN'S PSYCHOLOGICAL DEVELOPMENT DURING MIDDLE CHILDHOOD

Developmental milestones are age-specific tasks that most children can do at a certain age range. The following sections provide a synopsis of these milestones for children in middle childhood.

Emotional Development

Middle childhood children are continuing to expand their awareness of their internal feelings and the causal connection between thoughts and feelings—for example, thinking about a prior happy experience can make you feel happier, whereas thinking about possible threats and dangers can make you feel fearful. In regard to typical fears of school-age children (Bauer, 1976; Carroll & Ryan-Wenger, 1999), as grade level increases there is a decrease in the frequency of occurrence of fears with imaginary themes (e.g., fear of ghosts and monsters), of bedtime fear (e.g., fear of the dark), and of frightening dreams. There is a corresponding increase in the frequency of realistic fears involving injury and physical danger (e.g., robbers or kidnappers breaking into the house). Such fears are considered an adaptive aspect of development with the primary focus of promoting survival. Fears decline steadily with age, especially for girls, who express more fears than boys throughout childhood and adolescence. Girls are likelier than boys to have trouble expressing anger. Personal relationships are so important to girls that they fear doing or saying anything that might cause a rupture. They imagine that if they express what is really on their mind, their mother or friend will get angry and reject them (Tyson, 1999).

Cognitive Development

According to Piaget (as cited in Phillips, 1969), children at the elementary school level tend to be at the *concrete operational stage* of cognitive development. Accordingly, they are developing the ability to reason logically and organize their thoughts coherently. However, they tend to think in terms of physical, concrete objects rather than hypothetical or abstract ideas, such as love and duty. Their thinking becomes less egocentric, meaning that they are able to think about and understand things from the viewpoint of others. However, they tend to be focused more on the present and less on the future consequences of their actions. Their growing verbal abilities enable them to express their inner feelings, although complex emotions such as guilt or resentment are difficult for them to comprehend (Landreth, Ray, & Bratton, 2009). They are moving away from magical thinking to a more accurate perception of reality and can now distinguish between fantasy and reality.

Their cognitive growth is especially noticeable in their ability to think about solutions and consequences before they react to a problem. Compared with preschool children, school-age children tend to be less easily frustrated, less likely to fly off the handle when things do not go their way, and less aggressive and also more caring about others, more likely to share and take turns, and better able to make friends (Shure, 1994).

Cognitive abilities such as concentration and sustained attention also improve significantly during the middle childhood years. Young elementary school children (ages 6–8) tend to have an attention span of 15 to 30 minutes, whereas older children (ages 9–12) are likely to have attention spans of 30 to 45 minutes. Thus, play therapists usually prepare several play activities to keep children this age engaged during a 50-minute therapy session. Their selective attention is also much better in middle childhood than earlier, meaning that they are capable of tuning out irrelevant distractions in order to pay attention to a task.

Play Development

Piaget (1962) identified three stages in the development of children's play that provide a guide to appropriate materials and activities. Until the age of 2 or 3, children's play is largely *sensory-motor* in nature, whereas *pretend/symbolic* play predominates in preschoolers ages 2 to 5. After age 5, "games with rules," including team games, become the preferred play activity of children, and this preference continues throughout adolescence and adulthood. This shift from egocentric, symbolic play to social play, which requires the players to follow rules and cooperate, illustrates how changes in play development prepare children for the tasks of adulthood.

Moral Development

Children are mainly egocentric in their thinking when they enter middle childhood. During this period they move from a self-centered "What's in it for me?" attitude (e.g., if you do something for me, I would do something for you) to wanting to gain social approval and conform to the expectations and rules of people close to them. Children this age are also in the process of forming a conscience, which is the depository of all they are learning about their family's values and standards. Occasionally, this conscience sends them a clear signal when they betray what they know is right. This shift, from doing what's right because of the presence of an authority figure and fear of punishment to doing what's right based on internal standards of conduct, is the basis of moral behavior (Schaefer & DiGeronimo, 2000).

Moral principles of right and wrong lead to social rules that shape and guide children's interactions with others. According to Piaget (1962), when school-age children follow rules while playing interactive games with peers, they learn fairness, justice, and equality. These qualities lay the foundation for ethical thinking and behavior (Damon, 1983). One of the most surprising findings from child development research is that children's basic notions of morality appear to arise less from adult instruction and more from interactions with peers while playing games. In these interactions, they come to realize they can make their own rules based on principles of reciprocity and fairness.

Social Development

Children in middle childhood have a strong need to be accepted by their peers. They are very aware of themselves and other people as members of a group, and they have a strong need to be accepted by their peers. Thus, an important developmental task for children in middle childhood is to acquire *social competence*, which includes a compilation of desirable social skills that permit them to relate effectively in social situations. Proficiency in conversation, empathy, reciprocity, cooperation, and ability to have fun are skills particularly important for peer acceptance, whereas bossiness, aggressiveness, and teasing are not appreciated by the peer group (Nash, 2014).

In middle childhood, a child's emotions of pride and guilt become clearly connected with personal responsibility. Pride motivates children to take on further challenges, and guilt prompts them to make amends and strive for self-improvement.

Children this age are also acquiring greater control of their impulses, which reduces emotional reactivity and lability. They continue to develop the capacity to feel empathy for another's experience or life situation. Their frequent peer interactions tend to foster growth in their emotional maturity.

During middle childhood, the formation of friendships is of great importance to children. A *friendship* is a mutually agreed on relationship in which children like each other's personal qualities and respond to one another's needs, desires, and interests. Once a friendship is formed, trust is a defining feature. As a result, a violation of trust is considered a serious breach of friendship. Friendships remain fairly stable over middle childhood. Friendships tend to be with same-age and same-gender peers (Serbin, Powlishta, Gulko, Martin, & Lockheed, 1993) and are usually based on proximity, common interests, or other perceived commonalities. These preferences are important to consider in the formation of play therapy groups for children this age.

In regard to sex differences, girls tend to have fewer but emotionally closer friends than boys, and they tend to form more exclusive cliques and shifting peer alliances. Boys' play, in contrast, is marked by larger play groups, more competitiveness, rule-governed team play, and a greater preference for outdoor physical activity (Hughes, 2010). Boys have a strict dominance hierarchy composed of rankings that represent the relative power of those in a group hierarchy.

For older school-age children, this is the period to develop "chumships." *Chumship* can be defined as an intimate, one-to-one relationship with a peer of about the same age, interests, and gender. According to Sullivan's (1953) interpersonal theory, children this age, for the first time, can form a close attachment to a same-sex friend—an attachment characterized by intimacy and reciprocity. Having a best friend prevents loneliness while promoting self-worth, social skills, and status. It also prepares children later in life for intimate adult relationships.

USING PLAY THERAPY IN MIDDLE CHILDHOOD

Middle childhood children face a myriad of problems that benefit from the use of play therapy alone or play therapy integrated with more traditional talk therapy (e.g., cognitive–behavioral or traditional counseling). This age group is no stranger to sexual abuse; physical abuse and neglect; parental divorce; death of a parent, grandparent, sibling, teacher, or pet; bullying; loss of friendships; medical issues and surgery; and relocation of the family home, along with additional stressors such as community violence, domestic violence, school shootings, and domestic acts of terrorism. Indeed, this age group is often barraged with stressors that tax their developmental level, physiology, and tenuous coping strategies.

For some children, use of play-based techniques integrated into their treatment help them express and process their fears and anxieties and mitigate their social skill difficulties. For other children, who have past unresolved traumas that trigger horrific images of situations too difficult to express, play therapy can allow for the nonverbal abreaction and catharsis necessary to master traumatic experiences.

Role-playing through puppets can be extremely beneficial in regular therapy as well as play therapy in allowing for the trying on of skills and problem-solving strategies as well as in helping change distortions in thinking about problems and situations. Use of group play therapy allows for a playful, flexible environment in which peers can learn cooperative play while building friendships. The chapters in this book will help clinicians understand how best to integrate play therapy into their work regardless of the type of treatment approach they are using.

PLAN OF THE BOOK

Greater knowledge of the developmental issues facing children in middle childhood will enable child clinicians to create more effective interventions for this age group by informing the choice of treatment goals and strategies. A broad range of play therapy interventions for specific disorders of these children are described in the chapters of this book.

The chapters are divided into four sections based on clinical problem. Part I presents play interventions for internalizing disorders, such as anxieties and fears. The four chapters in this part address trauma from sexual abuse as well as from natural and human-made disasters through use of cognitive–behavioral play therapy and the use of play therapy in overcoming anxiety. Part II presents play interventions for externalizing disorders, with five chapters that address such disruptive behavior problems as aggression and attention-deficit/hyperactivity disorder. Treatment approaches include cognitive–behavioral, Theraplay, narrative therapy, and group play therapy models. Part III presents play interventions to strengthen relationship skills and includes chapters on peer pair counseling and child–parent relationship therapy. Finally, Part IV presents play interventions for autism spectrum disorder. The three chapters in this section cover different levels of functioning in children who are on the spectrum.

The goal throughout this volume is to highlight developmentally appropriate play therapy practice for clients in middle childhood. Each chapter provides practical applications that can be immediately implemented, together with a discussion of the theory and research underlying each approach. Case illustrations are included to bring the information to life. Our plan throughout is to demonstrate how to think developmentally in play therapy. The editors firmly believe that a consideration of developmental factors is critical to successful psychotherapy with children. *Developmentally appropriate practice* refers to play interventions that are compatible with an individual client's interests, needs, and abilities.

In recent years, the play therapy literature has expanded to include books on how to apply developmentally appropriate play therapy for infants and toddlers (Schaefer, Kelly-Zion, McCormick, & Ohnogi, 2008), preschoolers (Schaefer, 2010), adolescents (Gallo-Lopez & Schaefer, 2005), and adults (Schaefer, 2003). The present volume on children in middle childhood ensures that therapists have detailed clinical guidelines for applying developmentally appropriate play therapy throughout the entire human life cycle. A distinctive feature of play therapy is that it is the only form of psychotherapy that is sensitive to the developmental needs of clients across such a broad age span.

REFERENCES

Bauer, D. H. (1976). An exploratory study of developmental changes in children's fears. *Journal of Child Psychology and Psychiatry, and Allied Disciplines, 17,* 69–74. http://dx.doi.org/10.1111/j.1469-7610.1976.tb00375.x

Carroll, M. K., & Ryan-Wenger, N. A. (1999). School-age children's fears, anxiety, and human figure drawings. *Journal of Pediatric Health Care, 13,* 24–31. http://dx.doi.org/10.1016/S0891-5245(99)90097-4

Collins, W. (Ed.). (1984). *Development during middle childhood: The years from six to twelve.* Washington, DC: National Academy Press.

Damon, W. (1983). *The social world of the child.* San Francisco, CA: Jossey Bass.

Davies, D. (1999). *Child development: A practitioner's guide.* New York, NY: Guilford Press.

Erikson, E. (1963). *Childhood and society.* New York, NY: Norton.

Gallo-Lopez, L., & Schaefer, C. E. (Eds.). (2005). *Play therapy with adolescents.* Lanham, MD: Rowman & Littlefield.

Hughes, F. P. (2010). *Children, play, and development.* Thousand Oaks, CA: Sage.

Landreth, G., Ray, D., & Bratton, S. (2009). Play therapy in elementary schools. *Psychology in the Schools, 46,* 281–289. http://dx.doi.org/10.1002/pits.20374

Nash, J. B. (2014). Social competence. In C. E. Schaefer & A. A. Drewes (Eds.), *The therapeutic powers of play* (2nd ed., pp. 185–195). Hoboken, NJ: Wiley.

Phillips, J. (1969). *The origins of intellect: Piaget's theory.* San Francisco, CA: Freeman.

Piaget, J. (1962). *Play, dreams, and imitation in childhood.* London, England: Routledge.

Russ, S. W. (2004). *Play in child development and psychotherapy: Toward empirically supported practice.* Mahwah, NJ: Erlbaum.

Schaefer, C. E. (Ed.). (2003). *Play therapy with adults*. Hoboken, NJ: Wiley.

Schaefer, C. E. (Ed.). (2010). *Play therapy for preschool children*. Washington, DC: American Psychological Association. http://dx.doi.org/10.1037/12060-000

Schaefer, C. E., & DiGeronimo, T. (2000). *Ages and stages: A parent's guide to normal childhood development*. Hoboken, NJ: Wiley.

Schaefer, C. E., Kelly-Zion, S., McCormick, J., & Ohnogi, A. (Eds.). (2008). *Play therapy for very young children*. Lanham, MD: Rowman & Littlefield.

Serbin, L. A., Powlishta, K. K., Gulko, J., Martin, C. L., & Lockheed, M. E. (1993). The development of sex typing in middle childhood. *Monographs of the Society for Research in Child Development, 58*, 1–95. http://dx.doi.org/10.2307/1166118

Shure, M. (1994). *Raising a thinking child*. New York, NY: Henry Holt.

Sullivan, H. S. (1953). *The interpersonal theory of psychiatry*. New York, NY: Norton.

Tyson, P. (1999, July/August). Taking a stand. *Sesame Street Parents*, pp. 89–91.

Vandermaas-Peeler, M. (2002). Cultural variations in parental support of children's play. *Online Readings in Psychology and Culture, 6*(1). http://dx.doi.org/10.9707/2307-0919.1054

I

PLAY INTERVENTIONS FOR INTERNALIZING DISORDERS

1

GAME-BASED COGNITIVE–BEHAVIORAL THERAPY FOR CHILD SEXUAL ABUSE

CRAIG I. SPRINGER AND JUSTIN R. MISURELL

Recent literature has highlighted the importance of using innovative and creative therapeutic interventions for increasing engagement in evidence-based treatment among children and families (Briggs, Runyon, & Deblinger, 2011; Sánchez-Meca, Rosa-Alcázar, & López-Soler, 2011; Schaefer & Drewes, 2009). These interventions include using art, music, puppets, bibliotherapy, role-plays, and therapeutic games, to name a few (Malchiodi, 2008). Incorporating developmentally appropriate activities such as these into treatment for children provides a number of benefits, including improving rapport, providing a mechanism for communication and learning, and facilitating emotional processing, among others (Sánchez-Meca et al., 2011; Swank, 2008). Additionally, these approaches may be particularly useful when working with children who have experienced sexual abuse, in which feelings of shame and embarrassment and reluctance to discuss one's abuse experiences are not uncommon and may impede engagement in traditional talk therapy (Briggs et al., 2011; Cavett & Drewes, 2012; Drewes & Cavett,

http://dx.doi.org/10.1037/14776-002
Play Therapy in Middle Childhood, A. A. Drewes and C. E. Schaefer (Editors)

2012; Springer & Misurell, 2012). To address the need to provide treatment following child sexual abuse (CSA) that is both engaging and effective, we developed game-based cognitive–behavioral therapy (GB-CBT). This treatment model integrates structured play therapy with traditional components of evidence-based CBT to provide children and families impacted by CSA with a safe, supportive, motivating, and nonthreatening forum to explore and process abuse-related material.

BASIC RATIONALE AND THEORY

GB-CBT for CSA is based on five principles: (a) use of data to inform practice and treatment strategies, (b) use of a directive and structured approach to therapy, (c) incorporation of fun and interactive techniques, (d) emphasis on experiential learning, and (e) building on strengths (Misurell & Springer, 2013; Springer & Misurell, 2012). As a data-informed practice, the therapeutic components of GB-CBT, such as psychoeducation, emotional regulation skill building, abuse processing, and personal safety skills, were based on the empirical treatment literature for CSA (Cohen, Mannarino, & Deblinger, 2006; Cohen, Mannarino, Deblinger, & Berliner, 2009; Saunders, 2012). GB-CBT makes use of frequent feedback gathered throughout the treatment process. Standardized behavioral measures are used to gather information about symptoms and family functioning prior to therapy. Symptom checklists are routinely used across sessions to monitor progress. Additionally, behavioral measures are readministered at the end of treatment to determine ongoing needs and to inform future recommendations.

GB-CBT is a directive and structured approach to treatment. The plan for each therapy session is organized in advance and contains behavioral expectations, incentives, psychoeducation, role-plays, and specific games and activities designed to facilitate treatment goals. Activities are organized in a predictable sequence. At the beginning of each session, behavioral expectations and reward systems are reviewed. Next, psychoeducation and role-plays are conducted, followed by therapeutic games. Sessions continue with opportunities to discuss and process therapeutic accomplishments and emotional reactions to material presented. As sessions conclude, behavioral expectations are assessed and the incentives for accomplishing goals are awarded.

GB-CBT incorporates several play-based activities to make treatment fun and engaging, thereby increasing client interest and receptivity to therapy. The primary therapeutic techniques used in GB-CBT are structured therapeutic games (STGs), which are structured, rule-governed, playful activities that both teach and provide opportunities for the use of skills (Springer & Misurell, 2010, 2012, 2015). Specific STGs were designed for each of nine evidence-based components of GB-CBT treatment (e.g., emotional regulation training, abuse processing, personal safety skills). Additionally, role-plays, or "skill-skits," as they are referred to in GB-CBT, are used to provide psychoeducation in a way that is enjoyable and captivating rather than dry and academic. Each of these structured play-based activities allows children to engage in a format that resembles the way they naturally communicate with others and thus may be more congruent with their interests and preferences so that they feel more comfortable. Rewards, tokens, and prizes are also implemented to increase children's excitement and motivation in therapy. Additionally, clinicians are directly involved in the games and play along with children and caregivers, helping to make the clinician more relatable and to reduce barriers to discussing emotionally charged material.

In GB-CBT, experiential learning is emphasized by involving clients directly in games and activities that provide multiple opportunities for practicing and rehearsing skills. Games and activities also provide clients with opportunities for observational learning, in which other clients as well as clinicians can serve as models. By the same token, experiential activities allow clinicians to observe whether clients can use skills appropriately, allowing clinicians to provide corrective feedback when necessary. Additionally, participating in experiential activities gives clients immediate opportunities to incorporate this feedback. Through observations, clinicians can also assess whether clients have gained mastery of the skills or whether additional practice is necessary. Furthermore, by participating in therapeutic activities that resemble everyday life experiences, clients are likely to feel comfortable when faced with similar situations in settings outside of therapy.

GB-CBT is a strength-based model, in which techniques and topics are used to develop and bolster clients' positive behaviors and internal resources such as knowledge and skills. In terms of techniques, positive reinforcement is used throughout treatment through the use of token economies, verbal and nonverbal praise, and constructive feedback. Additionally, caregivers are encouraged to use parenting techniques that use incentives such as token economies in their home and are provided education about the value of increasing desired behaviors and use of skills through positive reinforcement. By emphasizing the important role of caregivers in treatment, the positive strengths and resources of families can be recruited to facilitate treatment goals. Therapeutic topics in GB-CBT focus on the development of skills and strengths rather than simply the alleviation of problems and deficits. Skills and strengths are developed by teaching a variety of social and emotional strategies for coping with challenges.

GB-CBT has been implemented through individual and group therapy. The GB-CBT individual model (GB-CBT-IM) has typically been administered in 90-minute sessions, each containing time spent with caregivers and children individually followed by a conjoint meeting with caregivers and children together. GB-CBT-IM consists of nine modules: (a) rapport building, (b) personal space and boundaries, (c) emotional identification and expression, (d) linking of feelings to experiences, (e) coping skills, (f) psychoeducation about CSA, (g) abuse processing, (h) personal safety skills, and (i) skills review and termination. By using a modular approach, treatment is tailored to individual needs on the basis of which topics are covered and the amount of time spent on them. For example, children who are proficient in personal space may not need to spend time discussing this topic, whereas children struggling with anxiety may require additional sessions focusing on developing coping strategies and relaxation skills before moving on to abuse processing. For this reason, length of treatment in GB-CBT-IM differs according to the presenting problems and ongoing therapeutic needs of clients. Children presenting with minimal symptoms may require six to eight sessions, whereas clients with complex trauma histories and elevated symptomatology may require 16 to 20 sessions of treatment. Overall, the average length of treatment in GB-CBT is between 10 and 12 sessions.

The GB-CBT group model (GB-CBT-GM) has typically been administered in 12 weekly 90-minute sessions. GB-CBT groups have been conducted with an average of approximately eight to 10 children. However, groups can be larger depending on client characteristics and the treatment center's staffing and needs. Groups are organized on the basis of developmental age and ability. For example, elementary school–age children have typically been assigned to groups of either 5- to 7-year-olds or 8- to 10-year-olds.

GB-CBT-GM can be conceptualized into two broad interventional components: (a) social and emotional skill building and (b) abuse-specific material. Each interventional component is subdivided into topics that are presented in a fixed sequence and build on one another. Treatment topics include rapport building and social skills, personal space, emotional identification and expression, linking feelings to experiences, anger management, psychoeducation about appropriate and inappropriate touching, the anatomical names of the parts of the body, child sexual abuse, abuse processing, personal safety skills, and relaxation and coping skills. A nonoffending caregivers' group parallels the topics covered in the children's group, in addition to providing parenting skills to help caregivers process their feelings about their children's abuse experiences and develop the skills necessary for helping their children and family recover from abuse (Springer, Colorado, & Misurell, in press). The GB-CBT-GM provides both children and caregivers with a supportive and cathartic peer environment that enables them to understand that what happened to them was not their fault, that they will be OK, and that they are not alone in their experiences.

DEVELOPMENTAL ISSUES

For treatment with children and families to be relevant and effective, it is important to consider clients' developmental needs, abilities, and interests. GB-CBT uses *structured therapeutic games*, games with a therapeutic structure containing behavioral expectations and incentives that are tailored to client goals and preferences and treatment topics that are designed to be accessible and relevant. Each STG was designed with particular attention to ability based on developmental level to ensure that tasks can be reasonably accomplished in a manner in which therapeutic goals are met. Considerations with regard to motor and cognitive skills, comprehension, and reading and writing abilities were factored into the creation of each STG. For instance, some games that require reading and writing ability were designed for older elementary school–age children and caregivers, whereas similar games for younger elementary school–age children involve verbal rather than written cues and responses. In other cases, older children and caregivers are asked to provide elaborate responses with minimal cues, whereas younger children are expected to provide basic responses to specific and detailed prompts.

The therapeutic structure in GB-CBT includes behavioral expectations, incentives, and rewards that differ depending on developmental level and interests. Although all elementary schoolchildren typically work on three behavioral goals, which include (a) following directions, (b) being polite, and (c) keeping their body in control, the level and type of education are differentiated between younger and older children such that younger children are provided with extensive examples to assist them in understanding, whereas older children are given opportunities to generate definitions of behavioral goals. In addition, expectations of what is necessary to successfully meet each behavioral goal are based on children's individualized abilities, needs, and functioning. For example, younger children who have difficulties sitting still for even short periods of time may be determined to have achieved the goal of controlling their body if they are able to sit still for a single activity, whereas older children who have demonstrated the capacity to sit still for most of the time may need to exhibit self-control throughout the majority of the session. Furthermore, the frequency and type of reinforcement also differ on the basis of children's developmental level. For instance, some children require more frequent reinforcement than others to motivate them to participate and engage in activities and acquire the targeted skills. Finally, the specific types of tangible and intangible rewards that are selected for use in treatment are based on client interests and age to ensure that they are motivating and appropriate.

Developmental factors are also considered when planning the presentation of topics and psychoeducational material in GB-CBT. For example, certain anger management and coping techniques, such as the Bear Hug and Cannonball, which involve diaphragmatic breathing, may be more suitable for younger children than more complex coping strategies such as the Cognitive Triangle, which teaches children about the interconnection of their thoughts, feelings, and behaviors. Developmental issues are also considered in the presentation of psychoeducational information. Psychoeducation about child sexual abuse for younger children includes a discussion of appropriate and inappropriate touching and the anatomical names of the private parts of the body. Whereas this information may be important to emphasize with younger children, clinicians working with older children may consider the topic of healthy sexuality in addition to a standard review of psychoeducation about sexual abuse. Furthermore, personal safety skills training may differ depending on age, because children of varying ages may be confronted with different risks and threats to their safety. For instance, older children may require more education about the safe use of technology and the risks of social media, whereas younger children may need more extensive education about appropriate personal space and physical boundaries.

PLAY INTERVENTION PROCEDURES AND SETTINGS

GB-CBT has been predominantly implemented and studied for treating CSA in an outpatient setting. Treatment has been administered to children and their caregivers through individual and group therapy modalities. Prior to beginning treatment, clients are screened using standardized behavioral measures to assess behavioral and emotional functioning and symptoms in an effort to determine appropriateness and to establish therapeutic goals. Clients have typically been included in treatment if they are at a minimum developmental age of 4 years, have experienced an incident of sexual abuse, and do not present with behavioral problems or symptomatology that would make them dangerous to themselves or others (e.g., suicidal or homicidal ideations, violent outbursts, significant sexualized behavior) or that would preclude them from fully engaging and participating in the therapeutic process (e.g., psychotic symptoms, severe hyperactivity or inattentiveness, impulsivity, defiance). The following sections provide an overview of GB-CBT clinical topics and provide examples of structured therapeutic games used in individual and group therapy formats.

Rapport Building

As with most forms of psychotherapy, developing a strong therapeutic relationship is paramount for clinical success. Strategies focus on establishing a safe and supportive climate that encourages openness and active participation through the use of playful and engaging techniques. In individual therapy with children ages 4 years and up and in caregiver group therapy, the Getting to Know You Stack card game is played. This game involves having clinicians and clients draw from a stack of cards and choose to answer questions contained on the cards. Each card contains two questions worth one or two points, which are based on level of difficulty. One of the questions is a basic question, such as, "What is your favorite color?" and the other is a more detailed, thought-provoking question, such as, "What do you want to learn in therapy?" Players are incentivized to answer the more detailed questions to earn more points and succeed in the game.

During group therapy, children ages 8 years and up play a fast-paced game, Conversation Scavenger Hunt, which serves as an icebreaker and encourages sharing information about oneself and learning about others. Prior to beginning play, children are provided with a worksheet containing two columns. In the left column, questions are presented asking players to generate information about themselves and their interests. An example of a question on the worksheet is, "What is my favorite TV show?" Once these questions are answered, players are asked to interview other group members to obtain their answers to the same questions. Players race to interview each other and complete their sheets. Play continues until all members have completed their interview worksheets. Placement can be assigned on the basis of the order in which players finish the game (e.g., first place, second place). In this way, children are motivated to meet and talk to one another within the context of a game.

Personal Space

Personal space is an important concept to discuss with most elementary schoolchildren but is particularly important with children who have experienced sexual abuse, because their understanding of what constitutes appropriate behavior may be distorted. Children may violate the personal space and boundaries of others, because these behaviors may have been normalized and reinforced during the course of their abuse experiences. It is necessary to define personal space and boundaries to help children recognize appropriate boundaries. This recognition will enable them to become aware of boundary violations and the impact such violations can have on themselves and others. In individual and group therapy with children between ages 4 and 7, Personal Space-O-Meter is played to facilitate knowledge of personal space. During this game, players are provided with items that can be used to connect (e.g., pipe cleaners, connector blocks) to construct a Personal Space-O-Meter (e.g., an arm-length chain) that can be used to test and demonstrate personal space. Players race to construct a Personal Space-O-Meter and then use it to have a conversation at an appropriate distance.

Another example of a fast-paced and high-energy game to practice personal space is Personal Space Invaders, which is played with children between ages 5 and 10 in individual and group therapy. This game involves Outer Space Adventurers (played by the children) who are under attack by Personal Space Invaders (played by clinicians). Children are provided with a stack of 10 foam cups and are asked to build a personal space orbit around themselves with the cups to protect them from the Personal Space Invaders. While they are building their orbits, Personal Space Invaders approach them and attempt to knock over their cups and destroy their orbits. Children are informed that to protect their personal space orbit and send the Personal Space Invaders away, they need to affirmatively tell them, "Give me personal space." This game provides multiple opportunities to practice assertiveness skills and requests for personal space.

Emotional Expression and Identification Skills

Emotional expression and identification skills are presented in GB-CBT to assist children and caregivers in learning how to recognize and share their feelings with others. By developing a large vocabulary of emotions, clients are able to have a rich and deep understanding of their own and others' life experiences. An individual and group therapy game for children between ages 8 and 10 that is used to expand feelings vocabularies is the Feelings Trivia Game. Players are provided with worksheets containing statements of possible life scenarios (e.g., being stuck at home with nothing to do) and are asked to generate lists of feelings that may be experienced in relation to these scenarios. The goal is to generate as many different feelings as possible across all scenarios within a specified period of time. A 4- to 7-year-old version of this game can be played in which the scenarios are read to children and responses are recorded by clinicians.

Another game that is used to enhance emotional expression and identification skills is Catch the Feeling, which is played in individual and group therapy with children ages 4 through 10. A cup filled with crumpled-up pieces of paper with feelings words written on them is emptied above each child. Children attempt to catch as many of the crumpled pieces of paper as possible. Once children have finished catching the pieces of paper, they read the feelings word listed on each piece of paper out loud and attempt to demonstrate the feeling through body language and facial expressions.

Linking of Feelings to Experiences

Once children master the skill of emotional identification, they are then capable of understanding how an important part of experiencing events is their own emotional reaction to them. Clinicians work with clients to identify experiences and the emotions they evoke, enabling clients to become increasingly aware of the multitude of emotions they encounter. An example of a game that can be played in individual and group therapy for children ages 5 to 11 is Cup of Feelings. In this game, several plastic cups, each labeled with a feeling, are arranged. Players take turns tossing a ping–pong ball into one of the cups. To earn a point for getting the ball into a cup, players must talk about a time when they experienced the emotion written on the cup.

Another game used to illustrate how feelings are associated with various situations is the Feelings Face–Situation Photo Matching Game. During this game, which is played in individual therapy with children ages 4 to 10, players are provided with two sets of cards. One set contains pictures of faces expressing various emotions, and the second set contains photographs depicting different situations. All cards are placed face down and spread out within their respective set. Players are asked to turn over one card from each set and must determine whether the feeling expressed in the face picture matches the photograph of the situation. If the cards match, then the player gets a chance to turn over two more cards in an attempt to find another match. If the cards do not match, then the next player gets a turn. Players compete to find as many matches as possible.

Coping Skills

Coping skills are an important aspect of treatment and are essential for assisting clients in managing difficult emotions that they may experience. In GB-CBT, coping skills can be subdivided into three discrete constructs: (a) stress and anger management, (b) relaxation skills, and (c) cognitive coping. Children are asked to discuss and express how they look and how their body feels when they are stressed or angry. Next, children are taught basic coping techniques in which they learn how to self-soothe. A group therapy game for children ages 5 to 10 that is used to practice these techniques is Handoff Madness. This game simulates a frustrating situation by giving players the difficult task of using spoons to pass a ping–pong ball across a room without dropping it. When the ping–pong ball falls to the floor, a frustrating situation is simulated, and players must use basic coping strategies to help them regain composure so that they can make another attempt at completing the task. Players are provided with incentives for successfully demonstrating basic coping strategies during the game.

Relaxation skills training begins with a discussion about the body's reaction to stress and anger (e.g., heart racing, sweaty palms, shortness of breath), how to identify when they are experiencing these emotions, and multiple strategies for monitoring and reducing their fight-or-flight reactions when these reactions are not serving a useful purpose. An example of a game used in individual and group therapy to practice identifying effective responding to stress and anger is Relaxercise. During this game, players simulate a state of increased physiological arousal through brief strenuous exercise and must use deep breathing and other self-soothing techniques (e.g., diaphragmatic breathing, mindfulness, progressive muscle relaxation) to reduce their heart rate in an effort to return their bodies to a relaxed state. At multiple points throughout this game, children check their pulse to understand the difference in their body between a relaxed and a stressed state.

Cognitive coping involves the interrelationship between three domains: thoughts, feelings, and behaviors. Children are taught that there are many ways of responding to life events and that if a response in one of the domains is changed, it necessitates changes in the other domains as well. Additionally, children are taught that they can monitor their thoughts and identify whether their thoughts are positive or negative. An individual therapy game that is used with children ages 9 to 11 to practice identifying the difference between positive and negative thoughts is the Thought Awareness Game. During this game, players are provided with a worksheet containing a series of self-talk statements and race to label each statement as either positive or negative. After completing the worksheet, clinicians review and discuss players' responses to each statement, and incentives are provided for insightful answers.

PSYCHOEDUCATION ABOUT CHILD SEXUAL ABUSE

Information about CSA is provided to enhance understanding about abuse and address cognitive distortions. Education includes distinguishing between OK and not-OK touches; discussing private parts; defining sexual abuse, its incidence, and reasons for its occurrence; normalizing postabuse feelings; and highlighting the utility and outcomes of treatment. A game used to practice distinguishing appropriate from inappropriate behavior is the OK/Not-OK Touch Game. During this game, which is used in individual and group therapy for children ages 4 to 10, players are asked to move to the side of the room designated as OK or not OK on the basis of whether they deem touches that are presented to be acceptable or unacceptable. For instance, if "mother hugs her child" is presented, players should go to the OK side of the room, whereas if the scenario is "someone at school grabs your butt," players should go to the not-OK side of the room. Incentives are provided for explaining the rationale for answers.

A game designed to provide and assess a broad range of child abuse–related knowledge is Life-Size Wheel of Knowledge. During this game, which is played in group and individual therapy, players race to answer questions pertaining to the categories of child sexual abuse, child physical abuse, and personal safety skills. Each player receives a worksheet containing a circle with six numbered wedges labeled with the aforementioned categories (two wedges for each category). Players roll a die and attempt to answer a question from the corresponding category in an attempt to complete the wedge with a successful answer. The game is finished when players are able to answer all six questions correctly, two from each category. Incentives are provided based on the order of player completion or on the amount of time it took to finish the game.

Abuse Processing

Gradual exposure to abuse-related material is an important part of the treatment process because it is thought to decrease anxiety associated with memories of the abuse and cues associated with it. Clients are provided with the rationale for confronting and discussing their abuse experiences and are reminded to use the coping skills they have acquired. Abuse processing can be subdivided into two types of disclosure: basic disclosure and advanced disclosure. Basic disclosure involves providing nonverbal or minimally verbal responses to acknowledge an aspect of the abuse experience, whereas advanced disclosure entails providing a detailed narrative of the abuse experience. A game used for basic disclosure in individual and group therapy is What's the Story? During this game, players provide single words (5- to 7-year-olds) or sentences (8- to 10-year-olds) to create stories about hypothetical children who have experienced abuse. Often, the contributions involve details from the player's own abuse experiences. Following the stories, players are asked to recall details of the stories they created.

A game used for advanced disclosure in individual therapy is the Unlock the Path board game. This game involves six levels in which players must talk, draw, and write or play out various aspects of the abuse (e.g., before, during, after), their therapy experiences, and their hopes for the future. The game results in the creation of a written narrative book containing text and pictures. Children play with their caregivers, who share their own experiences of the abuse as well while providing their children with support and encouragement.

It is important to note that incentives are not provided during the disclosure portions of games for several reasons. First, incentives may encourage or be perceived as encouraging children to provide additional details, incidents, or disclosures that might contain embellishments or may not be factual. This caution is particularly important to consider because cases of sexual abuse may be involved in criminal or family court litigation. Second, some children may view incentives to confront the abuse as manipulative, resembling the dynamics present during their sexual victimization.

Personal Safety Skills

Because caregivers have the primary responsibility of keeping children safe, they are provided with education about the importance of supervision and proactive steps they can take to minimize their children's future risk. Children are also provided with information about risk factors and steps they can take to minimize risk and receive necessary assistance from adults. Children are taught to trust their instincts and to use a "yell, go, tell" sequence when they are confronted with a situation in which they feel uncomfortable. They are also educated about the process of grooming and about Internet and technology safety. A game titled "You're Not the Boss of Me" is used in individual and group therapy to help children distinguish between acceptable and unacceptable requests and respond in a protective manner by notifying another adult when an unacceptable request is made. During this game, the player's "boss" instructs him or her to do various tasks. The player first verbally decides on the appropriateness of the task and on this basis decides whether to complete the task (e.g., type a letter) or use the "yell, go, tell" sequence to ask the clinician for help avoiding the inappropriate act (e.g., touch a private part) that the boss instructed him or her to do.

Another game used to assist children ages 5 to 10 with asking adults for help is the Emergency Scenarios Game, in which children are presented with 10 situations in which they must decide whether to ask a firefighter, teacher, or police officer for help. Once they ask the appropriate professional for assistance in a clear manner, they are able to move on to the next scenario. This game is completed in group therapy as a race between individual players or teams.

Skills Review and Termination

The final therapeutic component of GB-CBT is skills review and preparing for termination. During this portion of treatment, clients review the topics that were covered over the previous sessions and then plan for the future. The What Have You Learned Game is used, consisting of cards with questions pertaining to the topics that were covered over the course of treatment; players take turns responding to earn points. This game serves to reinforce knowledge of what was learned and provides a guide for clinicians to review any skill areas that need to be reviewed. The Guess Who Card Shuffle is a game played in group therapy by children and caregivers to prepare for termination. This game involves anonymously drawing the name of another group member and then writing a compliment to that person about how he or she contributed positively to the group. Players read out their responses, and all players attempt to guess who that player was talking about. A point is awarded for each correct guess. This game highlights the important contribution that each person made in the group. Treatment concludes with a graduation, in which therapeutic successes are celebrated.

EMPIRICAL SUPPORT

To date, three empirical studies examining the effectiveness of the GB-CBT approach for CSA have been published (Misurell, Springer, Acosta, Liotta, & Kranzler, 2014; Misurell, Springer, & Tryon, 2011; Springer, Misurell, & Hiller, 2012). Initial empirical investigations of both the group (n = 48) and individual (n = 45) GB-CBT models involved single group designs with pre- and posttreatment outcome measures (Misurell et al., 2011, 2014). Preliminary findings suggest that GB-CBT is effective in improving children's internalizing symptoms (e.g., depression, anxiety), externalizing behaviors (e.g., oppositionality, impulsivity), trauma-related symptoms (e.g., nightmares, flashbacks, intrusive thoughts), and sexually inappropriate behaviors. Furthermore, children exhibited improvements in terms of their knowledge of abuse and personal safety skills, two constructs that may serve as protective factors against future victimization. Clinical significance analyses were also conducted that examined the degree to which each individual exhibited change on a variety of outcome measures. These analyses revealed that the majority of children exhibited meaningful clinical change across a wide range of outcome measures.

A subsequent empirical study for the group model (n = 91) examined whether improvements were observed at the end of treatment and were maintained 3 months following treatment (Springer et al., 2012). The findings of this study indicated that children had clinical gains on a variety of measures, including internalizing symptoms, externalizing behaviors, trauma-related symptoms, and sexually inappropriate behaviors at both posttreatment and 3-month follow-up. Similarly, improvements in knowledge of abuse and personal safety skills were also observed at posttreatment and were maintained 3 months following treatment. Furthermore, clinical significance testing suggested that the majority of individuals involved in this study experienced meaningful improvements both at posttreatment and at 3 months following treatment. However, it should be noted that to date, the clinical outcome studies investigating GB-CBT do not include comparison groups.

Research examining GB-CBT for CSA has been conducted in urban outpatient settings in the northeastern United States. The vast majority of children involved in the empirical studies have been economically disadvantaged African Americans and Latinos. Research on treatment engagement has found attendance and retention rates to be lower in economically disadvantaged communities (Gopalan et al., 2010). However, families participating in GB-CBT-IM exhibited an 82% attendance rate, which is higher than the typical rate for community mental health services (58%; Guck, Guck, Brack, & Frey, 2007). In addition, attendance data also revealed that the study's attrition or treatment dropout rate was 27%, which is lower than other attrition rates commonly cited in the literature for similar populations (Miller, Southam-Gerow, & Allin, 2008). Additionally, findings demonstrated that families had high levels of client satisfaction (92%), and the vast majority of children and families (86%) indicated that their clinicians exhibited culturally competent practice. These results are promising and support the assertion that GB-CBT can facilitate the development of strong therapeutic relationships and enhance treatment engagement.

CASE ILLUSTRATION INCLUDING CAREGIVER INVOLVEMENT

Charlotte was a 9-year-old, biracial girl of African American and Latino descent who was initially referred for services after she had disclosed an extensive history of sexual victimization by her stepfather. Specifically, Charlotte reported to her mother that her stepfather had repeatedly fondled her vagina and buttocks and made her fondle his penis. These incidents reportedly occurred while Charlotte's stepfather was in a supervisory role and her mother was at work. Following her disclosure, Charlotte's 8-year-old half-sister, Kara, the daughter of Charlotte's stepfather, also disclosed that he had performed oral sex on her. In addition to her history of sexual abuse, Charlotte's biological father had not been involved in her life since birth, which she experienced as a rejection. She also harbored resentment toward her mother for not protecting her from her stepfather, anger toward Kara for her relationship to the perpetrator, and self-blame. Furthermore, Charlotte's family was under significant financial pressure because her mother had left work because of a physical disability and was struggling to support her five children.

Prior to the start of treatment, Charlotte and her mother were administered a battery of clinical measures to assess Charlotte's behavioral and emotional functioning. The measures indicated that Charlotte was experiencing a number of trauma-related difficulties, including intrusive thoughts, hyperarousal, flashbacks, and avoidance behaviors in relation to the abuse. Based on her presentation, Charlotte was recommended for GB-CBT individual therapy.

At the beginning of treatment, Charlotte presented as an intelligent, agreeable, and precocious child who appeared more mature than her stated age. Initial sessions focused on rapport building, personal space, and emotional expression skills, during which Charlotte and her mother were highly engaged and receptive. Charlotte's thoughtfulness and maturity were evidenced by her insightful responses during games designed to discuss emotional experiences and practice coping skills. Similarly, her mother participated in the therapeutic process each session by collaborating on treatment planning, providing observational reports about Charlotte's functioning, and playing conjoint child–caregiver games.

As treatment transitioned from a focus on social and emotional learning skills to sexual abuse–related topics, Charlotte became increasingly resistant. During the period sessions were focused on sexual abuse, Charlotte engaged in disruptive behavior at home and in school, which was seemingly her attempt at avoiding anxiety associated with discussing the abuse. She was reportedly fighting with her siblings and peers and defied her mother's and other adults' requests. These behaviors caused significant distress for the family and threatened to derail the focus of treatment. To manage her behavioral difficulties, Charlotte's mother was provided with education about using effective parenting strategies, including token economies, selective attention, and removal of privileges. Despite these challenges, Charlotte and her mother continued to participate in abuse processing games. However, her trauma-related symptoms persisted, and her aggression toward Kara intensified. Thus, a decision was made to refer Charlotte to participate in a GB-CBT group that her sister Kara was also scheduled to attend.

In group therapy, Charlotte had an opportunity to review the skills she had previously learned in individual therapy, which enabled her to demonstrate her competencies and serve as a role model for her peers. She was also able to develop empathy for the other children, including Kara, who struggled to cope with their own histories of abuse. Over time, Charlotte appeared to reconcile her resentment toward Kara and directly provided support for her sister and their shared abuse experiences. Furthermore, she exhibited posttraumatic growth by being supportive and caring of Kara and expressing an interest in helping other children who had experienced similar trauma. Concurrently, Charlotte's mother participated in a GB-CBT caregiver group in which she learned parallel skills through therapeutic games, helping her realize that others could understand and relate to the difficulties that she was having in relation to her children's abuse experiences and their subsequent behavioral and emotional problems as a result of their abuse experiences.

By the conclusion of group therapy, Charlotte and her mother appeared to exhibit increased knowledge of coping strategies and personal safety skills and were able to discuss the abuse with minimal difficulty. However, posttreatment assessment measures indicated that Charlotte continued to struggle with hyperarousal and recurrent thoughts about the abuse. For this reason, Charlotte and her mother returned for an additional GB-CBT booster session 1 month following completion of the group. During this session, Charlotte and her mother reported that her symptoms had been spontaneously dissipating as time elapsed from group completion and that she was no longer experiencing symptomatology or feeling resentment toward her mother and sister. After a brief review of coping strategies and personal safety skills, Charlotte's treatment was concluded.

CONCLUSION AND FUTURE DIRECTIONS

GB-CBT for CSA is an integration of structured play therapy with traditional, well-established cognitive–behavioral components of treatment. The model represents an attempt to maximize treatment engagement and enjoyment while also ensuring that treatment is as effective as possible. To date, GB-CBT has been conducted primarily in an outpatient setting serving urban, culturally diverse, and economically disadvantaged children. However, the model has also been successfully implemented in other settings, including inpatient units and residential treatment facilities. Efforts to disseminate the model are under way; the authors have been conducting professional workshops and presentations at conferences and universities. Additionally, a comprehensive treatment manual detailing the complete curriculum for both individual and group modalities has recently been published (Springer & Misurell, 2015).

Future research on GB-CBT should involve randomized controlled trials that control for extraneous factors such as the passage of time on the impact of treatment outcome. Additionally, the core of the GB-CBT curriculum that focuses on social and emotional learning is directly applicable to a wide range of childhood disorders including social anxiety, specific phobias, oppositional behaviors, and attention-deficit/hyperactivity disorder, among others. Further development of the GB-CBT model should include efforts to create programs and curricula that specifically address a variety of behavioral disorders and difficulties.

REFERENCES

Briggs, K. M., Runyon, M. K., & Deblinger, E. (2011). The use of play in trauma-focused cognitive–behavioral therapy. In S. W. Russ & L. N. Niec (Eds.), *Play in clinical practice: Evidence-based approaches* (pp. 168–200). New York, NY: Guilford Press.

Cavett, A. M., & Drewes, A. A. (2012). Play applications and trauma-specific components. In J. A. Cohen, A. P. Mannarino, & E. Deblinger (Eds.), *Trauma-focused CBT for children and adolescents: Treatment applications* (pp. 124–148). New York, NY: Guilford Press.

Cohen, J. A., Mannarino, A. P., & Deblinger, E. (2006). *Treating trauma and traumatic grief in children and adolescents*. New York, NY: Guilford Press.

Cohen, J. A., Mannarino, A. P., Deblinger, E., & Berliner, L. (2009). Cognitive–behavioral therapy for children and adolescents. In E. B. Foa, T. M. Keane, M. J. Friedman, & J. A. Cohen (Eds.), *Effective treatments for PTSD* (2nd ed., pp. 223–244). New York, NY: Guilford Press.

Drewes, A. A., & Cavett, A. M. (2012). Play applications and skills components. In J. A. Cohen, A. P. Mannarino, & E. Deblinger (Eds.), *Trauma-focused CBT for children and adolescents: Treatment applications* (pp. 105–123). New York, NY: Guilford Press.

Gopalan, G., Goldstein, L., Klingenstein, K., Sicher, C., Blake, C., & McKay, M. M. (2010). Engaging families into child mental health treatment: Updates and special considerations. *Journal of the Canadian Academy of Child and Adolescent Psychiatry, 19*, 182–196.

Guck, T. P., Guck, A. J., Brack, A. B., & Frey, D. R. (2007). No-show rates in partially integrated models of behavioral health care in a primary care setting. *Families, Systems, & Health, 25*, 137–146. http://dx.doi.org/10.1037/1091-7527.25.2.137

Malchiodi, C. A. (2008). *Creative interventions with traumatized children*. New York, NY: Guilford Press.

Miller, L. M., Southam-Gerow, M. A., & Allin, R. B., Jr. (2008). Who stays in treatment? Child and family predictors of youth client retention in a public mental health agency. *Child & Youth Care Forum, 37*, 153–170. http://dx.doi.org/10.1007/s10566-008-9058-2

Misurell, J. R., & Springer, C. I. (2013). Developing culturally responsive evidence-based practice: A game-based group therapy program for child sexual abuse (CSA). *Journal of Child and Family Studies, 22*, 137–149. http://dx.doi.org/10.1007/s10826-011-9560-2

Misurell, J. R., Springer, C. I., Acosta, L., Liotta, L., & Kranzler, A. (2014). Game-based cognitive–behavioral therapy individual model (GB-CBT-IM) for child sexual abuse: A preliminary outcome study. *Psychological Trauma: Theory, Research, Practice, and Policy, 6*, 250–258. http://dx.doi.org/10.1037/a0033411

Misurell, J. R., Springer, C. I., & Tryon, W. W. (2011). Game-based cognitive–behavioral therapy (GB-CBT) group program for children who have experienced sexual abuse: A preliminary investigation. *Journal of Child Sexual Abuse, 20*, 14–36. http://dx.doi.org/10.1080/10538712.2011.540000

Sánchez-Meca, J., Rosa-Alcázar, A. I., & López-Soler, C. (2011). The psychological treatment of sexual abuse in children and adolescents: A meta-analysis. *International Journal of Clinical and Health Psychology, 11*, 67–93.

Saunders, B. E. (2012). Determining best practice for treating sexually victimized children. In P. Goodyear-Brown (Ed.), *Handbook of child sexual abuse: Identification, assessment, and treatment* (pp. 173–197). New York, NY: Wiley.

Schaefer, C. E., & Drewes, A. A. (2009). The therapeutic powers of play and play therapy. In A. A. Drewes (Ed.), *Blending play therapy with cognitive behavioral therapy: Evidence-based and other effective treatments and techniques* (pp. 3–15). New York, NY: Wiley.

Springer, C. I., Colorado, G., & Misurell, J. R. (in press). Structured therapeutic games for non-offending caregivers of children who have experienced sexual abuse. *Journal of Child Sexual Abuse*.

Springer, C. I., & Misurell, J. R. (2010). Game-based cognitive–behavioral therapy (GB-CBT): An innovative group treatment program for children who have been sexually abused. *Journal of Child & Adolescent Trauma, 3*, 163–180. http://dx.doi.org/10.1080/19361521.2010.491506

Springer, C. I., & Misurell, J. R. (2012). Game-based cognitive–behavioral therapy individual model for child sexual abuse. *International Journal of Play Therapy, 21*, 188–201. http://dx.doi.org/10.1037/a0030197

Springer, C. I., & Misurell, J. R. (2015). *Game-based cognitive–behavioral therapy for child sexual abuse: An innovative treatment approach*. New York, NY: Springer.

Springer, C. I., Misurell, J. R., & Hiller, A. (2012). Game-based cognitive–behavioral therapy (GB-CBT) group program for children who have experienced sexual abuse: A three-month follow-up investigation. *Journal of Child Sexual Abuse, 21*, 646–664. http://dx.doi.org/10.1080/10538712.2012.722592

Swank, J. M. (2008). The use of games: A therapeutic tool with children and families. *International Journal of Play Therapy, 17*, 154–167. http://dx.doi.org/10.1037/1555-6824.17.2.154

2

PLAY THERAPY TO HELP SCHOOL-AGE CHILDREN DEAL WITH NATURAL AND HUMAN-MADE DISASTERS

AKIKO OHNOGI AND ATHENA A. DREWES

School-age children can easily be negatively impacted by natural and human-made disasters, such as earthquakes, tornadoes, hurricanes with severe flooding and evacuations, fires, acts of terrorism, school shootings, and unusual community events (e.g., explosions, construction disasters). The unfortunate consequences of these traumas on school-age children, as well as adolescents, are well documented (Davis & Siegel, 2000; Jeney-Gammon, Daugherty, Finch, Belter, & Foster, 1993; Jones & Ollendick, 2005; Lack & Sullivan, 2007; Lengua, Long, & Meltzoff, 2006; Terranova, Boxer, & Morris, 2009).

Children fall back on coping strategies to help them get through traumatic events. Depending on their developmental level and previous resources and resiliency, school-age children may cope through avoidance and distraction, self-blame, wishful thinking, cognitive restructuring, and problem solving. Younger children and those with posttraumatic stress disorder (PTSD) use more strategies than older children and those not suffering from PTSD (Stallard, Velleman, Langsford, & Baldwin, 2001). Children with PTSD are

http://dx.doi.org/10.1037/14776-003
Play Therapy in Middle Childhood, A. A. Drewes and C. E. Schaefer (Editors)

more likely to use distraction, social withdrawal, emotional regulation, and blaming others. This chapter offers a developmental perspective along with a review of recent brain research to help clinicians use play-based techniques and play therapy to help school-age children impacted by trauma build coping strategies.

BASIC RATIONALE AND THEORY

Following disasters, large numbers of children can become affected in a variety of ways. Physical loss can be compounded by less tangible losses, which are often least understood and can be more easily denied by those experiencing them. Intangible losses include loss of community because of relocation, disrupted services, loss of schools, loss of the support of friends when it is desperately needed most, and emotional unavailability of parents. There is the sense of loss of control over one's life and over the fury of nature or the actions of people. Looking at the surrounding devastation over and over again only adds to victims' feelings of impotence and helplessness. The loss of predictability and the realization that one's life can be dramatically altered in a few short hours result in feelings of vulnerability. As Terr (1990) observed,

> "Psychic trauma" occurs when a sudden, unexpected, overwhelmingly intense emotional blow or a series of blows assaults the person from outside. Traumatic events are external, but they quickly become incorporated into the mind. A person probably will not become fully traumatized unless he or she feels utterly helpless during the event or events. (p. 8)

Community reactions following disasters of various types are similar. At the time of the event, between 12% and 25% of people usually remain calm and can take some purposeful action. Another 10% to 25% are more than likely to become psychiatric casualties, displaying extreme anxiety. A larger proportion of the community, up to 75%, can seem immobilized by inertia and frozenness (Lack & Sullivan, 2007; Terranova, Boxer, & Morris, 2009). As a result, many disaster survivors tend to be overlooked amid the chaotic conditions because they are immobilized and in a stunned state. The reactions of school-age children are likely to mirror the reactions of their parents.

Children and their families become caught up in the need to survive, with parents not in tune with their children's emotional needs. Once basic survival needs are met (e.g., food, water, shelter, clothing), and with the progress of recovery, parents begin to deal with their own emotional issues, leaving little energy and time to address the emotional needs of their children.

Adding to the impact of trauma is that children's responses to disaster events and trauma are unique and different from those of their parents or other adults. School-age children's direct experience of the particular disaster, their perception of the parent's and significant adults' (e.g., teachers, neighbors) responses, and the child's developmental level at the time of trauma are critical factors that contribute to the child's coping response (Ohnogi, 2006).

School-age children are more in touch with the frightening reality of the event and may become confused and even frightened by the feelings they experience. These feelings can be overwhelming at times and in turn impair learning and concentration. Concerns about the safety of their families and other victims, feelings of vulnerability about the world and their life's future, and specific fears around reminders of the event may develop. Feelings of guilt and responsibility about the event may arise that may not be verbalized to spare the parent negative feelings or worry. Physical difficulties with sleep, somatic complaints, and traumatic play are common responses for school-age children. As a result, behaviors may show changes; children may become more aggressive and reckless or more withdrawn and inhibited.

IMPACT OF TRAUMA ON THE CHILD'S BRAIN

The severity of the trauma effect is dependent on various factors, such as age of the child, prior history of trauma, distance from the traumatic experience, personal resilience in coping with past events (Courtois, Ford, & Cloitre, 2009), and degree of support (Ohnogi, 2010; Perry, 2002; Silverman & La Greca, 2002). Factors that increase stress-related reactivity (e.g., family chaos) make children more vulnerable, whereas factors that provide structure, predictability, nurturing, and a sense of safety decrease vulnerability and increase coping abilities (Perry, 2002).

As a child's brain is developing, the effects of trauma differ depending on when in development the trauma occurred (e.g., infancy, early childhood, adolescence), the nature of the trauma (e.g., lack of sensory stimulation from neglect, hyperarousal due to persisting activation of the stress response), and the pattern of the trauma (e.g., one-time experience, ongoing trauma). The symptoms a child exhibits depend on multiple factors, including age of the child. Table 2.1 shows some of the typical trauma symptoms in traumatized school-age children categorized by developmental domain (emotional, behavioral, social, physiological, and cognitive).

Unless the traumatized child has appropriate support in dealing with his or her trauma reactions, the probability of the reactions generalizing to other stimuli resembling the traumatic memory will increase with repeated activation, turning into symptoms that will begin to elicit complex, multisystem symptomatology (Perry, 2006). All academic learning and healing

TABLE 2.1
Symptoms Common in Traumatized School-Age Children

Developmental domain	Symptoms
Emotional	Irritability, anxiety, affect regulation difficulties, dysphoria, anticipation or feeling that the disaster is happening again, general numbness to emotional topics, feelings of responsibility for what happened, survivor's guilt, confusion, intrusive recollections, reexperiencing of the disaster during play or dreams
Behavioral	Persistent avoidance of associated stimuli, numbing of general responsiveness, hyperactivity, impulsivity, aggressiveness, clinginess, nightmares, school avoidance, avoidance of reminders of the disaster, repeated retelling or playing out of the event
Social	Focus on threat-related cues (often nonverbal), disorganized attachment, withdrawal from activities and friends
Physiological	Increased muscle tone, fine and gross motor delays, increased heartbeat, hyperarousal, hypervigilance, startle response, sleep difficulties
Cognitive	Language problems, attention difficulties, memory problems, poor concentration

from a trauma require an interactive and experiential approach and must take into account individual differences and the child's development. Trauma exposure impacts school-age children's ability to learn because of brain changes in the prefrontal cortex and hippocampus. Their ability to regulate emotions and overall emotional health is impacted, along with cognitive–linguistic capacities. Posttrauma reactions to their experiences may include heightened worry about safety and worry about recurrence of the traumatic event. Changes in behavior, distrust of others, changes in ability to read social cues, somatic complaints, emotional numbing, irritability, angry outbursts, withdrawal, absenteeism, reexperiencing of the event, hyperarousal, and avoidant behaviors may be seen (Perry, 2001).

As a means of coping, school-age children may disconnect from internal states when feeling overwhelmed and may have difficulty sharing feelings with others. Consequently, some children may appear shut down, inattentive, and bored or listless. Others may present as hyperactive, impulsive, aggressive, reactive, or silly. Some children go back and forth between these response styles in an unpredictable way. Facial expressions and emotional communication may vary among guarded and constricted, intense and quickly changing, and easily overwhelmed and reactive to even mild stressors. In educational settings, children may have difficulty with executive functions such as processing information and following directions; may appear bored, inattentive, or impulsive; may have trouble asking for or accepting help from others or dealing with delays; may have poor frustration tolerance; and may be unable to be self-sufficient (Perry, 2002).

School-age children experiencing trauma display dysregulation of neurobiological stress systems (De Bellis et al., 1999; Perry, 2002). The behaviors seen are often maladaptive strategies to cope with elevated levels of stress. Subsequently, the development of effective coping strategies is needed, with the understanding that the children will likely need more time than nontraumatized children to consistently and effectively use strategies to reverse long-standing hyperarousal (Perry, 2002). Because trauma is often encoded in the nonverbal limbic (emotions) system of the brain, early on in the coping skills phase physically based relaxation strategies (e.g., yoga, progressive muscle relaxation, movement, blowing bubbles) may be more useful than cognitive-based and play-based strategies (Perry, 2002).

Use of play in healing from trauma in a safe environment changes the trauma network in a child's brain. Four properties of play—symbolization, quality, projection, and displacement—provide psychological distance from the trauma experience, allowing the child to feel safe while engaged in posttrauma play. Ariel (1992) stated that play acts as a device for regulating one's level of arousal around sensitive, emotionally laden themes. Modification of negative emotions attached to trauma memories through play and play-based techniques helps children feel more self-efficacious (Högberg, Nardo, Hällström, & Pagani, 2011; Stern, 1985). Through affect regulation and feelings identification, children are able to change intruding memories to distant memories, enabling them to process the trauma memory and decreasing automatic fear reactions when thinking of the trauma experience (Högberg et al., 2011).

Children can gain power over negative emotions associated with trauma memory through affect regulation, relaxation, and cognitive coping skills. Repetition of coping skills reduces negative emotions, enhances mastery, and facilitates gradual assimilation, resulting in more coherent and organized memories (Perry, 2002). Consequently, through development of healthier coping skills, children are able to lessen somatic experiences, increase their insight into emotional processes, enrich their emotional vocabulary, alter emotions associated with trauma memories, imagine new realities by developing a sense of mastery, feel more powerful, and regain control and a sense of self-worth. Thus, with the play therapist's support, children can work through the trauma experience through habituation by engaging in repetitive play and coping skill practice, cognitive restructuring by association with new thoughts and understanding, deconditioning by association with pleasant stimuli, and mastery by becoming empowered over emotions linked to play themes.

DEVELOPMENTAL ISSUES

In light of school-age children's limited ability to articulate their distress, often crisis intervention is given to parents, who in turn are expected to reassure their children. However, treatment should be individualized to each child and not left entirely up to parents. Therefore, individual therapy may become essential for some troubled children postdisaster, as well as inclusion in crisis-oriented groups and family therapy, which should also be available.

Through initial patterned neural activation, neural reorganization can occur (Perry, 2009). Use of patterned activities such as music, movement and yoga (for breathing), and drumming or therapeutic massage can help with state regulation. Incorporating somatosensory integration activities into sessions encourages children's awareness of and control over rhythm, which can improve links between higher and lower brain regions (Perry & Szalavitz, 2006). Once self-regulation, relaxation, and affective stabilization improve, then children may be ready to proceed to relational problems using more traditional play and art therapies. And once dyadic relationship skills are established, more insight-oriented therapeutic techniques and modalities (e.g., trauma-focused cognitive–behavioral therapy [CBT]) can be used (Perry & Hambrick, 2008). Neural systems respond to prolonged and repetitive activation by altering their neurochemical and microarchitectural (e.g., synaptic sculpting) organization and functioning (Perry, 2000). Therefore, repetitive play-based activities, such as drumming, jumping rope, movement and dance, and yoga enhance limbic system functioning and facilitate and enhance emotional regulation (Perry, 2002).

PLAY INTERVENTION PROCEDURES AND SETTINGS

The initial goal of trauma treatment is to restore a sense of emotional and physical safety so that children can work on gradually healing and returning to a healthy homeostasis. Trauma to the brain stem and diencephalon cannot be treated with verbal spoken language, because the primary processes of those regions involve movement and the senses. Thus, communication in that region of the brain relies on eye contact, facial expressions, touch, movement, rhythm, and sound. The play therapist must be a calm presence to create a safe and trusting environment.

Thus, interventions must be sequenced to heal the brain from the bottom up and from right to left through consistent, predictable, patterned, repetitive, and positive treatment. The necessary 20 therapeutic powers of play (Schaefer & Drewes, 2012) or a combination of these powers must be effectively used in the chosen treatment.

Because the core elements of a positive developmental experience need to be relevant (developmentally matched), repetitive (patterned), relational (safe), and rhythmic (resonant with neural patterns), interventions with traumatized children must begin at the lowest disorganized brain level and activate the disorganized brain region, as well as being patterned and fun. Because the higher brain structures (cortex) are not operating properly in dealing with a trauma, the interventions need to be focused initially on the lower brain structure, gearing the treatment to more sensory and emotional experiential interventions rather than use of verbalization and cognition (as in the more traditional verbal therapies). Thus, it is important to assess the brain region that has been affected and changed as a result of the trauma, identify the child's strengths to enhance remediation and resilience, and plan the specific play therapy interventions that can also be woven into standardized trauma treatments (e.g., trauma-focused CBT) to most effectively treat the trauma symptoms. Specifically, trauma treatment goals should work on affect regulation, stress management, cognitive reprocessing, and gradual exposure. These goals are promoted by finding ways to self-soothe and self-regulate, understanding and expressing emotions, developing healthy defenses, achieving mastery to counteract helplessness, recalling and narrating (through play) the real or imagined trauma, and managing anxiety related to memory or present fears. If the child is dealing with the death of a loved one, he or she will need to work on grief-focused healing through acknowledging what has been lost in the relationship, exploring unfinished business with the person who died, and memorializing the person and committing to other relationships in the present.

The therapist needs to plan interventions that provide therapeutic support through pleasurable interactions in a relational context. Examples of intervention activities are soothing, calming sensory activities such as receiving gentle touch (e.g., Theraplay) or massage, listening to music that is soothing but also has a repetitive beat, rocking, doing breathing exercises (e.g., blowing bubbles, practicing mindfulness techniques, blowing a pinwheel), chewing, singing songs, touching textures of all kinds, finger painting, and playing with clay, sand, or mud.

Diencephalon activities that help in treating trauma symptoms are sequenced motor activities in play through positive relational situations. Examples include gross and fine motor play such as jumping rope; swinging; rocking; crawling through tubes; navigating blanket mazes; playing with balls, bean bags, or hula hoops; throwing and catching; kicking; playing hand clapping games; dancing; and playing hopscotch. Yoga and tai chi, which use physical movement and breathing, regulate emotional and physiological states and are especially practical for school-age and older children.

Depending on which part of the brain has been affected (i.e., depending on the age of child when the trauma occurs) and what types of reaction the child is exhibiting (i.e., symptoms), the most effective and appropriate form of intervention will differ. The following types of interventions are most effective in addressing certain symptoms:

- Intrusive reexperiencing of the trauma or mild avoidance can be addressed using trauma-focused, structured, directive play therapy. For example, if the child is having intruding thoughts and images of the trauma, imagery and psychoeducational activities to "rewrite" images and thoughts to appropriate and positive ones, such as drawing the negative images being replaced by positive images, is helpful.
- Increased arousal can be addressed by non-trauma-focused, structured, directive relaxation and coping activities. For example, if the child is exhibiting heightened physical anxiety and arousal, structured physical relaxation activities to calm the nervous system, such as Raggedy Ann and Tin Man or Cooked and Uncooked Spaghetti (controlled tightening and relaxation of various muscles), are helpful.
- Dissociation and extreme avoidance can be addressed through structured directive grounding or strength-focused activities such as 3-2-1 (focusing on various senses by looking, smelling, hearing, tasting, and feeling three objects, then two objects, then one object), creation of hope songs, or nondirective play therapy to express memories and experiences through use of a sand tray, expressive arts, or play.

In addition, the following interventions promote recovery:

- Symptoms can be normalized using a trauma reaction puppet show or bibliotherapy.
- Affect can be regulated and hyperarousal managed by imagining a safe, protective bubble and engaging in deep breathing; blowing out negative emotion bubbles and breathing in safe, calm feelings; or touching a safe rock.
- Intrusive reexperiencing can be managed by imagining an emotion balloon (blowing out negative thoughts and feelings as one blows up a balloon); playing 3-2-1; tapping the head and simultaneously rubbing the stomach; imagining a safe place (meditation); positive imaging; or repeating a protective mantra.
- Accurate cognitions can be increased by creating a body tsunami, participating in a trauma response puppet show, playing the

Trash the Negative Thought game, or demonstrating trauma effects on the brain using toys.

- Effective coping can be increased by creating a coping bracelet, drawing, developing an informational radio show, or playing Go Fish for positive coping skills.
- Social support can be built by playing Rock–Scissors–Paper Support Train, creating a rock garden, drawing and using support coupons, writing thank you letters to support people, and cutting out a support people chain and writing names of the people who have helped and can help.
- Hope can be fostered by creating a village, singing a song and changing the words to reflect hope, and playing Hope Clay (i.e., creating and putting worries into a container made out of play dough).
- A trauma narrative can be developed by telling a story with a positive ending, role-playing, or creating a picture book.
- Grief-focused work involves picking out miniatures associated with losses, memorializing the loved one with clay sculptures, or making a drawing of unfinished business.

Traumatized school-age children express various trauma themes in their play. Common themes are nurturing and healing, grief and loss, aggression, rescue and destruction, and real-life scenarios. When assessment indicates that unstructured play interventions are most helpful for a particular child, it is important to have a wide range of toys for the child to be able to pick and choose from so that he or she can express the multiple emotions and experiences that he or she is dealing with, as toys are a child's words in self-expression and communication. The following are examples of toys that can help with the expression and processing of emotions:

- soft stuffed rabbit—nurturance or relief;
- hard, scowling monster—threat or fear;
- soldiers, police cars, food—feelings of safety and protection;
- construction tools, doctor kit—healing and reconstruction;
- monsters, scary animals (e.g., snake, bugs)—negative emotions;
- magic wand, greenery—creation of hope; and
- houses, people, vehicles (including boats for tsunami survivors), animals (including sea creatures for tsunami survivors)—resumption of normal life.

Care must be taken, however, that the child is not being retraumatized through the play interventions, whether structured or nondirective. Re-creation of the trauma experience in play can be either retraumatizing or adaptive (Gil, 2006; Terr, 1990). If the child is becoming retraumatized during the play, he or she will show no facial expression changes, very little body movement, no interaction with the play therapist, no change in the story line, and inflexible play; the child will seem stuck, without relief or resolution, and will seem anxious, helpless, or pressured after the play therapy session. The therapist should closely monitor the child for retraumatization and consider intervening if the story line seems to be stuck; there are repetitive play disruptions; the child exhibits significant negative feelings of anxiety, terror, or powerlessness without release; the play becomes compulsive; the play is not facilitating mastery; or the play is not moving toward resolution after a reasonable time.

EMPIRICAL SUPPORT

Research shows that adverse experiences in early life cause long-term changes in multiple brain systems (Anda, 2002). Increasing frequencies of early adverse childhood experiences correlate highly with enduring brain dysfunction and deleterious effects on health and quality of life (Anda, 2002). In addition, the child is at increased risk of emotional, behavioral, academic, social, and physical problems throughout the lifespan.

Studies of coping strategies in dealing with human-made disasters span a variety of disaster types and study designs. Weisenberg, Schwarzwald, Waysman, Solomon, and Klingman (1993) studied coping behavior and PTSD in 492 children who took shelter in a sealed room during a Scud missile attack. They found that the more severe stress reactions were found in children who placed greater emphasis on coping activities directed at the threat and less emphasis on avoidance and distraction. Effective coping was more likely to be seen in children in higher grade levels (7th and 10th) compared with lower grade levels (5th). Stallard et al. (2001) studied 97 children at 6 to 8 weeks after a traffic accident and found that younger children and those with PTSD used more coping strategies than older children and those not suffering from PTSD. The younger children and those with PTSD used distraction, social withdrawal, emotional regulation, and blaming others to cope.

A comprehensive interview study of 46 children who had experienced a residential fire 3 months previously found avoidant coping related to heightened levels of fear. After the terrorist attacks of September 11, 2001, several studies looked at coping in affected children. Lengua et al. (2006) studied a sample of children 1 month following 9/11 and found that posttrauma avoidant coping predicted a higher degree of PTSD symptoms.

Although many studies have found posttrauma negative effects, it should be noted that not all children develop symptoms, and over time many difficulties show a pattern of spontaneous improvement (Berliner, 2011). And some children who experience natural or human-made disasters do not present with symptoms. These asymptomatic children may be resilient and may never develop behavioral or emotional difficulties regardless of whether they receive treatment. Several protective factors have been found that may mitigate the formation and persistence of symptoms following trauma, including family support, willingness to participate in treatment, and innate ability to persevere in the face of adversity (Goodyear-Brown, Fath, & Myers, 2012).

Often the professional literature related to children who experience disaster focuses more on the reactions of adults or reports of the parents about their children that may minimize the children's reactions (Terr, 1990). Current studies of coping of children in relation to natural and human-made disasters support the importance of investigating coping in relation to posttraumatic stress reactions and note that avoidant coping strategies are a risk factor for PTSD (Lack & Sullivan, 2007; Pfefferbaum, Noffsiger, Wind, & Allen, 2014; Terranova et al., 2009). School-age children often express posttraumatic symptoms behaviorally; such symptoms may include regressive behaviors, anxiety, and depression (Davis & Siegel, 2000; Giaconia et al., 1994). In addition, because school-age children may not be able to abstractly interpret their somatic and affective feelings, they may describe these experiences as physiological symptoms (e.g., stomachache, headache; Cook-Cottone, 2004).

There have been recent efforts to make child treatment more appealing and engaging and less cognitive, especially in dealing with trauma, through the integration of creative interventions such as art, music, play, and drama with evidence-informed practices for treating disorders and problems of childhood trauma (Drewes & Cavett, 2012; Reddy, 2012; Reddy, Files-Hall, & Schaefer, 2005; Russ & Niec, 2011; Springer & Misurell, 2015). Practitioners have specifically written about the value of integrating play therapy techniques with traditional CBT for treating childhood trauma (Drewes, 2009; Drewes & Cavett, 2012; Lowenstein, 2008; Steele & Malchiodi, 2008; Webb, 2007).

Play has therapeutic powers (Schaefer & Drewes, 2012) to increase children's engagement, reduce their defenses, and provide them with the ability to communicate in a comfortable and developmentally appropriate manner through both verbal and nonverbal means (Knell & Desari, 2009). CBT provides structure, direction, focus, and skill development, which are necessary for symptom reduction and development of skills (Drewes, 2009). An integration of play therapy and CBT allows for the marriage of two complementary approaches, which together capitalize on the benefits of each to create a model for delivering highly effective and well-researched treatment in an engaging and relevant manner (Springer & Misurell, 2015).

CASE ILLUSTRATION INCLUDING CAREGIVER INVOLVEMENT

Keiko was an 8-year-old girl who resided in Tokyo and was visiting relatives in Iwate, on the coast of northern Japan. She was eating a snack of rice crackers while watching her favorite TV program, *Pokémon*, and cuddling with her grandparents when the Tohoku earthquake struck on March 11, 2011. Although she was prepared through practice to seek shelter when she felt tremors, she had no experience or reference points that taught her what to expect from a tsunami, such as the ear-shattering sirens and need to run to higher ground. After what seemed like hours (in reality a few seconds), her grandfather scooped her up (Keiko knew it was her grandfather because he smelled of fish, which was how he always smelled, being a fisherman) and started running uphill into the mountains. Keiko had her eyes closed the whole time and thus saw nothing. However, she heard something roaring and crashing, a horribly loud and frightening sound whose origin she had no idea of, and she did not want to open her eyes to see.

Keiko spent the night at a school with her grandparents and about 50 other people. They were unable to reach her parents as no one's cell phone was working. The following day, to her relief, Keiko's father came to the school and embraced her immediately. She was devastated, however, when her father informed her, crying, that her mother had been swallowed up by the sea the day before by something called a "tsunami"; this was apparently what that horrific roaring sound was. Keiko had never seen her father cry before.

Keiko was brought in for treatment in Tokyo by her father 9 months after the trauma. Her father reported during an initial parent consultation that Keiko had not been herself since the tsunami. She was jumpy, cried easily, had mood swings, could not concentrate in school, did not want to play with friends, would not let her father out of her sight, would suddenly begin screaming, did not want to take baths, trembled even while watching TV, sometimes refused to eat, woke up with nightmares, had difficulty hearing, had sudden temper tantrums without any apparent provocation, hyperventilated, often stared intently at her father, refused to visit her grandparents, and constantly talked about Pikachu (from *Pokémon*) coming to get her.

Her father was puzzled, as he informed the play therapist, because Keiko had no trouble speaking to him about missing her mother or about what she and her grandparents did to escape from the tsunami. During most of this consultation session, Keiko's father was constantly fighting tears, often having to stop talking to collect himself. He reported that the various concerning behaviors occurred whenever Keiko saw anything related to *Pokémon*, tasted food similar to rice crackers, or heard loud sounds. Keiko would also become extremely upset when her father was not smiling. It also came to light that Keiko would calm down whenever she smelled fish, touched something coarse, or jumped up and down. Although she refused to visit her grandparents in Iwate, speaking to her grandfather via video call also seemed to have a positive effect on her demeanor.

Various activities targeting the father–daughter attachment were incorporated into the treatment. These activities were structured and nurturing to help soothe Keiko's overactive limbic system. Hand massaging using lotion, thumb wrestling, creating a song together and dancing to it, choosing and placing various hats and masks on each other, taking turns hiding and finding various objects in the room, blowing bubbles at each other, and tossing scarves into the air were some of the activities. They helped to activate positive emotions, decrease automatic negative reactions, strengthen Keiko's and her father's sense of attachment to each other, increase a sense of safety and protection, and foster hope that their future together would be OK.

When Keiko was instructed to engage in unstructured play therapy, her demeanor and body posture visibly changed. At first, Keiko seemed excited about the various toys in front of her, looking from one to another with a smile on her face. However, immediately her smile was replaced with a blank look, and she stopped moving, became silent, and seemed to freeze. Keiko was unresponsive to the play therapist's tracking and reflecting comments. Suddenly, as if snapping out of a trance, Keiko started to visibly sweat, tremble, and hyperventilate; she screamed "Go away!" and flailed her arms in front of her. She then curled up into a ball on the floor.

Because Keiko presented the need for sensory play activities to readjust the balance of her central nervous system functioning before being able to effectively use play activities to work on her emotions and cognitions regarding the trauma, the play therapist started treatment incorporating various structured activities targeting her brainstem and diencephalon. These activities included the following:

- focusing on visual, auditory, tactile, olfactory, oral, and vestibular objects and movements—search the room for all the small dog stickers, listen to various songs and dance to them, close eyes and touch various objects, smell cotton balls infused with various aromas, eat snacks stimulating different taste buds, change the distance between herself and the play therapist;
- controlling breathing and body movement—breathe in hope and breathe out negative emotions to surround herself with a safe imaginary bubble, tense various parts of the body and then release;
- managing intrusive reexperiencing by focusing on other things—tap head and rub stomach, imagine a safe place while repeating a mantra of protection and then drawing it; and

- keeping objects close for use when experiencing negative reactions—handkerchief smelling of her father, favorite candy, smooth pebble, picture of her dog, song she likes on her new cell phone.

Keiko's brainstem and diencephalon seemed to steadily benefit from the sensory and attachment treatment, and her trauma symptoms decreased and eventually dissipated. Keiko no longer hyperventilated, was jumpy, or trembled. She did not cling to her father or stare at him, and she attended school more regularly. Her emotions were more stable, and she no longer had crying or screaming outbursts. She ate without too much fuss and was able to hear without problems. She still had difficulty with concentration in school and motivation to play with friends and do things that used to be of interest. She would not go near the TV or take baths very often, still had occasional temper tantrums and nightmares, continued to refuse to visit her grandparents, and still talked about Pikachu coming to get her.

The therapist then switched to a combination of structured activities accessing her limbic system and cortex using nondirective play therapy. Keiko made use of clay, sand, drawing, role-play, and miniature activities focused on decreasing her misattributions and distorted cognitions, allowing expression of both positive and negative emotions, stimulating the various senses while connecting them to emotions and thoughts, building a repertoire of effective coping skills, and saying good-bye to her mother. Keiko especially seemed to benefit from playing with clay, noting the texture, color, smell, shape, and sound the clay made when she transformed it into something to calm herself as she came to understand her emotional reactions and change her cognitions through the creative process.

For her nondirective play, Keiko concentrated on two activities that she devised. One was jumping from one sofa to the other in the play therapy room, trying not to touch the floor between the sofas. The two sofas were considered "safe land," and the floor in between was the "dangerous sea." The play therapist was instructed to "try to touch me" whenever Keiko was not on safe land. Keiko seemed to derive not only pleasure but also a sense of accomplishment, control, and capability to protect herself from being able to go from one safe land to the other without touching the dangerous sea or being caught. The other play activity she chose was curing a large stuffed alligator with a doctor kit. The alligator, who was "mommy to a little girl alligator," had multiple injuries occur to it, and Keiko would try to cure the alligator. Initially the alligator would end up being in pain and dying no matter what Keiko the doctor tried. Gradually the story line changed to the alligator going between pain and no pain and still being hurt but not dying. Eventually, as treatment progressed, Keiko the doctor succeeded in consistently curing the alligator, and finally the alligator figured out ways to keep itself from getting hurt to begin with.

For a family intervention, Keiko and her father were asked to use miniatures and other toys and materials to create "our village." Although the play therapist initiated this activity, soon Keiko sought to do the activity herself. At first, their village was very sparse, with only a few adults, no children, a few broken buildings, nothing to eat, and barren dirt, surrounded 360° by a huge sea full of monsters, zombies, sharks, and aliens. Slowly but surely, as treatment progressed, their village added people, buildings, vegetation, and food, and the sea became smaller and smaller with less danger in it.

Toward the end of treatment, Keiko and her father's village now had multiple soldier, police, firefighter, and monster figures protecting the village; plenty of food and water to be shared; mountains; trees and plants blooming; doctors, nurses, doctor kits, and ambulances at the hospital; many children and teachers at the school; angels, glitter, and stars "using magic to keep the village safe"; cars, trains, buses, and planes for transportation to "be able to get anywhere quickly"; houses and buildings that were "real sturdy and nothing can move them"; and a miniature brain named Shoko (Keiko's mother's name) in the middle of the village as a "symbol of the village." The sea next to the village had boats and sea creatures in it, and Keiko stated that it was "safe up until this line here," where she placed fences dividing the sea in two, with the far side being "dangerous with all these enemies" (a few sharks and zombies).

Keiko's story line for her village had changed from her original story line, in which people were fatally engulfed by the sea, to one in which they were able to swim back to land or were saved by ships. Sea creatures, which were once horrific monsters out to eat all humans, had returned to being fish and dolphins that were helping people survive. The sea, initially depicted as the enemy with a mind to kill and maim, was changed to something that provided food and calm. Pikachu, which was initially depicted using a monster figure because the play therapist did not have one, was replaced by a Pikachu doll that Keiko brought in; once the main threat to human existence, Pikachu returned to being a hero saving people from enemies.

By this time, all of Keiko's remaining symptoms were gone. She was now able to concentrate in school, played with friends, started to do things that used to be of interest, watched TV including *Pokémon*, bathed daily, no longer had temper tantrums or nightmares, and started to mention wanting to visit her grandparents. Her father, who had taken the recommendation of the play therapist to receive his own therapeutic support, matched Keiko's healing with his own progress.

CONCLUSION AND FUTURE DIRECTIONS

A child's brain is plastic, responsive to both positive and negative influences. Positive experiences, such as safety and security, help develop resiliency, whereas traumatic experiences affect neural development and the originally intended brain structure if the child is left unsupported.

A traumatic experience is one that overwhelms the child, negatively disrupting his or her homeostasis. The lower brain makes decisions and reacts first; it cannot wait for the cortex to do so, as the cortex becomes easily overwhelmed and temporarily shuts down. In effect, children use the upper brain when calm and the lower brain when in fear. Threat increases reactive responses and decreases thoughtful responses, as responses are governed by emotions and reactions. The ability to communicate with words dramatically decreases as the brain mobilizes to fight or flee. Trauma induces a whole-brain stress response that triggers compensatory reactions creating a new state of equilibrium.

Hyperreactivity and an oversensitive state of fear become a trait, a new homeostasis of anxiety; affected children are more easily threatened, show maladaptive behavior and cognition, and experience social and physiological problems. Overactivation of the survival mechanism leads to inhibition of cortical neural sprouting, including activity in limbic and cortex areas, resulting in an inability to deal with low-intensity stress and significantly inhibiting cognitive and emotional development. Early exposure to trauma can have significant effects on neural development. This new trauma-induced homeostasis is more energy consuming and maladaptive, and responses can be unproductive or harmful in a nonthreatening safe environment, leading to neuropsychiatric symptoms if left unintervened.

The key principle of effective play therapy is that each intervention is geared toward realtering the brain homeostasis to its former state through provision of appropriate neuropsychiatric regulation in a safe and secure environment and relationship. Through a safe, supportive therapeutic relationship, the stress response regulates, enhancing neural activation of the cortex and ensuring that the change is not solely on a surface level.

Because a developing brain is open to opportunities as well as vulnerabilities, the therapeutic powers of play through appropriate play therapy interventions can be used to alter the destructive changes to the brain caused by a trauma in reparative, healing ways. With repeated exposure to positive therapeutic intervention under a safe and secure relationship, the regions in the brain affected by the trauma can heal.

To fully ameliorate the neurological impact of psychosocial trauma on the developing brain of a child and to effectively treat the resulting developmentally specific trauma, play therapists providing treatment to traumatized children should apply their knowledge of basic principles of brain function and development in play therapy. For this to happen, more training for play therapists to work specifically with clients who have experienced natural and human-made disasters is necessary.

REFERENCES

Anda, R. (2002, November). *The wide-ranging health effects of adverse childhood experiences*. Paper presented at the 18th annual meeting of the International Society for Traumatic Stress Studies, Baltimore, MD.

Ariel, S. (1992). *Strategic family play therapy*. West Sussex, England: Wiley.

Berliner, L. (2011). Child sexual abuse: Definitions, prevalence and consequences. In J. E. B. Myers (Ed.), *The APSAC handbook on child maltreatment* (3rd ed., pp. 215–232). Los Angeles, CA: Sage.

Cook-Cottone, C. (2004). Childhood posttraumatic stress disorder: Diagnosis, treatment, and school reintegration. *School Psychology Review, 33*, 127–139.

Courtois, C. A., Ford, J. D., & Cloitre, M. (2009). Best practices in psychotherapy for adults. In C. A. Courtois & J. D. Ford (Eds.), *Treating complex traumatic stress disorder: An evidence-based guide* (pp. 82–103). New York, NY: Guilford Press.

Davis, L., & Siegel, L. J. (2000). Posttraumatic stress disorder in children and adolescents: A review and analysis. *Clinical Child and Family Psychology Review, 3*, 135–154. http://dx.doi.org/10.1023/A:1009564724720

De Bellis, M. D., Keshavan, M. S., Clark, D. B., Casey, B. J., Giedd, J. N., Boring, A. M., . . . Ryan, N. D. (1999). Developmental traumatology, Part II: Brain development. *Biological Psychiatry, 45*, 1271–1284. http://dx.doi.org/10.1016/S0006-3223(99)00045-1

Drewes, A. A. (Ed.). (2009). *Blending play therapy with cognitive behavioral therapy: Evidence-based and other effective treatments and techniques*. Hoboken, NJ: Wiley.

Drewes, A. A., & Cavett, A. (2012). Play applications and skills components. In J. A. Cohen, A. P. Mannarino, & E. Deblinger (Eds.), *Trauma-focused CBT for children and adolescents: Treatment applications* (pp. 105–123). New York, NY: Guilford Press.

Giaconia, R. M., Reinherz, H. Z., Silverman, A. B., Pakiz, B., Frost, A. K., & Cohen, E. (1994). Ages of onset of psychiatric disorders in a community population of older adolescents. *Journal of the American Academy of Child and Adolescent Psychiatry, 33*, 706–717. http://dx.doi.org/10.1097/00004583-199406000-00012

Gil, E. (2006). *Helping abused and traumatized children: Integrating directive and nondirective approaches*. New York, NY: Guilford Press.

Goodyear-Brown, P., Fath, A., & Myers, L. (2012). Child sexual abuse: The scope of the problem. In P. Goodyear-Brown (Ed.), *Handbook of child sexual abuse: Identification, assessment, and treatment* (pp. 3–28). Hoboken, NJ: Wiley.

Högberg, G., Nardo, D., Hällström, T., & Pagani, M. (2011). Affective psychotherapy in post-traumatic reactions guided by affective neuroscience: Memory reconsolidation and play. *Psychology Research and Behavior Management, 4*, 87–96. http://dx.doi.org/10.2147/PRBM.S10380

Jeney-Gammon, P., Daugherty, T. K., Finch, A. J., Jr., Belter, R. W., & Foster, K. Y. (1993). Children's coping styles and report of depressive symptoms following a natural disaster. *Journal of Genetic Psychology, 154*, 259–267. http://dx.doi.org/10.1080/00221325.1993.9914739

Jones, R. T., & Ollendick, T. H. (2005). Risk factors for psychological adjustment following residential fire: The role of avoidant coping. *Journal of Trauma & Dissociation*, 6, 85–99. http://dx.doi.org/10.1300/J229v06n02_08

Knell, S. M., & Desari, M. (2009). CBPT: Implementing and integrating CBPT into clinical practice. In A. A. Drewes (Ed.), *Blending play therapy with cognitive behavioral therapy: Evidence-based and other effective treatments and techniques* (pp. 321–352). Hoboken, NJ: Wiley.

Lack, C., & Sullivan, M. (2007). Attributions, coping, and exposure as predictors of long-term posttraumatic distress in tornado-exposed children. *Journal of Loss and Trauma, 13*, 72–84. http://dx.doi.org/10.1080/15325020701741906

Lengua, L. J., Long, A. C., & Meltzoff, A. N. (2006). Pre-attack stress-load, appraisals, and coping in children's responses to the 9/11 terrorist attacks. *Journal of Child Psychology and Psychiatry, and Allied Disciplines, 47*, 1219–1227.

Lowenstein, L. (Ed.). (2008). *Assessment and treatment activities for children, adolescents and families: Practitioners share their most effective techniques*. Toronto, Ontario, Canada: Champion Press.

Ohnogi, A. (2006). Play based psychological interventions with traumatized children: Work with tsunami orphaned Sri Lankan children. *International Journal of Counseling and Psychotherapy* (Vol. 4). Tokyo, Japan: Institute for Advanced Studies of Clinical Psychology.

Ohnogi, A. (2010). Using play to support children traumatized by natural disasters: Chuetsu earthquake series in Japan. In A. Kalayjian & D. Eugene (Eds.), *Mass trauma and emotional healing around the world: Rituals and practices for resilience and meaning-making* (pp. 37–54). Santa Barbara, CA: Praeger.

Perry, B. D. (2000). Traumatized children: How childhood trauma influences brain development. *The Journal of the California Alliance for the Mentally Ill, 11(1)*, 48–51. Retrieved from http://www.aaets.org/article196.htm

Perry, B. D. (2001). The neurodevelopmental impact of violence in childhood. In D. Schetky & E. Benedek (Eds.), *Textbook of child and adolescent forensic psychiatry* (pp. 221–238). Washington, DC: American Psychiatric Press.

Perry, B. D. (2002). Childhood experience and the expression of genetic potential: What childhood neglect tells us about nature and nurture. *Brain & Mind, 3*, 79–100. http://dx.doi.org/10.1023/A:1016557824657

Perry, B. D. (2006). Applying principles of neurodevelopment to clinical work with maltreated and traumatized children: The neurosequential model of therapeutics. In N. B. Webb (Ed.), *Working with traumatized youth in child welfare* (pp. 27–52). New York, NY: Guilford Press.

Perry, B. D. (2009). Examining child maltreatment through a neurodevelopmental lens: Clinical applications of the neurosequential model of therapeutics. *Journal of Loss and Trauma, 14*, 240–255. http://dx.doi.org/10.1080/15325020903004350

Perry, B. D., & Hambrick, E. (2008). The neurosequential model of therapeutics. *Reclaiming Children and Youth, 17*, 38–43.

Perry, B. D., & Szalavitz, M. (2006). *The boy who was raised as a dog*. New York, NY: Basic Books.

Pfefferbaum, B., Noffsiger, M. A., Wind, L. H., & Allen, J. R. (2014). Children's coping in the context of disasters and terrorism. *Journal of Loss and Trauma, 19*, 78–97.

Reddy, L. A. (2012). *Group play interventions for children: Strategies for teaching prosocial skills*. Washington, DC: American Psychological Association. http://dx.doi.org/10.1037/13093-000

Reddy, L. A., Files-Hall, T. M., & Schaefer, C. E. (Eds.). (2005). *Empirically based play interventions for children*. Washington, DC: American Psychological Association. http://dx.doi.org/10.1037/11086-000

Russ, S. W., & Niec, L. N. (2011). *Play in clinical practice: Evidence-based approaches*. New York, NY: Guilford Press.

Schaefer, C. E., & Drewes, A. A. (Eds.). (2012). *The healing powers of play: 20 core agents of change* (2nd ed.). Hoboken, NJ: Wiley.

Silverman, W. K., & La Greca, A. M. (2002). Children experiencing disasters: Definitions, reactions, and predictors of outcomes. In A. M. La Greca, W. K. Silverman, E. M. Vernberg, & M. C. Roberts (Eds.), *Helping children cope with disasters and terrorism* (pp. 11–33). Washington, DC: American Psychological Association.

Springer, C. I., & Misurell, J. R. (2015). *Game-based cognitive–behavioral therapy for child sexual abuse*. New York, NY: Springer.

Stallard, P., Velleman, R., Langsford, J., & Baldwin, S. (2001). Coping and psychological distress in children involved in road traffic accidents. *British Journal of Clinical Psychology, 40*, 197–208. http://dx.doi.org/10.1348/014466501163643

Steele, W., & Malchiodi, C. A. (2008). Interventions for parents of traumatized children. In C. A. Malchiodi (Ed.), *Creative interventions with traumatized children* (pp. 264–281). New York, NY: Guilford Press.

Stern, D. (1985). *The interpersonal world of the infant*. New York, NY: Basic Books.

Terr, L. (1990). *Too scared to cry*. New York, NY: Harper & Row.

Terranova, A. M., Boxer, P., & Morris, A. S. (2009). Factors influencing the course of posttraumatic stress following a natural disaster: Children's reactions to Hurricane Katrina. *Journal of Applied Developmental Psychology, 30*, 344–355. http://dx.doi.org/10.1016/j.appdev.2008.12.017

Webb, N. B. (2007). *Play therapy with children in crisis: Individual, group, and family treatment* (3rd ed.). New York, NY: Guilford Press.

Weisenberg, M., Schwarzwald, J., Waysman, M., Solomon, Z., & Klingman, A. (1993). Coping of school-age children in the sealed room during Scud missile bombardment and postwar stress reactions. *Journal of Consulting and Clinical Psychology, 61*, 462–467. http://dx.doi.org/10.1037/0022-006X.61.3.462

3

PLAYFUL TRAUMA-FOCUSED COGNITIVE–BEHAVIORAL THERAPY FOR SCHOOL-AGE CHILDREN

ANGELA M. CAVETT

Trauma-focused cognitive–behavioral therapy (TF-CBT), an empirically validated treatment for children ages 4 to 18 years, is based on the research of its developers, Judith Cohen, Anthony Mannarino, and Esther Deblinger. They identified components of therapy that were found to be necessary in the treatment of children who were traumatized. Their manuals were integrated into *Treating Trauma and Traumatic Grief in Children and Adolescents* (Cohen, Mannarino, & Deblinger, 2006).

Children who have experienced one or more traumas often benefit from TF-CBT. The TF-CBT components are **p**sychoeducation, **p**arenting skills, **r**elaxation, **a**ffective expression and modulation, **c**ognitive coping and processing, **t**rauma narrative, **i**n vivo mastery, **c**onjoint parent–child sessions, and **e**nhancing future safety, referred to by the mnemonic PRACTICE. Playful TF-CBT uses play therapy techniques consistent with each of the components to engage the child in a developmentally appropriate approach (Cavett, 2009a, 2009b, 2009c; Cavett & Drewes, 2012; Drewes & Cavett, 2012).

http://dx.doi.org/10.1037/14776-004
Play Therapy in Middle Childhood, A. A. Drewes and C. E. Schaefer (Editors)

TF-CBT is typically a short-term therapy (i.e., 12–16 weeks) in which the child is seen for 60- to 90-minute sessions once per week. For children with complex trauma, the duration of treatment is lengthened (e.g., to 28 sessions) so that he or she can acquire the skills needed in each component. The initial sessions, which address the components that are not directly related to trauma, allow the child to develop necessary skills so that when the trauma narrative is told, the child processes negative affective and cognitive experiences using cognitive coping skills to integrate the narrative.

BASIC RATIONALE AND THEORY

TF-CBT is a research-based model based on affective, cognitive, and behavioral concepts. A child who has been traumatized may have affective symptoms (e.g., depressive feelings, affective dysregulation), cognitive symptoms (e.g., feelings of responsibility for the father hitting the mother), and behavioral symptoms (e.g., aggression, avoidance). Research was used to identify therapeutic components found to be necessary in effective therapy for traumatized children. Components were included in TF-CBT if they contributed to reduction of affective or cognitive symptoms or problematic behaviors.

The sequence of sessions is based on the research as well. Typically, the first several (approximately four) sessions are spent on the PRAC components: **p**sychoeducation, **p**arenting skills, **r**elaxation, **a**ffective expression and modulation, and **c**ognitive coping and processing. The next few sessions (approximately Sessions 5–8) address developing the trauma narrative and processing it. For children who require in vivo exposure, this exposure is also done during these sessions. Once the child has developed the trauma narrative with the therapist, the next sessions (approximately Sessions 9–12) are conjoint sessions with the parent and child that allow the parent to hear the trauma narrative with the child and discuss ways to enhance future safety. (The parent may be a foster parent, relative, or other caregiver; the term *parent* is used for the remainder of the chapter to refer to the primary caregiver.)

Parents are included in TF-CBT for each of the PRACTICE components over the course of therapy. Often the child and parent are involved in sessions separately or together, varying with the needs of the child. The model is flexible to allow for parental involvement that best meets the child's needs. For instance, the parent may meet first with the therapist to discuss psychoeducation or relaxation skills or the trauma narrative, followed by the child alone and then both together to discuss that component. This time alone with the therapist allows the parent to learn skills to assist the child and to discuss any concerns that will impact therapy with the clinician. The model allows for parent substitutes or modifications based on the individual case. For instance, if a parent is not able to provide the cognitive coping skills for a child because of the parent's belief that the child was partially to blame for the sexual abuse, someone else, such as a grandparent, can fill that supportive role.

Children with complex trauma require changes in the timing of the components. For all children in therapy, the relationship with the therapist must be central, and this is especially true for children with complex trauma. Building trust in the therapist requires time and interactions that support the relationship. Describing the course of treatment and how the components will help the child build skills and process the trauma is essential for the child and caregivers as they commit to therapy. With children who have had multiple traumas, safety planning becomes evident throughout the treatment. When children have had a single trauma, safety planning can often be done later in treatment. If the child is not in a safe environment, or if there are risks that need to be reduced first, these considerations take priority. Safety planning for children with complex trauma builds a foundation on which the other components are built.

DEVELOPMENTAL ISSUES

Traditionally, children in the preoperational stage (age 2–7 years) and even the concrete operational stage (7–11 years) were not considered flexible enough in their thinking to apply cognitive–behavioral therapy (CBT) strategies. The flexibility of thinking of CBT was considered a verbal endeavor. Without cognitive changes, affective and behavioral changes were not considered possible. However, playful TF-CBT allows for concepts to be played with in the same manner in which words are used with adults. Concrete objects (e.g., dolls, drawings) and directive TF-CBT play therapy interventions allow the child to process trauma and make affective, cognitive, and behavioral changes.

School-age children typically are in the preoperational and concrete operational stages of cognitive development. As children develop, they are more able to use symbols cognitively to represent their experiences. Children in the preoperational stage can represent thoughts through their images and play. *Representation* refers to children's use of symbols to represent their worlds. Even very young children (2–3 years) can use symbols, including toys, in this manner, first as an object itself (2½ years) and later as both an object and a representation of something else (3 years). Therefore, for children in the young school-age range (6–7 years), the dollhouse can represent both a toy dollhouse and their own home.

Early school-age children in the preoperational stage can use symbolic but concrete representations for communicating their experiences. Their thoughts can be represented through images and play. Limits in cognitive development for school-age children, particularly centration, irreversibility, and egocentrism, contribute to the greater effectiveness of play therapy over CBT without play. School-age children can make comparisons between observable objects. In play therapy to help children with affective expression and modulation, for instance, a child may see two puppets act out a similar situation with different behavioral responses, one more aggressive than the other. The child can consider different aspects of the responses. Although school-age children may have difficulty verbally discussing behavioral options for responding to situations, they often can consider those options when they see them acted out by the puppets. This activity can be extended to discussion in the home environment of the two characters and their behavioral responses between sessions. Although preoperational children tend to be egocentric, meaning that they have difficulty taking the perspective of others, they are able to see different perspectives through play.

Children ages 8 to 11 are typically in the concrete operational stage are able to use cognitive strategies such as reversibility when applied to concrete situations. TF-CBT and play can be helpful during this stage for allowing the child to use concrete objects to explore their thinking. For example, children who were abused may represent themselves in a drawing or art project as damaged by the abuse but then repaired. Taping a drawing of a broken child back together and talking about what has helped in the process allows children in the concrete operational stage a way to process the healing of survivors of abuse. Children in this cognitive stage are also able to think more logically (i.e., if A > B and B > C, then A > C). Using concepts such as balancing coping skills with the intensity of the emotion, such as in Kenney-Noziska's (2008) Balancing Out Your Feelings, allows children to consider whether they have coping skills that are adequate and which coping skills may be more helpful for different amounts of an emotion. Interventions such as Rainbow Thinking and Distorted Mirror (Cavett, in press) include the use of concrete representations allowing children to challenge their own thinking. By using cognitive strategies such as Rainbow Thinking, the child learns to differentiate between black-and-white thinking that is abuse related and rainbow thinking that is more accurate and healthy. Distorted Mirror is a cognitive strategy that allows school-age children to consider their self-perceptions as accurate or distorted depending on whether they were created from abusive or healthy relationships. By using concrete toys during these interventions, playful TF-CBT allows children deeper understanding of the concept.

THERAPEUTIC SETTINGS FOR PLAYFUL TF-CBT

TF-CBT is often implemented in community mental health clinics, private practices, and other outpatient settings. TF-CBT may be used in mental health settings in which the therapist is able to provide consistent sessions for the duration of treatment. Because it is component based, the therapist needs to be able to provide care to address each of the components. TF-CBT is conceptualized as a combination of individual and family therapy that is based on the needs of the child and that teaches the components and related skills to both the parent and child.

TF-CBT may also be used with children in residential, long-term inpatient treatment or group home settings (Cohen, Mannarino, & Navarro, 2012). Children in residential care may benefit from TF-CBT, following assessment and adjustment to the setting, if they have a history of trauma. As with all children using TF-CBT, factors such as suicidality, psychosis, and self-injury must be stabilized before implementation. The timing of sessions is an important factor to consider for children in residential settings because it is necessary that the PRAC components be implemented before the trauma narrative is developed, and it is strongly recommended that children be able to finish processing their trauma narrative. For children in residential treatment, discharge can be a significant factor impacting the timing of TF-CBT components, and its timing must be strongly considered.

TF-CBT may be implemented in schools (Rivera, 2012). The school's administrators must understand how TF-CBT can fit into their current structure. It has been suggested that because children are often in school, it would be a natural fit to have TF-CBT implemented there. Many children who have been traumatized have symptoms including behavioral problems and decreased academic performance that impact the schools.

The process of implementing TF-CBT in schools begins with identifying children who have been traumatized and formally requesting parental permission to begin treatment. Parents must be encouraged to engage in the treatment if at all possible. In the school, TF-CBT may be implemented in a group. For instance, a child may complete the PRAC components in a group, create their trauma narrative in individual sessions, and return to the group to share the narrative, followed by final sessions related to in vivo exposure and safety planning. The main reason for providing children with TF-CBT in schools is that children are required to be present in school and may not have access to community outpatient services. However, often school counselors do not have the resources, including time required for each child who needs TF-CBT, to implement it in the schools given their total job description. Therefore, children are often referred to mental health clinics in the community.

PLAY ASSESSMENT, TREATMENT PLANNING, AND INTERVENTION

Play therapy interventions allow TF-CBT to be individualized for each child in an engaging manner that uses the interests and developmental stage of the child to inform how each of the TF-CBT components is implemented. Assessment is done before treatment begins in TF-CBT. Often therapists use the Traumatic Events Screening Inventory—Child Version (Ippen et al., 2002) or the Child Behavior Checklist (Achenbach, 1991) to assess presenting problems. Assessment also includes identifying the child's and family's strengths. Child strengths (e.g., cognitive, affective modulation, social, creative, or artistic) may not be noticed on standardized testing but must be incorporated into treatment. Play therapy assessments such as Puppet Sentence Completion (Cavett, 2010; Knell, 1992; Knell & Beck, 2000) allow for deeper understanding of the child's feelings and thoughts about self and his or her world and experience. The Puppet Sentence Completion task allows the child to complete sentence stems using puppets. Sentence stems may be listed in the assessments or created by the therapist to gather information about certain beliefs or experiences.

Treatment planning based on standardized testing and trauma-specific problems allows the therapist to connect the presenting problem to the treatment. Often in standard therapy, children are expected to accept the therapeutic goals determined by their parent and therapist. The problems have been determined by adults in the child's life, including the parent, teacher, social worker, and therapist. When using Stepping Up to Success (Cavett, 2010), the therapist creates a treatment plan that involves the child in creating a play- or art-based treatment plan that expresses the child's feelings and beliefs about what needs to change in their lives. Paper is used to create steps, and each step is labeled with a presenting problem. Strategies to address each problem are written on paper footprints and glued to the steps.

Psychoeducation

Psychoeducation is an important component for the child and parent to learn what is normal for victims of trauma and the process of healing after a trauma. When play is integrated into psychoeducation, the child is better able to integrate the concepts. Play therapists may use puppets, dolls, or toy figures that are similar to the characters in the books used for psychoeducation to allow for integration. Through acting out the scenes in the books, children begin to gain mastery over the sense of powerlessness of the traumatized character or child. Bibliotherapy is useful for psychoeducation; stories that can be generalized across traumas include *Brave Bart: A Story for Traumatized and*

Grieving Children (Sheppard, 1998). In *Brave Bart*, a little kitten, Bart, has had something happen that is upsetting, but he relies on an old cat to help him work through the past trauma.

The child and parent learn about trauma and how people often respond to trauma to normalize the symptoms. The family should learn about the components of TF-CBT and how therapy progresses from general skills to those directly related to the trauma. An intervention created to help communicate the sequence of steps in TF-CBT treatment is Nested Boxes (Cavett, 2010). With Nested Boxes, the therapist labels a nested box for each component of therapy, with the smallest box representing the trauma narrative. The therapist uses the nested boxes to describe how each of the PRACTICE skills is learned in sequence, with the trauma narrative occurring after the PRAC skills have prepared the client with necessary coping skills. The boxes are put back together beginning with the outer ones as the therapist describes how each skill is used to process the trauma narrative, represented by the smallest box.

How the general skills are used later to develop the trauma narrative and process it is discussed during psychoeducation. Children who have been traumatized share common symptoms. Often the child and parent are confused by or frustrated with the child's symptoms. Psychoeducation allows for changes in the child's and parent's perceptions of the child. Psychoeducation counters views of the child that are inaccurate or based in myths about trauma. For therapists not trained in play therapy, psychoeducation may be done with worksheets and verbal relay of information between therapist and parent. However, for the child to understand and integrate the content, play therapy techniques can be used.

Children's responses tend to be dependent on how involved adults, especially caregivers, are in the therapy. By using both individual and family sessions, TF-CBT allows both the child and parent to learn about each of the components so that the skills will be transferred from therapy to home and other environments. When the therapist uses play therapy techniques with both parent and child, the parent learns to communicate with the child at the child's developmental level.

Parenting Skills

Including parents in teaching skills (e.g., relaxation) ensures that the child has support in learning and using the skills. Parenting skills, including strategies such as time-out, are used in TF-CBT. Parents are encouraged to provide nurturing and support as well as structure and appropriate consequences to guide their children. To help promote the parent–child relationship, play therapy interventions such as Nightly Snuggle (Lowenstein, 2006) and Positive Placemats (Cavett, in press) are used. Nightly Snuggle describes how to have a positive interaction while snuggling at bedtime. Positive Placemats is an intervention in which the child and parents create paper or cloth placemats and write positive statements on each family member's placemat at mealtime.

Typically, parents are seen as having a parallel process to that of the child. Parents are impacted by their child's trauma, and the work done in TF-CBT often results in improvements for both. While children are preparing through the PRAC sessions for the creation of the narrative, parents are also learning skills to become prepared for the trauma narrative and how to help process it.

Relaxation

Relaxation allows the child to learn techniques related to decreasing physiological reactivity and affective modulation. This component has several domains, including imagery, progressive muscle relaxation, mindfulness meditations, and anchoring. Spiritual experiences related to the child's culture may also be used for this component. For example, drumming may be incorporated into the process for Native American children, who may have a family member assist them in learning culture-specific songs and chants.

As with each of the domains, the best approach to teaching the child about relaxation is through play therapy. The play therapy interventions allow the child to be relaxed in the process of learning. To attempt to teach didactically or to a child who does not feel engaged in the process defeats the purpose. Parent and child may be taught several relaxation strategies across the range of similar strategies. Breathing exercises are used, and several child-friendly playful interventions address breathing, including Personalized Pinwheels (Goodyear-Brown, 2005). With Personalized Pinwheels, children create a pinwheel with a drawing on each spoke to remind them of coping skills that work for them. For instance, one spoke may have bubbles drawn on it to remind them that they feel more relaxed after a bubble bath.

Anchoring is used to help children be mindfully aware of the here and now. It allows for the focus to be turned to the safe present environment. Teaching children how to calm themselves and remain in the present is critical in work with traumatized children. *Anchors* are mindfulness techniques that help the child become focused on and fully engaged in the moment. In play, children are often focused and fully engaged in the moment. For example, children may play in the sand at the end of a session while the therapist reflects on the child's actions, allowing for a developmentally appropriate form of anchoring. Several anchoring techniques can be shared with the child, including Categories A to Z, Cross Hopping (Hoch-Espada, 2007), and Rocks in the River (Cavett, in press). With Categories A to Z, the child and therapist (and parent if present) look around the room and name things that begin with each letter of the alphabet in order. With Cross Hopping, the child jumps from square to square in an X created with masking tape on the office floor. This helps the child focus on the jumping happening in the here and now. Rocks in the River uses small plastic "rocks," and the child focuses on hopping from one to another to get to the other side of the river. Colored plastic rocks can be used with the therapist naming the color to hop to, or the child can use any of the rocks.

Active anchors such as pogo sticking, foursquare, or wheelbarrowing from the office to the waiting room allow for movement that heals the body. The therapist may ask children anchoring questions (e.g., How does the ground feel below your hands? Does your face feel flushed as your head is upside down?) as they wheelbarrow. Verbal anchoring does not allow the depth of experience that play allows; this concept is true across all the components of TF-CBT.

Progressive muscle relaxation (PMR) is another type of strategy that can be done playfully with children. Several PMR scripts, interventions, or CDs can be helpful for children, including Spaghetti (Belknap, 2006) and the book *A Boy and a Bear* (Lite, 1996). In *A Boy and a Bear*, a boy and a bear climb up a hill and stop to do relaxation together on a rock. With Spaghetti, the image of spaghetti raw or cooked is used in a playful dance of tighten and relax. Several books related to cognitive strategies for mindful meditation include *Moody Cow Meditates* (MacLean, 2009) and *Mindful Monkey, Happy Panda* (Alderfer & MacLean, 2011). A comfort bottle can be created after reading *Moody Cow Meditates*, allowing the child to practice mindfulness meditation. In *Mindful Monkey, Happy Panda*, the panda describes the process of being mindful to the monkey.

Teaching parents strategies for relaxation is important. The parent who learns playful, engaging methods of relaxation can engage the child. If children feel that they must or are being forced to do relaxation, the result is counterproductive. Parents should be encouraged to practice the playful relaxation interventions regularly, at least once per day for a few minutes. The practice should be a fun activity that involves both parent and child. If the child is not interested, the parent can be encouraged to change the activity to something that would be interesting to the child. Parents should also be encouraged to initially use the techniques only when the child is playfully engaged in them. After the child learns how to use the strategy, it may be applied at times when the child has more negative affect.

Affective Expression and Modulation

Often children come to therapy with a limited feelings vocabulary, perhaps limited to *happy*, *sad*, *angry*, and *scared*. Parents may also be limited in their feelings vocabulary. Learning about different feelings and how to identify them in each other is critical. Therapeutic interventions are used to help children understand facial expressions, physiological reactions, and feelings in themselves and others. In addition to learning about the range of feelings, children learn about the intensity of affect. For older children, using subjective units of distress can be beneficial for describing intensity of affect. In school-age children, interventions such as the Feelings Abacus (Cavett, 2010) are used. With the Feelings Abacus, the child uses an abacus constructed to allow for feelings magnets to be used alongside the beads, which are used to show "how much" each feeling is felt by the child.

In cases of extreme trauma, including neglect, the child may need to build affective skills over time. For example, a child who had experienced multiple traumas, including severe neglect as an infant and toddler, could not imitate feelings while playing feelings charades or in other settings. This inability was reflected in his inability to show feelings other than a blank face or anger. Over the course of therapy, he was able to build this skill. First, he played feelings charades with his mother showing feelings, with him guessing the feeling and using a therapeutic toy, Meebie, to show the feeling himself. The Meebie (http://www.orkidtoys.com) is a purple stuffed animal with hook-and-loop detachable facial parts for learning about emotions. Eventually, the child was able to start to imitate the feelings using a mirror to check his facial expression and being coached on how to move parts of his face. Children may also use clay to make faces and mold them into different expressions. The tactile experience allows for deeper integration of the concepts related to affective facial expression.

O'Connor (1983) developed the Color Your Life intervention, which matches colors with feelings. A code is made of color–feeling associations. Gingerbread person cutouts (Drewes, 2001) are used to show the feelings of the child. This intervention may be adapted to have multiple people represented (Gil, 2006). For instance, early in TF-CBT a child may use the Color Your Life intervention to learn about names for feelings while expanding his or her feelings vocabulary. While doing the trauma narrative, the intervention may be used to show the feelings of the child and other people who were involved in or impacted by the trauma.

Sensory-based active interventions related to feelings identification and modulation are essential because experiences, including trauma, are based in the body. Written exercises about feelings limit the depth at which the information is processed to the cognitive level. When actions (play) are not only allowed but encouraged, the child learns about feelings in an integrated manner. Teaching strategies related to identifying and modulating affect through written interventions is limited in several ways. Children typically do not want to do a homework-type task. Worksheet activities also seem limited in that they may have a "right" answer that the child learns for that sheet. It is questionable whether written assignments related to feelings are understood at an emotional level. Play therapy techniques often allow for gross motor movement. These techniques include Feelings Bowling (Cavett, 2009a), Floating Feelings (Dyson, 2010), and Feelings Ring Toss (Cavett, 2009a). With each of these activities, toys such as a ring toss are adapted to represent different feelings. For instance, the red bowling pins in a child's plastic bowling game can reflect anger. When the child gets the ring around the ring toss game or knocks down the pins, the feeling it represents is discussed. Activities such as Hunting for Feelings (Cavett, 2009a), which was developed for a 12-year-old boy who enjoyed hunting (which is culturally normative in rural North Dakota), involved the therapist throwing a Folkmanis puppet such as a turkey into the air or moving a fox among the "bushes" (i.e., baskets of toys) and allowing the child to "hunt" it with an air gun. When he hit his target, he talked about a feeling that the therapist suggested. This child was not impressed with talk about feelings or therapeutic games, but this activity, developed based on his interests, allowed him to feel understood and engaged. TF-CBT allows for culturally sensitive adaptations that allow children to process each of the components.

Several books are available that may be included with play therapy for feelings identification. Such books include *Double-Dip Feelings: Stories to Help Children Understand Emotions* (B. S. Cain, 1990), which describes feeling more than one way at a time, and *The Way I Feel* (J. Cain, 2000), which helps children understand feelings identification.

Cognitive Coping and Processing

Teaching cognitive coping skills begins with a cognitive triangle showing the child the relationships between feeling, thinking, and behaving. This teaching may be done through play therapy techniques such as the Three-Headed Dragon (Drewes, 2011) for young school-age children or the Magnetic Cognitive Triangle (Cavett, 2010). The Three-Headed Dragon allows for teaching about feelings, thoughts, and behaviors using the three heads of a dragon puppet to represent each concept. The Magnetic Cognitive Triangle is created with a magnetic board and magnets representing feelings, thoughts, and behaviors that are manipulated by children in session to describe their experience. When teaching about how the child is impacted by the parent's perceptions and affective experience, the Mirrored Cognitive Triangles (Cavett, in press) intervention may be beneficial. Mirrored Cognitive Triangles shows how the feeling, thinking, and behaving of the parent impacts the child's experience. Kenney-Noziska (2008) developed a fun gross motor intervention to describe the cognitive triangle, which can be seen on Liana

Lowenstein's YouTube channel (Lowenstein, 2014). This activity allows children to learn about the connections between feelings, thinking, and behaving. Interventions such as Positive and Negative Thinking (Kenney-Noziska, 2008) allow understanding of the impact of thoughts. Positive and Negative Thinking involves strips of paper describing thoughts that the child categorizes as positive or negative thoughts in a game format with the help of the therapist. Each of the cognitive coping skills is first used with day-to-day experiences and applied later to trauma narratives.

Trauma Narrative

The child will likely take several sessions to tell of the traumatic experience through the trauma narrative. The child may say it verbally and have the therapist transcribe it or may write or type it himself or herself. The trauma narrative may take the form of a song or rap, poem, play, or scrapbook. Often school-age children are able to express detail through using play to tell their trauma narrative. This play may be done with a time line, sand tray, or dollhouse (to represent a building such as a police station or hospital) and figures. A talking stick may be beneficial for Native American and other children as they tell and process their trauma narrative while creating a talking stick of their life or trauma (BigFoot & Schmidt, 2012). Children may use body drawings to process feelings and their experience during the trauma.

Play therapy interventions such as Rebuilding Mr. or Mrs. Potato Head: Processing Traumatic Sensory Memories (Cavett, 2010) may be used to encourage school-age children to include sensory information in their trauma narratives. In this intervention, the child puts together Mr. or Mrs. Potato Head while describing a sensory experience associated with the trauma. An intervention for helping children learn to tolerate the narrative is Change the Channel (Goodyear-Brown, 2002) through which the child learns cognitive control by drawing pictures of soothing, relaxing scenes and scenes that are more anxiety provoking. The therapist processes changing thoughts as the child uses a remote control and the therapist "changes the channel" using the drawings.

The therapist encourages the child throughout the sharing of the narrative. Having the child discuss the most difficult or upsetting aspects is important because the deeper the trauma narrative is and the more cognitive distortions are expressed, the more cognitive changes can occur. The therapist helps the child clarify the experience, including feelings, thoughts, and sensory experiences. It is important for the therapist to monitor feelings using subjective units of distress throughout the narrative. A strategy such as the Feelings Abacus (Cavett, 2010) may be beneficial in this process. The therapist includes anchoring and relaxation strategies throughout sessions to help the child manage the affective and cognitive experience as the trauma is reexperienced.

The child prepares the narrative with the therapist, repeating what was done in earlier sessions to have mastery over the exposure. As the child plays out scenes, the therapist uses reflective listening and praise. Through the play, the child develops a trauma narrative that is well beyond that which could be done with words. Even simple concepts such as "dad was behind the door waiting for us, and when he heard us talking he came out" are difficult for a child to communicate verbally. However, these concepts are fairly simple to share when they are acted out in the dollhouse, allowing the child to feel heard. When the experiences are understood, they add affective and cognitive elements more than through verbal narratives.

In Vivo Mastery

In vivo mastery of innocuous stimuli is done through an exposure hierarchy. This intervention may involve aspects of play, especially in the early stages when the exposure may be to toys that miniaturize the innocuous stimuli. For instance, for a child afraid of school bathrooms following sexual assault in a school bathroom, the child may begin with exposure to toy buildings that represent schools. Drawing the stimulus is helpful during early exposure. As the child gains mastery, exposure to the real stimulus must occur (i.e., entering a school bathroom). A play therapy intervention Pop Goes the Weasel (Cavett, 2010) helps children learn that they can decrease feelings of anxiety or startle with repeated exposure.

Conjoint Parent–Child Sessions

Eventually the child shares the narrative with the parent. While the child is writing the narrative, the parent is working with the therapist to learn how to support and assist the child when the narrative is shared with the parent.

At this stage of therapy, parents often feel protective of their children, whom they realize have had negative things happen to them. Parents need to feel the therapist is partnering with them to provide a therapeutic experience that is helpful, respectful, and healing. Parents often need assurance that the therapist will hear the child's experience in a way that promotes healing and that this process progresses over many sessions. The therapist–parent team monitors the child's symptoms and responses. The therapist provides information about normative responses to the trauma narrative, including informing the parent that the child's negative behaviors may increase temporarily during development of the trauma narrative. Often children resist therapy at this time. The therapist and parent need to communicate during the process to provide support for continuing the process and strategies to help the child cope with the process in a healthy way. The sharing of the narrative with the parent is typically a very powerful and healing experience.

Enhancing Future Safety

Enhancing future safety is a component that is often done at the end of the therapy sequence with children with a single trauma. This step may be adapted for children with complex trauma or others who need to have safety addressed to promote safety in their environments. Safety includes physical safety but also must include emotional and affective safety. For children in environments where safety is uncertain, such as in families with ongoing domestic violence, helping the parents and community (e.g., social services) ensure safety is critical.

Play therapy interventions for teaching about safety introduce the concept of potential dangers and how to be safe. They teach children responses that promote their safety. Handouts have been a traditional method of teaching children and parents about safety. Developing a written treatment plan has also been a critical component of teaching safety concepts to the child and family. However, few children are engaged by such handouts, and it is questionable whether handouts result in substantial change in children's behaviors or ability to adapt to and promote their own safety. Play therapy interventions allow for child engagement and teach the concepts in a manner that promotes learning the key concepts.

To learn about safety, puppets or dolls may act out different scenarios and react to an emergency or potentially dangerous situation. Repetition through play is more tolerated by children than verbal repetition of safety rules. Repetition through play allows for deeper learning. Role-play through scenarios depicting common human-made and natural disasters allows children to have fun while practicing what they can do. Props such as a director's board or a written script may enhance the activity and ensure that key points are addressed. The termination of TF-CBT may be processed with play therapy interventions such as the Family Shield (Brickell, 2010). The Family Shield is an artistic creation based on symbols that children feel reflects the strengths that they and their family have and the progress made in therapy.

EMPIRICAL SUPPORT

TF-CBT is based on components found necessary in the research on efficacious treatment of children and adolescents who had been traumatized (Cohen et al., 2006). It is the most researched treatment for children who have been traumatized. TF-CBT was found to be more effective than child-centered therapy (Cohen, Deblinger, Mannarino, & Steer, 2004), and studies support maintenance of the results 1 year after treatment (Deblinger, Mannarino, Cohen, & Steer, 2006). There are numerous studies supporting the effectiveness of TF-CBT (Cohen, Deblinger, Mannarino, & Steer, 2004; Cohen & Mannarino, 1996, 1997, 1998; Cohen, Mannarino, & Knudsen, 2005; Deblinger & Heflin, 1996; Deblinger, Lippmann, & Steer, 1996; Deblinger, McLeer, & Henry, 1990; Deblinger, Stauffer, & Steer, 2001; Deblinger, Steer, & Lippmann, 1999; King et al., 2000).

CASE ILLUSTRATION INCLUDING CAREGIVER INVOLVEMENT

Andrew was a 6-year-old biracial (African American–White) boy who was referred by his mother after they went to a domestic violence shelter to escape violence toward both him and his mother by his stepfather. Although the abuse of his mother had been ongoing for several years, his stepfather had recently begun slapping Andrew as well. Andrew had witnessed the violence toward his mother and seemed to have developed a sense of responsibility for protecting her. He began to assert himself verbally and by placing himself between his mother and stepfather. His stepfather had slapped him on two such occasions, telling him that he could not protect his mother and making verbal statements that minimized Andrew's value.

Andrew's mother completed the Child Behavior Checklist, and results showed elevations on the Total Problems score ($T = 71$, > 98th percentile), Externalizing Problems score ($T = 66$, 95th percentile), and Internalizing Problems score ($T = 66$, 95th percentile). His testing was consistent with the presenting problems articulated by his mother in the clinical interview. He met the criteria for oppositional defiant disorder, attention-deficit/hyperactivity disorder (ADHD), and generalized anxiety disorder. He was not referred for medication for ADHD initially, because trauma and change may have resulted in his meeting ADHD criteria. He had symptoms of posttraumatic stress disorder but did not meet criteria for diagnosis using the *Diagnostic and Statistical Manual of Mental Disorders* (5th ed.; American Psychiatric Association, 2013). Andrew's problems with behavior and mood were likely related to his history of trauma, and TF-CBT was implemented.

Andrews's mother was an integral part of therapy. She was able to learn about the expectations for therapy at the beginning of therapy and each of the treatment components throughout. This familiarity was beneficial as it allowed her to use the skills and to reinforce the use of skills by Andrew. Andrew's mother also learned skills directly related to parenting. Like most parents of traumatized children, she felt guilt and shame related to her "allowing" Andrew to be exposed to domestic violence and physical abuse. The

Playful TF-CBT therapist was able to work through some of the concerns she expressed related to her feelings and also referred her to an individual therapist, who worked with her at a deeper level to process her own feelings related to being a victim of domestic violence and herself a survivor of childhood abuses. In part because of her feelings of shame and guilt, she allowed Andrew to "get away with" behaviors that she felt she would have responded to had she not felt guilty about his exposure to abuse. TF-CBT with Andrew's mother allowed her to see that she needed to provide structure, including consequences for his behavior, to offer him a better future. The extremes of *too much* or *not at all* were addressed in the parenting skills sessions with Andrew's mother. Play therapy techniques were also implemented in the parenting component. Andrew's mother learned to appreciate him and hear his voice through structured play therapy interventions.

Psychoeducation included learning about domestic violence and physical abuse. Psychoeducation was woven throughout the therapy as needed because of the need for safety planning. Initially Andrew played My Safe Neighborhood (Cavett, 2010) with the therapist. This activity consisted of acting out different scenarios in the play using toys, including buildings (dollhouse, smaller dollhouse used as a domestic violence shelter, police station, school), toy vehicles (police cars, ambulances, school buses), and doll figures. His mother worked with the therapist and a domestic violence staff member to construct a safety plan, and elements of it were shared through the play with Andrew. Toward the end of therapy, Andrew read *When Mommy Got Hurt* (Lee & Sylwester, 1996) to discuss his feelings about domestic violence and how to stay safe.

Play therapy was instrumental in teaching relaxation skills to Andrew. He and the therapist read the book *Moody Cow Meditates* (MacLean, 2009) and made a relaxation bottle together. They constructed an Anger Menu (Cavett, 2010) to discuss ways he could express his anger that were acceptable and to explore relaxation and meditation strategies that worked for him. His therapist used a dragon puppet (Folkmanis) to act out Drakley the Dragon Says (Belknap, 2006), a playful progressive muscle relaxation script that he not only did but enjoyed.

Andrew's mother practiced several strategies with him, and he was able to choose which one he used each day for their special relax-and-unwind time. He learned about feelings identification in himself and others using feelings charades and movable hook-and-loop facial features (e.g., angry eyes, closed eyes, tears, scars) on a Meebie therapeutic toy. His mother practiced reflective listening with him and was able to learn to manage her own affective responses when he had sad and angry feelings. Andrew and his therapist played a Cognitive Coping game (Lowenstein, 2014) to learn about how feelings, thoughts, and behaviors are connected and impact each other.

Andrew first did a verbal narrative that was fairly brief:

> My name is Andrew, and I am 6 years old. I like to play video games. My favorite food is chicken nuggets. I live with my mom. We live in a shelter. My dad hit her. Now we cannot see him. He was mean to us.

As he was able to use play, he was able to expand his narrative. His therapist, who was transcribing his narrative, checked in with him, verbally reflecting what he showed in his play and having him provide any feedback or correction to what she observed. For example, he played that his dad was lying on the couch and mentioned that the TV was on. His therapist noted this, stating, "Your dad was lying on the couch watching TV." He corrected her, saying, "No, he wasn't watching TV. The TV was on, but he was sleeping then."

The therapist and Andrew reviewed his previous narrative each session, and he acted out the scenes, adding more depth by including more of his feelings, thoughts, and sensory experiences. His trauma narrative then included the previous portion and a new portion that he played out each session. After several times of playing out the narrative, the therapist asked him to add his feelings and thoughts at times during his playing out of the narrative. She asked him, "What were you feeling when [an event occurred (e.g., your mom pointed at the protein bars)]?"

As the narrative was read again during the fifth narrative development session, the therapist asked Andrew what he was feeling and thinking and added his feelings and thoughts to the narrative. The final version of the narrative follows; the timing of the therapist's prompts about feelings (F) and thoughts (T) are noted (sentences with no notation were spontaneously noted by Andrew):

> My name is Andrew, and I am 6 years old. I like to play video games. My favorite food is chicken nuggets. I live with my mom. We live in a shelter. My dad hit my mom. Now we cannot see him. He was mean to us, and he hurt us. This is the worst time he hurt us: I was playing with Bear [the dog] in my room. (F) I was happy and calm. (T) I like playing with Bear. *[Andrew used dolls and the dollhouse to act out the following events while talking through the trauma.]*
>
> Mom was sleeping, but she got up. Dad was on the couch sleeping with the TV on. Mom came into my room and told me that I had better be quiet. I told her that I was hungry. She said that we didn't have any cereal. She went into the kitchen. She said, "Andrew, come here." I went into the kitchen and saw what she was pointing at. (F) I felt worried. I ate the protein bars when she was sleeping. The wrappers and crumbs were on the table. I told her that I was hungry. She said, "You know that dad will get mad if you eat his protein bars." (F) I felt worried and scared. Dad

woke up and came into the kitchen. (F) I felt scared. I think, "He is going to hurt my mom." He was yelling, "Shut the — up! I told you I was tired. You never do what I tell you to do, and I can never get any sleep here! Maybe I need to sleep somewhere else." (F) I felt worried and scared and wanted to hide. (T) I wanted to hide, and I thought, "I think he is going to hurt me and mom. I hope he does not see the protein bar."

He looked around the kitchen and saw that I ate his protein bars. My mom tried to stand in front of the food. She didn't want him to see it. I felt worried. (T) I thought he was going to hurt her. He pushed my mom and said, "That little — keeps eating my food!" (F) I felt bad that it was my fault he was going to hurt her. If I would not have eaten them, he would still be sleeping. My mom tried to tell him to calm down and told him that I could eat food. (F) I felt worried because he was still mad. He punched her in the mouth. I felt angry and upset and scared. (T) I thought, "I need to keep her safe. He is going to hurt her. It is my fault because I didn't be good." I tried to step between them and told him, "Don't hurt mommy!" but he kept hitting her. I felt mad. He yelled, "You are just a little piece of —." I felt hurt and scared and sad. He pushed me and I fell back. (F) I felt worried. (T) I thought, "I wish I would not have made him mad." My mom tried to stand in between us, and he hit her again. She was crying and screaming. I felt sad. He stomped by her and slapped me. (F) I felt angry and sad. He went back into his room and slammed the door. (F) I felt mad and angry at him. My mom sat and cried. I felt sad and worried. I thought, "I can't take care of her. He hurt her."

The depth of a trauma narrative with play allows for greater sharing of what happened and how the child experienced it. Play allows the child to think through the experience and re-create it with toys, which allows for a sensory experience that seems to facilitate verbalizations as well. However, it also carries an intensity of experience and emotion that require the clinician to be able to tolerate the telling of the narrative, sensitivity and compassion to empathize and support the child, and clinical skills to help the child process the experience. Often trauma narratives are brief and lack detail if the child does not feel the therapist can "handle" hearing (or seeing in play) the child's experience. The gradual exposure to the domestic violence played out in miniature in therapy allowed Andrew some mastery over the experience.

Andrew used the play therapy intervention Cognitive Triangle (Lowenstein, 2014) to discuss feelings, thoughts, and behaviors early in therapy. This intervention was used to help him explore trauma-specific thoughts as well. His mother listened to his narrative, and they discussed the roles in the family. His mother was able to assure him that parents feed children and that although boundaries can be set around people having some food or other items that they do not need to share, his breaking that rule did not mean his dad had the right to hurt him or his mother. They discussed times she had to set limits with him in the past week and how she could give consequences that were appropriate without being abusive.

A Best Friend puppet show was used to explore self- and other blaming. In the puppet show, different scenarios were discussed, and who was to blame for them was identified. Several scenarios included his best friend (in puppet form) doing things both positive and negative. Andrew acknowledged that the behaviors his best friend was responsible for included only his own behavior. Andrew was able to say that he knew his best friend would not be to blame if his own father hit him, even if the friend had done something wrong.

Andrew and his mother played the Safe Neighborhood intervention again and specifically explored who would help with certain safety scenarios. He and his mother constructed a Family Shield discussing how they were there for each other and how his mother was responsible for keeping him safe. They noted other adults who supported them, including staff at the shelter and the police and judge who signed a restraining order. They were able to identify several family strengths, including having a sense of humor and loving and respecting each other.

CONCLUSION AND FUTURE DIRECTIONS

TF-CBT with play therapy interventions allows clinicians to use the most empirically supported treatment in a developmentally sensitive manner. The TF-CBT components (Psychoeducation, Parenting Skills, Relaxation, Affective Expression and Modulation, Cognitive Coping and Processing, Trauma Narrative, In Vivo Mastery, Conjoint Parent–Child Sessions, and Enhancing Future Safety) were based on factors supported by research on effective treatment of children.

School-age children benefit from therapy that allows them deeper expression of feelings, thoughts, and experiences. They also develop a better understanding of coping skills (e.g., relaxation) when the techniques are fun, engaging, and active. Often current treatment of childhood trauma uses child-centered play therapy. Over the course of the future, collaboration between the TF-CBT and play therapy fields will likely allow for abundant play therapy techniques to be included and appreciated by those researching treatment for children who have been traumatized. Play therapists will likely benefit from understanding the research that was the foundation for TF-CBT and ways the model may inform their practices. Bridges between researchers and clinicians will likely result in better treatments for children.

REFERENCES

Achenbach, T. M. (1991). *Manual for the Child Behavior Checklist/4–18 and 1991 profile*. Burlington: University of Vermont, Department of Psychiatry.

Alderfer, L., & MacLean, K. L. (2011). *Mindful monkey, happy panda*. Somerville, MA: Wisdom.

American Psychiatric Association. (2013). *Diagnostic and statistical manual of mental disorders* (5th ed.). Washington, DC: Author.

Belknap, M. (2006). *Stress relief for kids: Taming your dragons*. Duluth, MN: Whole Person Associates.

BigFoot, D. S., & Schmidt, S. R. (2012). American Indian and Alaska Native children: Honoring children—mending the circle. In J. A. Cohen, A. P. Mannarino, & E. Deblinger (Eds.), *Trauma-focused CBT for children and adolescents: Treatment applications* (pp. 280–300). New York, NY: Guilford Press.

Brickell, N. (2010). Family Shield. In L. Lowenstein (Ed.), *Creative family therapy techniques: Play, art, and expressive activities to engage children in family sessions* (pp. 289–292). Toronto, Ontario, Canada: Champion Press.

Cain, B. S. (1990). *Double-dip feelings: Stories to help children understand emotions*. Washington, DC: American Psychological Association.

Cain, J. (2000). *The way I feel*. New York, NY: Scholastic.

Cavett, A. M. (in press). *Play-based cognitive–behavioral therapy interventions for children*. West Conshohocken, PA: Infinity Press.

Cavett, A. M. (2009a, October). *Playful trauma-focused cognitive behavioral therapy*. Paper presented at the Association for Play Therapy International Conference, Atlanta, GA.

Cavett, A. M. (2009b). Playful trauma-focused cognitive behavioral therapy with maltreated children and adolescents. *Play Therapy*, *4*, 20–22.

Cavett, A. M. (2009c, September). *Playful trauma-focused cognitive behavioral therapy with traumatized children*. Retrieved from http://www.lianalowenstein.com/cavett.pdf

Cavett, A. M. (2010). *Structured play-based interventions for engaging children and adolescents in therapy*. West Conshohocken, PA: Infinity Press.

Cavett, A. M., & Drewes, A. (2012). Play applications and trauma-specific components for young children. In J. A. Cohen, A. P. Mannarino, & E. Deblinger (Eds.), *Trauma-focused CBT for children and adolescents: Treatment applications* (pp. 124–148). New York, NY: Guilford Press.

Cohen, J. A., Deblinger, E., Mannarino, A. P., & Steer, R. A. (2004). A multisite, randomized controlled trial for children with sexual abuse-related PTSD symptoms. *Journal of the American Academy of Child & Adolescent Psychiatry*, *43*, 393–402. http://dx.doi.org/10.1097/00004583-200404000-00005

Cohen, J. A., & Mannarino, A. P. (1996). A treatment outcome study for sexually abused preschool children: Initial findings. *Journal of the American Academy of*

Child & Adolescent Psychiatry, 35, 42–50. http://dx.doi.org/10.1097/00004583-199601000-00011

Cohen, J. A., & Mannarino, A. P. (1997). A treatment study for sexually abused preschool children: Outcome during a one-year follow-up. *Journal of the American Academy of Child & Adolescent Psychiatry, 36*, 1228–1235. http://dx.doi.org/10.1097/00004583-199709000-00015

Cohen, J. A., & Mannarino, A. P. (1998). Interventions for sexually abused children: Initial treatment findings. *Child Maltreatment, 3*, 17–26. http://dx.doi.org/10.1177/1077559598003001002

Cohen, J. A., Mannarino, A. P., & Deblinger, E. (2006). *Treating trauma and traumatic grief in children and adolescents*. New York, NY: Guilford Press.

Cohen, J. A., Mannarino, A. P., & Knudsen, K. (2005). Treating sexually abused children: 1 year follow-up of a randomized controlled trial. *Child Abuse & Neglect, 29*, 135–145. http://dx.doi.org/10.1016/j.chiabu.2004.12.005

Cohen, J. A., Mannarino, A. P., & Navarro, D. (2012). Residential treatment. In J. A. Cohen, A. P. Mannarino, & E. Deblinger (Eds.), *Trauma-focused CBT for children and adolescents: Treatment applications* (pp. 73–102). New York, NY: Guilford Press.

Deblinger, E., & Heflin, A. H. (1996). *Treating sexually abused children and their nonoffending parents: A cognitive behavioral approach*. Thousand Oaks, CA: Sage.

Deblinger, E., Lippmann, J., & Steer, R. (1996). Sexually abused children suffering posttraumatic stress symptoms: Initial treatment outcome findings. *Child Maltreatment, 1*, 310–321. http://dx.doi.org/10.1177/1077559596001004003

Deblinger, E., Mannarino, A. P., Cohen, J. A., & Steer, R. A. (2006). A follow-up study of a multisite, randomized, controlled trial for children with sexual abuse-related PTSD symptoms. *Journal of the American Academy of Child & Adolescent Psychiatry, 45*, 1474–1484. http://dx.doi.org/10.1097/01.chi.0000240839.56114.bb

Deblinger, E., McLeer, S. V., & Henry, D. (1990). Cognitive behavioral treatment for sexually abused children suffering post-traumatic stress: Preliminary findings. *Journal of the American Academy of Child & Adolescent Psychiatry, 29*, 747–752. http://dx.doi.org/10.1097/00004583-199009000-00012

Deblinger, E., Stauffer, L. B., & Steer, R. A. (2001). Comparative efficacies of supportive and cognitive behavioral group therapies for young children who have been sexually abused and their nonoffending mothers. *Child Maltreatment, 6*, 332–343. http://dx.doi.org/10.1177/1077559501006004006

Deblinger, E., Steer, R. A., & Lippmann, J. (1999). Two-year follow-up study of cognitive behavioral therapy for sexually abused children suffering posttraumatic stress symptoms. *Child Abuse & Neglect, 23*, 1371–1378. http://dx.doi.org/10.1016/S0145-2134(99)00091-5

Drewes, A. A. (2001). Gingerbread Person Feelings Map. In H. G. Kaduson & C. E. Schaefer (Eds.), *101 more favorite play therapy techniques* (pp. 92–97). New York, NY: Jason Aronson.

Drewes, A. A. (2011, April). A *skill-building workshop: Effectively blending play-based techniques with cognitive behavioral therapy for affect regulation in sexually abused and traumatized children*. Paper presented at the annual conference of the Canadian Association for Child and Play Therapy, Guelph, Ontario, Canada.

Drewes, A. A., & Cavett, A. M. (2012). Play applications and skills components. In J. A. Cohen, A. P. Mannarino, & E. Deblinger (Eds.), *Trauma-focused CBT for children and adolescents: Treatment applications* (pp. 105–123). New York, NY: Guilford Press.

Dyson, P. (2010). Floating Feelings. In L. Lowenstein (Ed.), *Assessment and treatment activities for children, adolescents, and families: Volume 2. Practitioners share their most effective techniques*. Toronto, Ontario, Canada: Champion Press.

Gil, E. (2006). *Helping abused and traumatized children: Integrating directive and non-directive approaches*. New York, NY: Guilford Press.

Goodyear-Brown, P. (2002). *Digging for buried treasure: 52 prop-based play therapy interventions for treating the problems of childhood*. Nashville, TN: Author.

Goodyear-Brown, P. (2005). *Digging for buried treasure 2: 52 more prop-based play therapy interventions for treating the problems of childhood*. Nashville, TN: Author.

Hoch-Espada, A. (2007). *Using TF-CBT with complex trauma*. Retrieved from http://mediasite.nctsn.org/NCTSN/Viewer/?peid=a097ce39-3d62-45d9-abde-4f19e160af20

Ippen, C. G., Ford, J., Racusin, R., Acker, M., Bosquet, M., Rogers, K., . . . Edwards, J. (2002). *Traumatic Events Screening Inventory—Parent Report Revised*. Washington, DC: National Center for PTSD & Dartmouth Child Trauma Research Group.

Kenney-Noziska, S. (2008). *Techniques, techniques, techniques: Play-based activities for children, adolescents, and families*. West Conshohocken, PA: Infinity Press.

King, N. J., Tonge, B. J., Mullen, P., Myerson, N., Heyne, D., Rollings, S., . . . Ollendick, T. H. (2000). Treating sexually abused children with posttraumatic stress symptoms: A randomized clinical trial. *Journal of the American Academy of Child & Adolescent Psychiatry, 39*, 1347–1355. http://dx.doi.org/10.1097/00004583-200011000-00008

Knell, S. M. (1992). *Puppet Sentence Completion Task*. Unpublished manuscript.

Knell, S. M., & Beck, K. W. (2000). The Puppet Sentence Completion Task. In K. J. O'Connor & C. E. Schaefer (Eds.), *Handbook of play therapy: Vol. 2. Advances and innovations* (pp. 704–721). New York, NY: Wiley.

Lee, I., & Sylwester, K. (1996). *When Mommy got hurt: A story for young children about domestic violence*. Oakland, CA: Storymine Press.

Lite, L. (1996). *A boy and a bear*. Plantation, FL: Specialty Press.

Lowenstein, L. (2006). *Creative interventions for bereaved children*. Toronto, Ontario, Canada: Champion Press.

Lowenstein, L. (2014). *Helpful thoughts: CBT activity*. Retrieved from https://www.youtube.com/watch?v=VNHPxkT0wIg&list=UU8GvOEKqaxtrHUzBSMGHCsg

MacLean, K. L. (2009). *Moody cow meditates*. Boston, MA: Wisdom.

O'Connor, K. J. (1983). The Color-Your-Life technique. In C. E. Schaefer & K. J. O'Connor (Eds.), *Handbook of play therapy* (pp. 251–258). New York, NY: Wiley.

Rivera, S. (2012). Schools. In J. A. Cohen, A. P. Mannarino, & E. Deblinger (Eds.), *Trauma-focused CBT for children and adolescents: Treatment applications* (pp. 29–48). New York, NY: Guilford Press.

Sheppard, C. G. (1998). *Brave Bart: A story for traumatized and grieving children*. Grosse Pointe Woods, MI: National Institute for Trauma and Loss in Children.

4

USE OF PRETEND PLAY TO OVERCOME ANXIETY IN SCHOOL-AGE CHILDREN

SANDRA W. RUSS AND KARLA K. FEHR

One of the earliest uses of pretend play in therapy was to reduce anxiety in children. Anna Freud (1927) used play as a way for children to express fears and resolve conflicts that caused anxiety. Her conceptualization was from a psychoanalytic tradition. Since that time, play has been used in therapy from different theoretical frameworks such as client-centered therapy and cognitive–behavioral approaches. Recently, therapists have been using play in ways that integrate different theories and techniques. Research supports these integrated approaches. We think that integration of approaches is a trend of the future, and in this chapter we present a case that illustrates an integrated approach to separation anxiety in a child.

http://dx.doi.org/10.1037/14776-005
Play Therapy in Middle Childhood, A. A. Drewes and C. E. Schaefer (Editors)

BASIC RATIONALE AND THEORY

Psychoanalytic and psychodynamic approaches view the play process as a way for children to reduce anxiety. According to Chethik (1989), the psychodynamic therapist first sets the stage for therapy by describing how play will be used for communication. As children come to feel safe in the situation, "meaningful" play is developed in which children express more of their affective life. Central fantasies emerge, often associated with anxiety, with some themes being repeated over and over, allowing for an unpleasant experience to be "digested" until it becomes manageable and anxiety is reduced (Erikson, 1963; Wälder, 1933). Kessler (1988) pointed out that one of the great legacies of the psychoanalytic tradition is the use of play in psychotherapy.

Pretend play has been incorporated into various other therapeutic approaches. For example, in client-centered play therapy, the therapist expresses an empathic understanding of the child's experience and frame of reference as expressed in his or her pretend play and communicates this to the child (Gaylin, 1999). In cognitive–behavioral play therapy (CBPT), cognitive and behavioral interventions are incorporated within a play therapy paradigm in which different scenarios that are relevant to the child's issues are presented to the child, and with modeling and rehearsal, the child is taught problem-solving skills and alternative behaviors (Knell, 1993a). In trauma-focused cognitive–behavioral therapy (CBT), pretend play is used to help the child imagine scenes for relaxation and to reenact traumatic experiences (Briggs, Runyon, & Deblinger, 2011).

Across these different approaches, four broad functions of play emerge as a vehicle for bringing about change in therapy (Russ, 2004; Russ & Fehr, 2013). First, because play is a natural way for emotion to be expressed, children in therapy can use pretend play to communicate troubling and conflict-laden feelings. Second, the therapist actively labels, accepts, empathizes with, and interprets the play expressions, which in turn helps the child feel understood and promotes the development of a therapeutic relationship with the child (Russ, 1995). For many children, the feeling of empathy from the therapist around the play facilitates change in their internal representations and interpersonal functioning.

A third major function of play, particularly from a psychodynamic perspective, is as a vehicle for insight and working through. In therapy, children reexperience major developmental or situational traumas that are expressed in play. During this process, the therapist labels the play and ties observations and interpretations to events in the child's life. The emotional resolution of conflict or trauma and negative feelings is a major mechanism of change. In many cases, especially with young children, cognitive insight does not occur.

As Messer and Warren (1995) suggested, emotional reexperiencing and emotional working through are responsible for changes in internal feelings and behavior.

A fourth major function of play in therapy is to provide the child opportunities to practice a variety of ideas, behaviors, interpersonal behaviors, and verbal expressions. Because the pretending is occurring in a safe environment with a permissive, nonjudgmental adult, the child can try out and rehearse expressions and behaviors without concern about real-life consequences. In addition, pretend play allows children to express scenarios that are important to them but are distanced a little through the pretend world (e.g., "The puppet is angry with Dad, but I am not angry with Dad"). Children can alter narratives in play and change the outcome of traumatic events. In some forms of play therapy, the therapist is quite directive in guiding the child to try new behaviors. For example, Knell (1993a) developed a CBPT approach that actively uses modeling techniques and a variety of cognitive–behavioral techniques.

DEVELOPMENTAL ISSUES

During normal development, children experience a variety of age- and stage-relevant tasks (Toth & Cicchetti, 1999). Many of these tasks and developmental issues are accompanied by fears and anxiety. The content of fears changes as children get older. Many of these fears are developmentally based fears that most children experience, such as concerns about experiencing loss, being hurt, being tested in school, or not being liked. Other fears and anxiety can emerge after external traumatic events such as illness, divorce, or an accident. Play is one way in which children can express and master these fears and anxiety. Children use play to develop problem-solving skills and to process emotions (Russ, 2004, 2014). Therapists can use these play processes to help children whose fears and anxieties are outside of the normal range.

Play also follows a developmental sequence. Children begin to discover pretend play around the age of 2 years (Hirsh-Pasek & Golinkoff, 2003). Children at this age begin to use objects in ways that are different from their usual uses. A button can become a flying saucer, or a block can become a telephone. Belsky and Most (1981) pointed out that play follows developmental stages in which a child moves from reacting to characteristics of objects to exploring objects to using objects symbolically. Pretend play becomes more frequent during the preschool years of ages 4 and 5.

As children become older, their play becomes more complex. Children engage in pretend play until 9 and 10 years of age. Dansky (1999) thought that in high-level play, children display many types of thinking, such as fantasy, metaphor, and problem solving. He theorized that acting in an "as if" frame in pretend play enables the child to engage in a mode of problem solving beneficial to the child. There are many individual differences in play ability. Using a measure of play, the Affect in Play Scale, with a variety of populations of children ages 4 to 10 years, we found many individual differences in the ability to pretend, use imagination, use fantasy, and express emotion in play (see Russ, 2014, for a review). In general, the better the child's ability to pretend and express feelings in play, the more able he or she is to use play to resolve problems and reduce fears.

MECHANISMS OF CHANGE TO REDUCE ANXIETY

How does play help a child reduce fears and anxiety? What occurs during the play experience that helps children process and manage negative emotions? There are several possible mechanisms at work.

In normal development and in child psychotherapy, children use pretend play to manage negative emotions. What are the cognitive–affective mechanisms that enable anxiety to be reduced in this way? According to D. G. Singer and Singer (1990), pretend play is reinforcing when it permits expression of positive affect and the appropriate control of negative affect. Research by Golomb and Galasso (1995) supports this idea. In a study with preschoolers, they found that when the affective valence of an imagined situation was negative, children would modify the theme to diminish their fear, such as imagining a friendly monster. In a positive affect situation, they concluded, children monitor and regulate affect in pretend play so as not to exceed a certain threshold while still having enough emotional involvement to enjoy the play.

Referring to Tomkins's (1970) concept of miniaturization, J. L. Singer (1995) asserted that pretend play helps children "cut down the large things around it to manageable proportions" (p. 191). By creating manageable situations in a pretend, safe setting, negative emotions can be expressed. J. L. Singer proposed that children can then increase positive affect and reduce negative affect through play. This conceptualization fits with the idea that play is one way in which children learn to regulate their emotions. Similarly, Strayhorn (2002) described fantasy rehearsal as helping children build up habit strength for the handling of conflict situations. In this view, a child can reduce fears and anxiety around separation and other issues by acting out adaptive ways of handling the separation and feelings around it in pretend play situations.

In child therapy, the therapist uses these natural play processes in a safe setting where the play can be guided. Some forms of therapy have a great deal of structure and guidance, and others follow the lead of the child. Exposure to negative emotions that the child has been avoiding is central to cognitive–behavioral treatments. Pretend play is one way that children can gain exposure in a controlled manner to these emotions and painful memories. Therapists who work with children with posttraumatic stress disorder (PTSD) or with traumatized backgrounds offer many clinical descriptions of the effective use of play to help children integrate traumatic experiences (Gil, 1991; D. G. Singer, 1993; Terr, 1990). Extinction of the fear and anxiety occurs over time.

In psychodynamic therapy approaches, the emotional reexperiencing and working through process involves more than extinction of emotion. It involves building a meaningful narrative around the emotion or trauma (Gaensbauer & Siegel, 1995). In addition, insight is applied to particular experiences and behaviors (Shapiro, Friedberg, & Bardenstein, 2006). Developing a coherent narrative was central to the structured play techniques used by Gaensbauer and Siegel (1995) with very young children who had experienced trauma. They thought that the mechanisms of change when play is used are similar to mechanisms of change in older children with PTSD. With young children, the therapist actively structures the play to re-create the traumatic event. Play then enables the child to organize fragmented experiences into meaningful narratives. The interpretive work by the therapist helps the child understand the personal meanings of the trauma. Also, there is a desensitization of the anxiety and fear and other negative emotions associated with trauma.

In their work with traumatized children, Gaensbauer and Siegel (1995) used toys that were relevant to the trauma for each particular child. For example, if the child had been in a car accident, they used cars, a hospital room, and so forth and asked the child to play out "what happens next." The therapist was active in acting out the events while being soothing and comforting. The parents were often involved in the reenactments as well. According to Gaensbauer and Siegel, these children would "repeatedly return to play vehicles that provide them an opportunity to express their unresolved feelings" (p. 303). They stressed that the key element that enables the child to use the play adaptively, rather than in a repetitive fashion, is the "degree to which the affects can be brought to the surface so that the child can identify them and integrate them in more adaptive ways" (p. 297).

Another mechanism of change is a corrective emotional experience. The relationship between the therapist and child is especially important for a corrective emotional experience to occur. Often, the child's learned expectations are not met when the therapist accepts the child's feelings and thoughts expressed in play. For example, a doll expresses anger to the mother doll, but the therapist, contrary to the child's expectations, is not angry or punishing. Rather, the therapist is accepting of the feelings and works to understand the reasons for the anger. After a number of these therapeutic events, a corrective emotional experience occurs (Kessler, 1966). The automatic connection between angry thoughts or feelings and anxiety or guilt gradually decreases (or extinguishes), and the child then becomes more comfortable with these feelings and thoughts. With some children, the therapist is directive and helps the child think about alternative ways of viewing a situation and generating problem-solving strategies, sometimes by role-playing and modeling coping strategies (D. G. Singer, 1993). Although this mechanism of change is not often associated with psychodynamic therapy, it is frequently part of an intervention within a psychodynamic conceptualization of a case (Shapiro et al., 2006). Whether the mechanism of change is exposure and desensitization, developing a new narrative around the event, developing new problem-solving strategies, or developing insight and working through, reducing fears and anxiety is an important therapeutic goal for many children.

PLAY INTERVENTION PROCEDURES AND SETTINGS

Play interventions usually occur in a private space—in a clinic, hospital, school, or private office setting. Age-appropriate toys are available. In more directive, structured approaches, the toys are relevant to the problem. For example, anxiety about hospitalization would include hospital- and medical-related toys as well as more unstructured toys (e.g., Legos, human and animal figures, dollhouse). The techniques used by the therapist may include reflection, summary statements, modeling of solutions, expression of feelings, and interpretation, depending on the therapeutic approach. In more directive, short-term approaches, the play is guided with active interventions by the therapist. However, in any approach, the therapist must be careful not to be so directive that the child becomes inhibited.

In real-world therapy today, the therapy is often an integrated approach, using techniques from a variety of theoretical traditions. A different mix of techniques provides the ability to tailor the therapy to the needs of the individual child. Examples of these techniques are given in the case example later in this chapter.

EMPIRICAL SUPPORT

Research has determined that focused play interventions can successfully reduce anxiety in children. Although the studies showing that focused play interventions reduce anxiety have not investigated the mechanisms that underlie the anxiety reduction, they point the way for research and practice. In two such studies, puppet play was used to reduce anxiety in children facing surgery (see Phillips, 1985). Johnson and Stockdale (1975) found less anxiety (as assessed using palmar sweat index level) for children in the puppet play group both before and after surgery. Similarly, Cassell (1965) found that anxiety was reduced before surgery for a puppet play group compared with a no-treatment control group. Although there were no differences in anxiety after the surgery, children in the puppet play group were less disturbed during the cardiac catheterization and were more willing to return to the hospital for further treatment.

An important study by Rae, Worchel, Upchurch, Sanner, and Daniel (1989) investigated the effects of play on the adjustment of 46 children hospitalized for acute illness. Children were randomly assigned to one of four experimental groups:

- In the therapeutic play condition, children were encouraged to play with medical and nonmedical materials. Verbal support, reflection, and interpretation of feelings were expressed by the research assistant.
- In the diversionary play condition, children were allowed to play with toys, but fantasy play was discouraged. The toys provided did not facilitate fantasy, nor did the research assistant.
- In the verbally oriented support condition, children were encouraged to talk about feelings and anxieties. The research assistant was directive in bringing up related topics and asked about procedures.
- In the control condition, the research assistant had no contact with the children.

All treatment conditions consisted of two 30-minute sessions. The main result was that children in the therapeutic play group showed significantly greater reduction in self-reported hospital-related fears than the other three groups. Because this study had comparison groups that controlled for non-fantasy-based play, as well as verbal expression with an understanding adult, one can conclude with more certainty that the fantasy play was the element that helped the child deal with the fears (Rae et al., 1989).

Focused play interventions have also been effective in reducing separation anxiety in children. In a carefully controlled study, Milos and Reiss (1982) used play interventions with 64 preschoolers who were rated as highly separation anxious by their teachers. The children were randomly assigned to one of four groups: three play groups—(a) a free-play group with appropriate toys, (b) a directed-play group with a scene set with the mother doll bringing the child to school, and (c) a modeling group in which the experimenter played out a separation scene—and (d) a control group who played with toys that were irrelevant to separation scenes (e.g., blocks, puzzles, crayons). All children received three individual 10-minute play sessions on different days. The results showed that all three thematic play groups were effective in reducing separation anxiety when compared with the control group. An interesting finding was that when the free-play and directed-play groups were combined, the quality of play rating was significantly negatively related to a posttest anxiety rating ($r = -.37$).

Barnett (1984) also looked at separation anxiety and expanded on the work of Barnett and Storm (1981) in which free play was found to reduce distress in children following a conflict situation. In Barnett's study, a natural stressor was used—the first day of school. Seventy-four preschool children were observed separating from their mothers and were rated as high anxiety or low anxiety. These two groups were further divided into a free-play condition and a no-play condition in which the children listened to a story. Half of the play session was solitary and half was with other children; the story condition was split in a similar way. Play was rated by observers and categorized in terms of types of play. Anxiety was measured by the palmar sweat index. The main result was that play significantly reduced anxiety in the high-anxiety group and had no effect for the low-anxiety group. For the high-anxiety children, solitary play was best in reducing anxiety. High-anxiety children spent more time in fantasy play than did low-anxiety children, who showed more functional and manipulative play. Barnett interpreted these findings to mean that play was used to cope with a distressing situation. These findings supported her idea that it is not social play that is essential to conflict resolution, but rather imaginative play qualities that the child introduces into playful behavior. The presence of peers increased anxiety in the high-anxiety group (Barnett, 1984).

These play intervention studies suggest that pretend play helps children reduce fears and anxieties and that there is something about play itself that serves as a vehicle for change. In therapy approaches that have a strong empirical base, such as trauma-focused CBT, the play component has not been isolated in the research (Briggs et al., 2011). Russ and Niec (2011) concluded that evidence-based approaches do integrate play into therapy, but the play element itself has not been isolated and evaluated. However, the positive results of the rigorous play intervention studies just reviewed suggest that the play components of these therapies are central to anxiety reduction.

Kazdin (1990) recommended that the field of child psychotherapy needs to consider combining treatment approaches if optimal results are to be obtained. Integrating play techniques from various approaches into targeted play interventions that focus on specific problems would be a good way forward in the play intervention area (Russ, 2004). Specific play modules could also be part of an overall therapy package. In author Russ's research program at Case Western Reserve University, we have been developing focused play intervention protocols that target specific kinds of problems, such as school anxiety (Pearson, 2008), sleep problems (Fehr, Russ, & Ievers-Landis, 2014), or constricted affect and imagination (Hoffmann, 2012; Moore & Russ, 2008). These interventions incorporate different play techniques, story stems, and toys that are relevant to the specific problem.

CASE EXAMPLE: COGNITIVE–BEHAVIORAL PLAY THERAPY FOR ANXIETY REGARDING SCHOOL ENTRY

The following case example describes a targeted play intervention for a child with separation anxiety carried out by author Fehr. It is based on cognitive–behavioral play therapy, which itself is an integrated approach. CBPT was developed for very young children (ages 2½–6 years) as children this young are often unable to verbalize their anxieties. However, we suggest that this protocol may be appropriate for use with school-age children up to 10 years old depending on the sensitivity of the topic and the difficulty children might have in directly discussing the situation.

Chase was an 8-year-old boy whose parents brought him to treatment because of separation anxiety. According to his parents, Chase was able to cope well with expected, daily separations. He attended school with no difficulties and was able to play at his friends' houses. However, he would become distressed when separation was unexpected. For example, his parents reported a recent situation at the grocery store in which Chase had become extremely distressed when his mother had turned a corner without him noticing. When he turned around, she was out of his sight, and he had been unable to be independent in the grocery store since that time. Further, they noted that initiation of separation was difficult at times, especially if the separation was to be for an extended period of time. Specifically, Chase was unable to walk independently into the school building, although he separated with no difficulties if a parent or teacher accompanied him into the building. He was also unable to spend the night at anyone else's house, including extended family.

Given the multiple concerns regarding separation anxiety, a cognitive–behavioral approach to treatment was initiated with particular emphasis on psychoeducation regarding anxiety, relaxation strategies, exposure challenges (i.e., practicing unexpected separations through playing hide-and-seek, having Chase practice turning around and then having his parent step out of sight, practicing sleeping at his grandparents' house while his parent slept in another room in the same house), and parental management and response to anxiety.

Although four to five sessions of CBT was effective at encouraging more age-appropriate independent sleeping behaviors and decreasing distress when Chase did not immediately see his parents, Chase remained unable to independently walk into school. When exposures were attempted, Chase became very distressed and remained in the car crying until someone walked him into the building. Further, Chase became increasingly avoidant in therapy sessions to discussing this topic. By the fifth session, when discussions about his thoughts and potential challenges to walking into school were attempted, Chase avoided responding in any way to his parents or the therapist and instead played or fiddled with the toys available in the room until the conversation was changed. At this point, a cognitive–behavioral play approach was initiated.

CBPT is a developmentally appropriate approach that uses cognitive–behavioral principles within pretend play and is recommended when children need to learn coping strategies or when the child's involvement in therapy is deemed important (Knell, 1993a, 1998). Successful case studies have described implementation of CBPT for children with selective mutism (Knell, 1993a, 1993c), phobias (Knell, 1993a; Knell & Dasari, 2009a), separation anxiety (Knell, 1993b; Knell & Dasari, 2009b), and encopresis (Knell, 1993a; Knell & Moore, 1990) and with children who have experienced traumatic life events such as divorce (Knell, 1993a) and sexual abuse (Knell & Ruma, 1996; Ruma, 1993). Some of the approaches described in case studies included both a CBPT child component and a behavioral parent management component, suggesting that including both child and parent treatment components may be a successful approach (e.g., Knell & Moore, 1990).

Based on CBPT principles, Pearson (2008) developed a three-session cognitive–behavioral play intervention (CBPI) that was effective at decreasing preschoolers' school anxiety compared with children in an active control group that played with puzzles and coloring sheets. This protocol was also adapted to create a structured three-session CBPI for young children with sleep difficulties (Fehr et al., 2014). The CBPI for sleep difficulties was piloted as part of normal clinical care with children presenting to a multidisciplinary pediatric sleep clinic and in a pilot study with 8 children (ages 4–5 years) who were randomized to receive parent information about behavioral sleep strategies or parent information plus the three-session CBPI. In the sleep clinic, positive results were obtained and generalized to the home setting to improve sleep habits and decrease distress and separation anxiety at bedtime, even after conducting only one CBPI session.

In the CBPI intervention pilot study, all children's sleep habits improved. However, sleep anxiety was reduced for children receiving the play intervention compared with children whose parents received only behavioral information (Fehr et al., 2014). These preliminary results provide support for the use of the CBPI when added to behavior management for these young children. Although these results are promising, a larger study is needed to confirm the results, and this study is currently in preparation.

In Chase's case, both the clinician and his parents believed that assisting him in being able to discuss and implement coping strategies to decrease distress when faced with independently walking into the school building was essential for an ultimately successful treatment outcome. Thus, the CBPI was explained to the parents, who were eager to add a component specifically addressing Chase's school anxiety to the treatment.

CBPI Sessions

The CBPI sessions were developed following the methodology of Pearson (2008) and Fehr et al. (2014). Children are provided with standardized toys, including a variety of structured toys relating to session content (for Chase, examples included a gender-matched doll, parent doll, car, and book bag) and unstructured toys that they can use for any other props they may need (e.g., blocks, animal figures).

Three standardized story stems are provided at each session, and each play script introduces a character and how he or she feels (e.g., scared, lonely). The child is instructed to play out how the doll can "feel better." The play facilitator's doll is introduced as the "older cousin" who "has some ideas about how to help." The play facilitator provides modeling and encouragement for coping strategies, focusing on positive coping self-statements and a problem-solving approach. Typically, two or three specific coping solutions of the child's preference are focused on to encourage generalization. Children are praised for their ideas and prompted to play out the coping strategies. At the end of each session, the child is allowed to make up a fourth story about anything he or she wants.

Chase's parents reported that the only situation that continued to elicit significant distress was walking into school independently. Therefore, the play sessions included standardized scripts focused on variations on this theme. During the first session, the play facilitator (author Fehr) introduced Chase to a boy doll who was in school missing his mother. Chase was hesitant to interact in this story and was unable to identify any coping strategies the doll could use. Suggestions of hugging a transitional object (i.e., special blanket) available in his backpack or reminding himself, "My mom will be back to pick me up after school, and I can give her a kiss then" were offered and modeled. He appeared interested in the modeling and offered that the doll could go home to feel better. This suggestion was praised and reframed as thinking about good feelings and memories at home to feel better.

After modeling these solutions through the play story, the second story was introduced. In this story, a boy is worried about getting out of the car in front of his school. In contrast to the first story, Chase was able to identify a number of solutions that the doll could use: asking his mother for a hug if he didn't have one already, holding on to his blanket instead, and thinking about good feelings and memories at home. These solutions were praised and modeled. Chase was encouraged to play out each coping strategy following the modeling, and he began engaging in the play story himself.

After reinforcement for his interaction and ideas, the third story was introduced in which a boy is standing at the door of the school building with his mother and he has to walk in the door by himself. With prompting, Chase was able to identify and independently play out the following coping strategies: holding on to his blanket, reminding himself that his mother would return after school, and thinking of pleasant thoughts. An additional coping self-statement that he is brave and completes the rest of his day on his own was offered, and he was able to incorporate this suggestion in the play with minimal prompting. Chase's willingness to engage and ability to identify and play out coping strategies was praised and reviewed. Of note, in the context of playing out this story, Chase's doll identified that he was worried about greeting the other children without the parent or teacher to help him initiate the interaction. Chase was then allowed to make up a story about anything he wanted to end the session positively, and Chase chose to play out a story about the doll and mother playing together on the playground on a nonschool day.

The stories created for the first session were chosen to ensure that they would be relevant to Chase's anxiety-provoking stimuli but not so overwhelming that he would be unable or unwilling to engage in the play narrative. In particular, the themes included separation (i.e., missing his mother), dealing with anxiety and worries (i.e., worrying in the car), and independent behaviors (i.e., walking through the school door alone). In each subsequent session, one story stem within each of these three theme areas was introduced. For example, in the second session, the story stems included a boy who is at school and feeling lonely without his mother (separation), a boy worrying about his mother while he is at school (anxiety and worry), and a boy who just walked into school and needs to greet his classmates (independent behaviors). This last story was developed on the basis of content during the first session indicating that part of Chase's fear of walking into school was related to independently greeting his classmates.

Furthermore, stories were graduated over time so that Chase's exact fear of walking from the car into school was not introduced until the third session. During the second CBPI session, Chase was much more engaged and willing to play out the story and coping strategies with encouragement and some prompting. He continued to provide the coping strategies practiced in the first session and included a few novel strategies as well. By the third session, Chase was very comfortable engaging in the play sessions and was independently able to identify and play out coping strategies for each of the presented scenarios.

His parents reported that his anxiety had seemed to decrease at school drop-offs as well. Specifically, they noted that although he still required someone to walk into the building with him, he did not appear to experience anticipatory anxiety on the way to school and was able to walk into the school building without being directly next to his parent or teacher. At the beginning of the fourth CBPI session, Chase and his parents reported a situation that occurred the previous week in which the family was running late to school so that when they arrived, the bell was already ringing. Chase was encouraged to run in so that he wouldn't be late, and Chase had done so! Chase and his parents reported that he walked into school independently the next two days as well. Although Chase had already met his goal, a final CBPI session was conducted focused on solidifying the coping strategies Chase had learned and reinforcing the positive feeling the Chase doll felt when he walked into school independently, even if he was a little nervous before getting out of the car. Follow-up with the family over the next 2 months indicated that treatment goals had been achieved and maintained, and treatment was discontinued.

Mechanisms of Change

It was clear that the first three CBPI sessions were instrumental in allowing Chase to feel more comfortable and confident in coping with separation from his parents during school, which subsequently allowed him to walk into school independently. There are five mechanisms of change that are likely responsible for the effectiveness of CBPT and the gains made with this child. First, CBPT directly teaches children coping skills. Knell (1998; Knell & Dasari, 2011) identified modeling, problem solving, verbalizing emotions, and relaxation skills as effective techniques within CBPT. In the first story, Chase was unable to identify any coping strategies. Throughout the session, positive coping statements and a problem-solving approach were directly modeled and encouraged, and Chase was able to implement the coping strategies taught into the following sessions independently.

Second, CBPT allows children to practice generating and using coping skills. Knell (1998) stated that one benefit of CBPT for young children is its experiential nature. Through the play story, children can practice their skills in place of real-life experience and thus become more adept at using the strategies. This technique can be beneficial as children may be more engaged and cooperative practicing these methods in a situation-specific story with the therapist as opposed to in the actual situation with parental coaching. The experiential nature of the play was thought to be particularly beneficial to Chase as he was progressively able to engage in the play and identify coping techniques with each scenario introduced over the three sessions.

Third, Knell (1998) described systematic desensitization as a change mechanism of CBPT. In play, children can confront their fears in a way that still allows them to maintain control. The pairing of the relaxing play with the anxiety-provoking stimulus, as well as the experiencing of the feared stimulus while the child remains in control of the situation, gives the child experience with the feared stimulus in a desensitizing way.

Relatedly, the fourth proposed change mechanism for CBPT is that children can gain mastery over fear through the play story (Knell, 1998). Pretend play provides an opportunity for children to integrate their fears and play out the fears in a safe environment (Erikson, 1963). Therefore, children can learn to master their fears and the situation through play. The play facilitator or therapist in CBPT ensures that the child will reach a positive outcome within the play session, thus increasing the sense of mastery. Systematic desensitization and mastery over the feared situation (i.e., walking into school independently) were observed as change mechanisms during the session with Chase. Specifically, his increasing comfort with and engagement in the separation-related play suggests that he was able to confront this fear while staying in control, providing an opportunity for mastery. It seems that this control was especially important for Chase as even discussing the situation had been overwhelming and too anxiety provoking prior to beginning the CBPI sessions.

Finally, CBPT encourages generalization of the skills to more than one setting. This consideration is especially relevant in CBPI as children are presented with multiple story stems that address a related issue. In this manner, children are required to generalize the newly learned coping strategies to several related situations. The practice of these strategies in numerous play situations increases the likelihood that children will generalize the skills to situations in their daily life as well. Chase did not play out any stories regarding coping with walking into the school building during a high-stress situation. However, his first successful walk into the building had been during the stressful situation of running late for school. This fact suggests that he was not only able to generate and practice internalized coping skills but also was able to generalize these skills in a new problem situation (i.e., being late for school) and relate the learned skills to the behavioral goal of entering school independently. Chase's ability to walk into school first independently during this high-stress situation likely was a result of practicing these coping skills ahead of time.

Generalization of CBPI

The change mechanisms in CBPT encompass a broad range of psychological approaches with empirical bases. Therefore, they are likely to prove effective when applied to a variety of children's problems as long as the particular children are able to use pretend play and their imagination. The original CBPI protocol included three weekly 20- to 30-minute sessions. Although Chase received four play sessions, three sessions were sufficient to achieve his treatment goal of walking into school independently.

In the CBPI sessions, standardized play scenarios are presented to address a variety of common anxiety-provoking situations for young children. For example, in the sleep protocol, each session includes a story about a child experiencing a nighttime fear, worrying about a bad dream, and separating from his or her parents. Although a variety of standardized story scripts are possible, it is important to ensure that the child is not exposed to any new fears during the course of treatment. To accomplish this in the standardized CBPI protocol, story stems are tailored within the standardized set on the basis of the fears endorsed by the child and his or her parent. When creating a story stem set for a particular concern, the desire to include a variety of story themes to increase generalization must be balanced with ensuring that the story content is relevant to the individual child, as was done in Chase's treatment.

CONCLUSION AND FUTURE DIRECTIONS

There is empirical evidence that play interventions can reduce fears and anxiety in children. Current treatment approaches are using a variety of play intervention techniques in an integrated fashion. This integration is optimal in allowing the intervention to be tailored to the individual child. Suggestions for future directions are as follows:

- Develop targeted play interventions for specific problems that follow a basic template but allow for flexibility in techniques based on different mechanisms of change.
- In research, identify specific play techniques that effect change.
- Determine for which children play-based interventions are most effective.
- When play is part of an empirically supported treatment, isolate the play component so that it can be evaluated.
- Conduct pilot studies with individual children to refine interventions.
- Disseminate research findings and play protocols to clinical settings.

REFERENCES

Barnett, L. A. (1984). Research note: Young children's resolution of distress through play. *Journal of Child Psychology and Psychiatry, 25*, 477–483. http://dx.doi.org/10.1111/j.1469-7610.1984.tb00165.x

Barnett, L. A., & Storm, B. (1981). Play, pleasure, and pain: The reduction of anxiety through play. *Leisure Sciences, 4*, 161–175. http://dx.doi.org/10.1080/01490408109512958

Belsky, J., & Most, R. (1981). From exploration to play: A cross-sectional study of infant free-play behavior. *Developmental Psychology, 17*, 630–639. http://dx.doi.org/10.1037/0012-1649.17.5.630

Briggs, K. M., Runyon, M. K., & Deblinger, E. (2011). The use of play in trauma-focused cognitive–behavioral therapy. In S. W. Russ & L. N. Niec (Eds.), *Play in clinical practice: Evidence-based approaches* (pp. 168–200). New York, NY: Guilford Press.

Cassell, S. (1965). Effect of brief puppet therapy upon the emotional responses of children undergoing cardiac catheterization. *Journal of Consulting Psychology, 29*, 1–8. http://dx.doi.org/10.1037/h0021670

Chethik, M. (1989). *Techniques of child therapy: Psychodynamic strategies*. New York, NY: Guilford Press.

Dansky, J. (1999). Play. In M. Runco & S. Pritzker (Eds.), *Encyclopedia of creativity* (pp. 393–408). San Diego, CA: Academic Press.

Erikson, E. (1963). *Childhood and society*. New York, NY: Norton.

Fehr, K., Russ, S., & Ievers-Landis, C. (2014, March). *Treatment of sleep problems in young children: Pilot of a cognitive–behavioral play intervention*. Poster presented at the Society of Pediatric Psychology Annual Conference, Philadelphia, PA.

Freud, A. (1927). Four lectures on child analysis. In *The writings of Anna Freud* (Vol. 1, pp. 3–69). New York, NY: International Universities Press.

Gaensbauer, T. J., & Siegel, C. H. (1995). Therapeutic approaches to posttraumatic stress disorder in infants and toddlers. *Infant Mental Health Journal, 16*, 292–305. http://dx.doi.org/10.1002/1097-0355(199524)16:4<292::AID-IMHJ2280160405>3.0.CO;2-3

Gaylin, N. L. (1999). Client-centered child and family therapy. In S. W. Russ & T. H. Ollendick (Eds.), *Handbook of psychotherapies with children and families* (pp. 107–120). New York, NY: Kluwer Academic/Plenum. http://dx.doi.org/10.1007/978-1-4615-4755-6_6

Gil, E. (1991). *The healing power of play*. New York, NY: Guilford Press.

Golomb, C., & Galasso, L. (1995). Make believe and reality: Explorations of the imaginary realm. *Developmental Psychology, 31*, 800–810. http://dx.doi.org/10.1037/0012-1649.31.5.800

Hirsh-Pasek, K., & Golinkoff, R. (2003). *Einstein never used flash cards: How our children really learn—And why they need to play more and memorize less*. New York, NY: Rodale.

Hoffmann, J. (2012). *A pretend play group intervention for elementary school girls*. (Unpublished doctoral dissertation). Case Western Reserve University, Cleveland, OH.

Johnson, P. A., & Stockdale, D. F. (1975). Effects of puppet therapy on palmar sweating of hospitalized children. *Johns Hopkins Medical Journal, 137*, 1–5.

Kazdin, A. (1990). Psychotherapy for children and adolescents. *Annual Review of Psychology, 41*, 21–54. http://dx.doi.org/10.1146/annurev.psych.41.1.21

Kessler, J. (1966). *Psychopathology of childhood*. Englewood Cliffs, NJ: Prentice-Hall.

Kessler, J. (1988). *Psychopathology of childhood* (2nd ed.). Englewood Cliffs, NJ: Prentice-Hall.

Knell, S. M. (1993a). *Cognitive–behavioral play therapy*. Northvale, NJ: Jason Aronson.

Knell, S. M. (1993b). Cognitive–behavioral play therapy. In S. W. Russ & T. H. Ollendick (Eds.), *Handbook of psychotherapies with children and families* (pp. 385–404). New York, NY: Kluwer Academic/Plenum.

Knell, S. M. (1993c). To show and not tell: Cognitive–behavioral play therapy in the treatment of elective mutism. In T. Kottman & C. Schaefer (Eds.), *Play therapy in action: A casebook for practitioners* (pp. 169–208). Northvale, NJ: Aronson.

Knell, S. M. (1998). Cognitive–behavioral play therapy. *Journal of Clinical Child Psychology, 27*, 28–33. http://dx.doi.org/10.1207/s15374424jccp2701_3

Knell, S. M., & Dasari, M. (2009a). CBPT: Implementing and integrating CBPT into clinical practice. In A. A. Drewes (Ed.), *The effective blending of play therapy and cognitive behavioral therapy: A convergent approach* (pp. 321–352). New York, NY: Wiley.

Knell, S. M., & Dasari, M. (2009b). Cognitive–behavioral play therapy for children with anxiety and phobias. In H. G. Kaduson & C. E. Schaefer (Eds.), *Short-term play therapy for children* (2nd ed., pp. 22–50). New York, NY: Guilford Press.

Knell, S. M., & Dasari, M. (2011). Cognitive–behavioral play therapy. In S. W. Russ & L. N. Niec (Eds.), *Play in clinical practice: Evidence-based approaches* (pp. 236–263). New York, NY: Guilford Press.

Knell, S. M., & Moore, D. J. (1990). Cognitive–behavioral play therapy in the treatment of encopresis. *Journal of Clinical Child Psychology, 19*, 55–60. http://dx.doi.org/10.1207/s15374424jccp1901_7

Knell, S. M., & Ruma, C. D. (1996). Play therapy with a sexually abused child. In M. A. Reinecke, F. M. Dattilio, & A. Freeman (Eds.), *Cognitive therapy with children and adolescents: A casebook for clinical practice* (pp. 367–393). New York, NY: Guilford Press.

Messer, S. B., & Warren, C. S. (1995). *Models of brief psychodynamic therapy*. New York, NY: Guilford Press.

Milos, M. E., & Reiss, S. (1982). Effects of three play conditions on separation anxiety in young children. *Journal of Consulting and Clinical Psychology*, *50*, 389–395. http://dx.doi.org/10.1037/0022-006X.50.3.389

Moore, M., & Russ, S. W. (2008). Follow-up of a pretend play intervention: Effects on play, creativity, and emotional processes in children. *Creativity Research Journal*, *20*, 427–436. http://dx.doi.org/10.1080/10400410802391892

Pearson, B. (2008). Effects of a cognitive–behavioral play intervention on children's hope and school adjustment. *Dissertation Abstracts International: Section A. The Humanities and Social Sciences*, *69*(06), 3316831.

Phillips, R. (1985). Whistling in the dark? A review of play therapy research. *Psychotherapy: Theory, Research, Practice, Training*, *22*, 752–760. http://dx.doi.org/10.1037/h0085565

Rae, W. A., Worchel, F. F., Upchurch, J., Sanner, J. H., & Daniel, C. A. (1989). The psychosocial impact of play on hospitalized children. *Journal of Pediatric Psychology*, *14*, 617–627. http://dx.doi.org/10.1093/jpepsy/14.4.617

Ruma, C. D. (1993). Cognitive–behavioral play therapy with sexually abused children. In S. M. Knell (Ed.), *Cognitive–behavioral play therapy* (pp. 197–230). Northvale, NJ: Aronson.

Russ, S. W. (1995). Play psychotherapy research: State of the science. In T. H. Ollendick & R. J. Prinz (Eds.), *Advances in clinical child psychology* (Vol. 17, pp. 365–391). New York, NY: Plenum Press.

Russ, S. W. (2004). *Play in child development and psychotherapy: Toward empirically supported practice*. Mahwah, NJ: Erlbaum.

Russ, S. W. (2014). *Pretend play in childhood: Foundation of adult creativity*. Washington, DC: American Psychological Association. http://dx.doi.org/10.1037/14282-000

Russ, S. W., & Fehr, K. K. (2013). The role of pretend play in child psychotherapy. In M. Taylor (Ed.), *The Oxford handbook of the development of imagination* (pp. 516–528). Oxford, England: Oxford University Press. http://dx.doi.org/10.1093/oxfordhb/9780195395761.013.0033

Russ, S. W., & Niec, L. N. (2011). Conclusions and implications for the use of play in intervention and prevention programs. In S. W. Russ & L. N. Niec (Eds.), *Play in clinical practice: Evidence-based approaches* (pp. 335–341). New York, NY: Guilford Press.

Shapiro, J., Friedberg, R., & Bardenstein, K. (2006). *Child and adolescent therapy: Science and art*. Hoboken, NJ: Wiley.

Singer, D. G. (1993). *Playing for their lives*. New York, NY: Free Press.

Singer, D. G., & Singer, J. L. (1990). *The house of make-believe: Children's play and the developing imagination*. Cambridge, MA: Harvard University Press.

Singer, J. L. (1995). Imaginative play in childhood: Precursor of subjunctive thoughts, daydreaming, and adult pretending games. In A. Pellegrini (Ed.), *The future of play therapy* (pp. 187–219). Albany, NY: State University of New York Press.

Strayhorn, J. M., Jr. (2002). Self-control: Toward systematic training programs. *Journal of the American Academy of Child & Adolescent Psychiatry*, *41*, 17–27. http://dx.doi.org/10.1097/00004583-200201000-00007

Terr, L. (1990). *Too scared to cry: Psychic trauma in childhood*. New York, NY: Harper & Row.

Tomkins, S. (1970). A theory of memory. In J. Antrobus (Ed.), *Cognition and affect* (pp. 59–130). Boston, MA: Little, Brown.

Toth, S. L., & Cicchetti, D. (1999). Developmental psychotherapy and child psychotherapy. In S. W. Russ & T. H. Ollendick (Eds.), *Handbook of psychotherapies with children and families* (pp. 15–44). New York, NY: Kluwer Academic/Plenum.

Wälder, R. (1933). Psychoanalytic theory of play. *Psychoanalytic Quarterly*, *2*, 208–224.

II

PLAY INTERVENTIONS FOR EXTERNALIZING DISORDERS

5

PLAYFUL COGNITIVE–BEHAVIORAL THERAPY FOR CHILDREN WITH SEXUAL BEHAVIOR PROBLEMS

DIANA GARZA LOUIS

The National Center on Sexual Behavior of Youth (2003) defined children with sexual behavior problems (SBPs) as "children 12 years old or younger who demonstrate developmentally inappropriate or aggressive sexual behavior" (p. 1). Examples of inappropriate sexual behavior include self-focused excessive masturbation and coercion or force toward others (Friedrich, 2007). Research has increasingly confirmed that SBPs in young and school-age children can be successfully treated with short-term interventions. Psychoeducation, cognitive behavior therapy (CBT), and a family-focused model that involves the caregivers and helps correct misinformation for both the caregivers and the child can be very effective (Gil & Shaw, 2014).

Playful CBT is a developmentally sensitive adaptation of CBT that addresses symptom reduction and modification of attitudes, beliefs, and expectations. Playful CBT can be used to direct and educate the child in making more positive choices and challenging inappropriate thoughts and behaviors using puppets, figures, art materials, toys, and games in the playroom.

http://dx.doi.org/10.1037/14776-006
Play Therapy in Middle Childhood, A. A. Drewes and C. E. Schaefer (Editors)

Integrating empirically supported CBT techniques with play therapy can help children improve their coping skills, improve emotional regulation, and reduce behaviors that are creating dysfunction in their normal sexual development. Because of the age range of this population (preschool through 12 years), interventions can be adapted to the developmental, social, and cognitive skill level of the child. In this chapter, we review normal versus problematic sexual behavior, describe precipitating factors that contribute to problematic sexual behaviors, discuss developmental issues, and suggest play therapy interventions that can be used with children with SBPs.

NORMAL VERSUS PROBLEMATIC SEXUAL BEHAVIOR

Children with SBPs are first and foremost children, and children have a natural inclination for sexual exploration and testing of limits as they progress from one developmental milestone to another (Goodyear-Brown, 2011). Engaging in inappropriate sexual behavior is often transient, and most children do not continue this behavior during adolescence and adulthood (Carpentier, Silovsky, & Chaffin, 2006). These children are quite responsive to short-term, community-based interventions.

When a child is referred for treatment of an SBP, it is important to distinguish between normal, age-appropriate sexual interests and problematic sexual behavior. Normal sexual behavior among children is usually spontaneous, intermittent, mutual, not distressing, and not reflective of preoccupation and usually does not involve advanced sexual behaviors such as oral sex or intercourse (Chaffin et al., 2006; Ewell, 2012; Widdifield, 2013). Common activities that are considered normal in children may involve sexual behavior such as playing doctor, looking at or touching peers' genitals, or telling "dirty" jokes (Barnes & Fortino, 2012). Usually participation in sexual play is voluntary, mutually enjoyable, and done between friends or acquaintances. The behavior usually stops if children are instructed to stop by an adult.

Johnson (2009b) indicated that normal sexual play often results in embarrassment but not usually in feelings of shame, anger, fear, or anxiety. It is important for the clinician to be knowledgeable of the range of sexual behaviors the child may present and determine whether the behaviors are within the norm of children his or her age. If the behavior is problematic, the clinician must determine how problematic the behavior might be to decide on the interventions needed.

Gil and Johnson (1992) identified a continuum of sexual behavior in children ranging from normal sexual exploration, to sexually reactive behavior, to mutual sexual behavior, to extensive mutual behavior, to molestation. This continuum helps clinicians determine the degree of the problematic behavior, the possible motivation that may be driving that behavior, and the context of the behavior when determining the severity of the problematic behavior. As noted above, normal sexual exploration is usually transient and nonintrusive and easily corrected when a child is instructed to stop. Sexually reactive or sexualized children may present an SBP because of the environment they live in or because they have been sexually victimized. Children who present extensive mutual sexual behaviors with a peer may be driven by the pleasurable sensations, sexual arousal, and orgasm that are derived from the behavior (Ewell, 2012); however, their behavior is not coercive or aggressive.

When the sexual behaviors are extensive, developmentally incongruent, premeditated, coercive, aggressive, obsessive, pervasive, and excessive in frequency and duration, then they are considered problematic. There are increased concerns if the child is molesting other children and corrective efforts by adults have not stopped the behavior, especially if the difference between the children's ages is 2 or more years (Chaffin et al., 2006; Gil & Shaw, 2014). These cases may need more specific interventions relating to the child's sexual behavior and attention to factors that may be contributing to this behavior such as family problems or mental health issues.

Letourneau, Chapman, and Schoenwald (2008) identified the following criteria for determining whether the sexual behavior is inappropriate:

- high frequency of the behavior;
- interference with the child's social or cognitive development;
- coercion, intimidation, or force;
- emotional distress;
- significantly different ages and development; and/or
- repeated secrecy after interventions by caregivers.

Duration of the inappropriate sexual behavior and the child's history, as well as the social and cultural contexts of the behavior, should also be considered to determine the level of intervention needed (Goodyear-Brown, 2011).

PRECIPITATING FACTORS FOR SEXUAL BEHAVIOR PROBLEMS

Maltreatment and family violence are highly correlated with SBPs (Gil & Shaw, 2014). Some of the variables that contribute to the development of an SBP are the cumulative stress that these children experience through poverty, inadequate parenting and supervision, family violence, sexual and physical abuse, and sexualized environments. Many of these children grow up in families that foster relating to others in a disturbed manner. The adults in their surroundings model poor emotional regulation, sexualized interactions, violence and coercion, and poor boundaries and provide poor supervision.

These children develop inadequate, aggressive, coercive, and sexualized behavior. Other contributing factors may include modeling of a caregiver's sexuality, access to pornography, and inappropriate television viewing or other media programming (Gil & Shaw, 2014).

Cultural and religious beliefs and customs regarding sexuality should also be considered when dealing with children and families of different cultures. Clinicians should be respectful of others' culture but make sure that those beliefs and customs are not harmful to others. Because of these factors, the Association for Treatment of Sexual Abuse's Task Force on Children With Sexual Behavior Problems (Chaffin et al., 2006) recommended that when assessing a child, clinicians be ecologically focused and consider the child's relationship and interactions with his or her environment, including family, peers, community, and school.

Many children with SBPs have other behavioral or emotional problems. Many have a diagnosis of attention-deficit/hyperactivity disorder, oppositional defiant disorder, conduct disorder, or attachment disorder, and many receive special education services because of learning disabilities or emotional disturbance. These children tend to internalize symptoms, have limited coping, have difficulty in their relationships with their caregivers, and have a stressful family environment (Ewell, 2012; Gray, Busconi, Houchens, & Pithers, 1997; Pithers, Gray, Busconi, & Houchens, 1998; Silovsky & Niec, 2002).

When children present with sexual behaviors, adults often have an automatic response and interpret the behaviors as problematic and reflective of abuse or deviance. Sometimes these children are presenting normal sexual behaviors. Caregiver overreaction to sexual behaviors could escalate these behaviors if the child is intrigued or reinforced by the caregiver's distress. Most children who have been sexually abused do not develop SBPs. However, children who have been sexually abused at a younger age, who have been abused by a family member, or whose abuse involved penetration are at greater risk of developing SBPs (Kellogg, 2010).

DEVELOPMENTAL ISSUES

Although clinicians use the word *sexual*, many children at this age are not motivated by the intent of sexual gratification (Bonner, Walker, & Berliner, 1999a). They may be imitating something they have seen or heard or behavior that is modeled by a caregiver. Developmentally appropriate behaviors that are frequently observed in children include trying to view another person's genitals or breasts, standing too close to other people, and touching their own genitals. These behaviors are all part of exploring, learning, and experimenting with normative sexual behaviors (Ewell, 2012). A *developmentally inappropriate behavior* is defined as a behavior that occur at a greater frequency or at a much earlier age than would be developmentally or culturally expected, that becomes a preoccupation for the child, and/or that recurs after adult intervention or corrective efforts have been made (Kellogg, 2010).

Children with SBPs are far less able than adolescents or adults to engage in complex cognitive processes such as planning (e.g., "I'll go play with Suzi. Maybe she'll let me touch her"), grooming ("Maybe if I let her play with my smartphone and spend time with her, she'll let me touch her"), or rationalizing ("She likes me to touch her"). The child's developmental stage needs to be considered; impulsive behaviors rather than compulsive behaviors are much more likely in a younger child than in an adolescent. When children present self-stimulation sexual behaviors, they may simply need to be redirected to an alternative behavior that is self-soothing. Redirecting can be simple and concrete ("I don't want you to do that") rather than attempting to teach the child cognitive coping strategies (Chaffin et al., 2006). Sexual fantasy is not quite developed until ages 11 to 13, according to Daleiden, Kaufman, Hilliker, and O'Neil (1998). Sexual thoughts in younger children are usually related to thoughts of past abuse or thoughts of touching other children, but even these thoughts are infrequent. Usually the sexual behavior is more impulsive and attributable to curiosity rather than being motivated by sexual arousal or seeking sexual satisfaction as an adolescent or adult might be.

Children with SBPs may not appear to have remorse regarding their behavior. In their developmental stage, young children may not have the cognitive skills or emotional development for empathy and remorse. They can, however, understand that their behavior is inappropriate and harmful to others and that secrets are not appropriate, and they have a clear understanding of right and wrong. Older children can conceptualize long-range consequences and have a clearer understanding of remorse and empathy (Goodyear-Brown, 2011). All of these factors should be considered when planning therapeutic interventions.

When dealing with SBPs, the safety of others is of extreme concern. Most children with SBPs are safe with other children at home and at school when the behavior is addressed and there is appropriate treatment and supervision. Some children may need more intensive or inpatient treatment and supervision if they are highly aggressive and intrusive in their sexual behavior and if they are unresponsive to outpatient treatment.

Friedrich (2007) maintained that the answer to children's SBPs is a relational solution. Attachment for these children is often insecure and disorganized, and caregivers often have a history of trauma. The caregivers often are inadequate in providing security and reassurance to these children, which leads the children to explore connections with others in a manner that may be inappropriate (Friedrich, 2007).

PLAY INTERVENTION PROCEDURES AND SETTINGS

Short-term interventions that include active caregiver involvement and the use of cognitive–behavioral strategies have been found to be the best interventions. Play therapy using puppets, toys, games, art, role-plays, and other playful activities can be blended with cognitive–behavioral strategies to educate and support the child and caregiver and promote learning new skills to identify, control, and manage sexual behaviors and emotional regulation (Goodyear-Brown, 2011). Best practices include treatment that is specific to the sexual behavior, is structured, and provides psychoeducation and practice of learned skills.

Developing skills that specifically address controlling and manipulating others is also part of the treatment goals. Making better choices, understanding how others feel, and apologizing to the person who was offended by the behavior are worked on if appropriate. Examples of play activities to address these goals may include using puppets to depict scenarios of behavior and interactions with others before and after the problematic behavior or role-playing apologizing to the victim and others affected by the problematic sexual behavior when the child is able to comprehend this concept. The sand tray can be used to depict scenarios in which the child demonstrates appropriate choices when encountering difficult situations or chooses appropriate activities versus sexual activities when experiencing sexual thoughts or feelings.

Parent training strategies and cognitive goal setting techniques have empirical evidence of being successful with children with SBPs. Interventions should address rules and supervision at home such as bathing and sleeping alone, preventing exposure to sexual materials, all family members using modesty, and respecting the privacy of all members of the family (Bonner, Walker, & Berliner, 1999b). Group therapy is recommended for children and caregivers. Benefits of group treatment include enhanced feelings of support, positive peer interactions, positive peer pressure, modeling, cost-effectiveness, and the opportunity for therapists to observe and assess the children's and caregivers' social interactions (St. Amand, Bard, & Silovsky, 2008).

Play activities individually with the caregiver and child or in group can include having a puppet show discussing rules, using the playhouse to depict sleeping arrangements, drawing pictures or making a collage of modestly dressed people, or playing the Space Invaders game (Johnson, 2009a) or the Responsibility Game (Garza Louis, 2009). Space Invaders has two sets of 80 brightly colored cards that address various sexual scenarios about boundaries violations. It can be played like Concentration or Go Fish. The Responsibility Game is a board game developed to assist in teaching, reviewing, and learning positive skills to help change children's inappropriate sexual behavior. The child moves around the board and answers questions related to rules, safe thinking and decisions, values and beliefs, and the impact of their sexual behavior on others. Issues can be addressed through activities with the child and caregivers individually, in group, or in family sessions. Through play, children explore, at a developmentally appropriate level, the impact of their behavior, strategies for coping with sexual thoughts and feelings, and ways to improve mastery and self-regulation.

Caregivers can address behavior, rules, sex education, and abuse prevention using playful interactions with their children. They can improve parenting skills, practice using praise, improve communication and positive interactions, and learn developmentally appropriate behavior management by establishing rules, rewards, time-outs, and consequences through role-plays and other playful activities.

Tailoring Treatment to Meet Developmental Needs

When working with children younger than 12 years old, clinicians should consider the developmental stage of the child to determine the focus of treatment and the concepts addressed. For younger children (ages 4–6), individual play sessions can be interactive, directive, and nurturing. Clinicians seek to reduce the focus of the sexual behavior and help the child develop better boundaries. Play activities can include cartooning of events, thoughts, and feelings. Feelings Charades are a good activity for identifying emotions and helping the child develop a broader spectrum of expressing feelings. Young children are unable to understand how their behavior affects others at this age, so storytelling of kids in similar circumstances and role-playing between children and caregivers help them develop external controls (Friedrich, 2007).

For children ages 7 to 10, therapy should be supportive and directive, reviewing sexual rules and discussing details of the sexual behaviors. Role-playing saying no to sexually intrusive thoughts or feelings, practicing self-control strategies, playing Space Invaders, and using art to depict scenes of past behaviors and future situations are good activities. At this age, self-report is unreliable, but children are developmentally able to connect thoughts, feelings, and behaviors, so attending to these issues is a good focus in sessions (Friedrich, 2007).

For children ages 11 to 12, cognitive–behavioral strategies in addressing sexual behavior can be used as interventions. At this age, children are able to explore fantasies, and the therapist can assess sexual preoccupation through the use of drawings. Self-reporting is more reliable at this age and can be used more frequently. Children at this age have greater cognitive skills and awareness and a better understanding of consequences. Art projects, feeling identification games, sand play, and psychoeducation regarding self-control and anger management are all positive interventions for children of this age.

Examples of play activities include role-playing, doing Feeling Charades or puppet shows of thought stopping (e.g., distracting themselves with video games), reading or writing stories about controlling anger or sexual thoughts and feelings or exploring being a trustworthy friend, or playing the Relaxation Game (Crisci, Lay, & Lowenstein, 1998) to help with emotional regulation are all playful interventions that address specific coping skills, behavior, and emotional management. The Relaxation Game is a board game in which the player moves around the board and follows the instructions on the square where he or she lands; examples include "take three deep breaths" and "tense and relax your hands."

Treatment Manuals

There are numerous treatment manuals that can be used for children with SBPs and their families. Bonner, Walker, and Berliner (2012a, 2012b) provided a treatment manual for CBT group treatment for children and caregivers, and Gil and Shaw (2014) developed a program design with excellent resources. Grant and Lundeberg (2009) published an excellent book with numerous activities for children with SBPs, as have Kahn (2007), Macfarlane and Cunningham (2003), and Gil and Johnson (1992). In addition, Bonner et al. (1999b) developed a treatment manual for dynamic group play therapy with caregiver involvement. Although play therapy is not specifically incorporated in some of these treatment manuals, using directive play therapy activities and blending play in addressing the specific interventions for SBPs can be very effective for this age range of children. Blending CBT with play therapy is a developmentally sensitive approach that can help younger children address sensitive issues in therapy.

Clinical Strategies

Evidence-based research indicates that specific issues should be addressed in treatment for children with SBPs (St. Amand et al., 2008). Examples of playful cognitive–behavioral strategies that can be modified to the child's developmental level are as follows:

- Rules
  - Have the child make a poster or collage with rules to help keep him or her safe regarding sexual behavior.
  - Have a puppet show with one character teaching the other about rules.
- Relaxation
  - Play the Relaxation Game (Crisci et al., 1998).

- Ask the child to create a scene in the sand tray or with art materials that depicts activities that are nonsexual, healthy, and fun.
- Sex education
  - Have the child identify body parts using a drawing of a child's body or make a cutout of a body and name the body parts appropriately (depends on the developmental stage and age of the child).
  - Use the Stories About Touching activity (Grant & Lundeberg, 2009). Make 10 cards each out of green, red, and orange paper. Review the stories, and have the child identify whether each story is about "good touching" (green card), "bad touching" (red card), or "secret touching" (orange card).
- Boundaries
  - Help the child define what boundaries are and make several concentric circles of differing sizes (like a target) with the middle circle representing the child. The child can identify people who have varying degrees of trust and limits regarding their interactions represented by the different-sized circles.
  - Play the Space Invaders game (Johnson, 2009a).
- Triggers
  - Ask the child to draw or make scenes in the sand tray or make a collage about things that cause sexual thoughts that could lead to inappropriate sexual behavior. Have the child draw three self-portraits depicting positive activities that can prevent inappropriate sexual behavior. Using a list of the things the child noted as causing sexual thoughts or feelings, have the child match which activity he or she can use as an intervention for each trigger.
- Emotional regulation
  - Have the child draw "feeling faces" and identify the feelings, giving an example of something that happened that resulted in each feeling.
  - Role-play or do a puppet show of ways to manage negative feelings in a more positive way in the future.
- Cognitive coping skills
  - Play the Responsibility Game (Garza Louis, 2009) or Space Invaders game (Johnson, 2009a).
  - Using puppets (an owl and a skunk, if available), make a puppet show using the "stinky thinking" and "wise owl thinking" puppets (Grant & Lundeberg, 2009) as prompts.

- My sexual behavior problems
  - Have the child write a story, song, or poem about the SBP he or she has had.
  - Ask the child to depict events through drawings, in the sand tray, with puppets, or in the playhouse.
- Impulse Control Game
  - Create a road map on a large piece of paper with several stop signs and crossroads. Ask the child to develop 10 cards with high-risk situations, for example, "A kid 2 years younger than me wants me to play with him" or "My aunt wants me to babysit." The child travels through the road map using a toy car, and at each crossroads stops, picks a card, and talks about the choices he or she can make at each crossroad.
- Impact of sexual abuse on others
  - Have the child create a story about someone who has been sexually abused.
  - Ask the child to do the Paper Dolls Exercise (Crisci et al., 1998), which involves cutting out a string of paper dolls to represent all the people whom the child believes have been affected by the abuse. The child identifies feelings represented by different-colored stickers and adhesive bandages representing pain or hurt, places the stickers or bandages on the paper, and talks about how the people were affected.
  - Older children can select various figures from the sand tray to identify each family member and others affected by his or her inappropriate sexual behavior and identify how each feels about the SBP.
- Abuse prevention
  - Have the child make a poster or collage or write an ad, song, or poem to help other kids learn about sexual abuse. Role-play high-risk situations and positive choices.
- Relationship skills
  - Have the child draw a picture of himself or herself being safe and responsible with friends and family. Using the playhouse, have the child create a story together with the caregiver that addresses making positive choices.

All of these activities can be done individually, in group, or jointly with a caregiver. Processing the activity with the caregiver is an integral part of improving communication and the relationship between them to help the child feel safe, validated, and supported.

EMPIRICAL SUPPORT

A review of the literature found no empirical studies using playful CBT for children with SBPs. Carpentier and colleagues (2006) studied 135 children with SBPs treated in a 12-session CBT group versus a client-centered play therapy group and compared them with 156 children with nonsexual behavior problems. The CBT group had significantly fewer incidents of inappropriate sexual behaviors posttreatment than the play therapy group (2% vs. 10%). Results of this study indicate that short-term, focused CBT with an educative model was most effective with children and their caregivers, although the play therapy group did appear to be an effective alternative (Bonner et al., 1999a).

St. Amand and colleagues (2008) did a meta-analysis of 11 studies with 18 treatment modalities and found that parenting and behavior management strategies were the most effective interventions for children with SBPs. Highly structured and interactive modalities that directly addressed the sexual behavior and had rule-based learning experiences with a psychoeducational and cognitive–behavioral format and practice time with caregivers had the best results. Review of rules, expression of feelings, self-control, boundaries, relaxation, behavior management, sex education, social skills, and abuse prevention have all been identified as primary topics to be addressed (Letourneau et al., 2008; Widdifield, 2013). Other studies have indicated a very low rate of recidivism for children and adolescents with SBPs: between 5.2% and 10.0%, according to Caldwell (2007), Chaffin (2008), and Chaffin et al. (2006).

Children with SBPs often are developmentally incapable of complex cognitions because of their age or developmental impairments or high stress in their lives (e.g., inadequate parenting, family violence, abuse, trauma). Directive play therapy interventions can address the necessary concepts regarding SBPs at a more appropriate developmental level in a playful and nonthreatening fashion that allows the child to process and incorporate the skills and concepts learned. Through play, children can understand complex problems, gain mastery of the concepts learned, and practice skills in a safe therapeutic environment. Incorporating play activities in sessions with caregivers increases their understanding of the child's developmental level and promotes greater communication with the child.

CASE ILLUSTRATION INCLUDING CAREGIVER INVOLVEMENT

Alex was an 11-year-old boy who was referred for treatment because of inappropriate sexual behavior toward his sister. Alex was pleasant and cooperative, articulate, well-mannered, and mature for his age. Alex was respectful and obedient toward his parents and somewhat serious and sedate compared with other children of his age. His family history was mostly unremarkable except that his biological father was in prison following a drug conviction. Before Alex's inappropriate sexual behavior was identified, he lived with his mother, stepfather, and sister, but when his SBPs came to light he was removed from his home by child protective services and placed with his maternal grandparents. Alex got along well with other children and was compliant and appropriate with adults; he had not had any serious behavior problems at home or at school.

Most of Alex's sessions were individual, although his mother attended a few sessions with him. The *Roadmaps* workbook (Kahn, 2007) was used as the primary treatment manual, and play activities were incorporated as part of his treatment. Alex identified "wrong touching" by drawing a profile of himself on a large piece of paper, identifying body parts, and identifying areas of the body that should not be touched by others. He identified and expressed feelings by playing Feelings Charades and the Responsibility Game. He developed a list of rules to post in his room and reviewed those rules with his mom. He practiced making good choices by playing the Impulse Control Game and creating a road map of high-risk situations. He practiced safety planning by creating scenes with figures in the sand tray and playing out high-risk situations.

Alex was able to describe his inappropriate behavior by writing a story about what happened, identifying anger and frustration as frequent feelings that had triggered some of his behavior in the past. Through his story, he admitted that he had seen some pornography online on one occasion and was curious about what he had seen. Alex had a good understanding of the concepts discussed, and he expressed remorse and regret for having participated in this behavior.

In sessions with his mom, Alex shared his list of rules in their home and discussed future situations that might occur and strategies to be safe. His mom viewed a video of Alex playing the Impulse Control Game in which he identified high-risk situations and ways of managing these situations in the future. His mom was very positive and engaged with Alex; she expressed that she had not realized he could come up with practical and realistic interventions for the high-risk situations. They created a family portrait together and discussed how Alex could show respect to his elders and others, including his sister. Alex was able to return home within a few weeks after presenting an apology letter to his sister in a family therapy session.

CONCLUSION AND FUTURE DIRECTIONS

Children with SBPs are being referred to clinical practices with more and more frequency. Better reporting of inappropriate sexual behaviors has contributed to this increase, as well as heightened awareness that some sexual behaviors are damaging to victims even when the sexual behavior is by another child. Unfortunately, the typical reaction to sexual behavior in children has become excessive and punitive, and children who have SBPs are responded to as perpetrators of crimes when in reality many offenses are within the realm of normal sexual development. Assessing the severity and intensity of the behavior helps clinicians determine the level of intervention to use in such cases.

Studies indicate that CBT is the best intervention for children under 12 years of age with SBPs. The treatment should focus on the inappropriate sexual behavior and should include caregivers to address issues of supervision and reduction of a sexualized environment in the home and to help them set clear and appropriate limits and boundaries. Blending play activities with CBT is an appropriate intervention given that many of these children are developmentally incapable of complex cognitions.

Through play interventions, children in this age range can address issues of body awareness, expression of feelings, rules, and boundaries and can increase their awareness of appropriate sexuality in a nonthreatening and developmentally sensitive manner. Involving caregivers in play activities improves communication, supervision, and relational skills between the caregiver and child and can have long-lasting, positive effects for both the caregiver and the child. To date, no evidence-based research studies are available using playful CBT with this population. More evidence-based research and long-term studies are needed to substantiate the benefits of using play interventions blended with cognitive–behavioral approaches in clinical settings.

Playful CBT that is focused on inappropriate sexual behavior can be easily integrated into a clinician's toolbox of play therapy interventions. Therapists should increase their awareness about what is normal and what is beyond the norm of sexuality at different developmental stages to avoid labeling and overreacting when these cases are brought to their attention. Children with SBPs need guidance and support in making good and safe choices when they have sexual thoughts and feelings, and they can develop into normal and healthy individuals through these therapeutic interventions. Playful CBT can have a positive impact on these children by providing a developmentally sensitive approach to addressing this sensitive issue.

REFERENCES

Barnes, K., & Fortino, J. (2012, October). *Understanding and treating the sexually acting out child.* Paper presented at the conference of the Association for Play Therapy, Cleveland, OH.

Bonner, B., Walker, E., & Berliner, L. (1999a). *Children with sexual behavior problems: Assessment and treatment—Final report* (Grant No. 90-CA-1469). Washington,

DC: Administration of Children, Youth, and Families, Department of Health and Human Services.

Bonner, B., Walker, E., & Berliner, L. (1999b). *Treatment manual for dynamic group play therapy for children with sexual behavior problems and their parents/caretakers*. Washington, DC: National Clearinghouse on Child Abuse and Neglect Information.

Bonner, B., Walker, E., & Berliner, L. (2012a). *Treatment manual for cognitive–behavioral group therapy for children with sexual behavior problems*. Oklahoma City, OK: National Center on Sexual Behavior of Youth, Center on Child Abuse and Neglect, University of Oklahoma Health Sciences Center. Retrieved from http://digitalprairie.ok.gov/cdm/singleitem/collection/stgovpub/id/10123/rec/2

Bonner, B., Walker, E., & Berliner, L. (2012b). *Treatment manual for cognitive–behavioral group therapy for parents/caregivers of children with sexual behavior problems*. Oklahoma City, OK: National Center on Sexual Behavior of Youth, Center on Child Abuse and Neglect, University of Oklahoma Health Sciences Center. Retrieved from http://digitalprairie.ok.gov/cdm/singleitem/collection/stgovpub/id/10122/rec/1

Caldwell, M. F. (2007). Sexual offense adjudication and sexual recidivism among juvenile offenders. *Sexual Abuse: Journal of Research and Treatment, 19*, 107–113.

Carpentier, M. Y., Silovsky, J. F., & Chaffin, M. (2006). Randomized trial of treatment for children with sexual behavior problems: Ten-year follow-up. *Journal of Consulting and Clinical Psychology, 74*, 482–488. http://dx.doi.org/10.1037/0022-006X.74.3.482

Chaffin, M. (2008). Our minds are made up—Don't confuse us with the facts: Commentary on policies concerning children with sexual behavior problems and juvenile sex offenders. *Child Maltreatment, 13*, 110–121. http://dx.doi.org/10.1177/1077559508314510

Chaffin, M., Berliner, L., Block, R., Cavanagh Johnson, T., Friedrich, W. N., Garza Louis, D., . . . Silovsky, J. F. (2006). *Report of the Task Force on Children With Sexual Behavior Problems*. Retrieved from Association for the Treatment of Sexual Abusers website: https://www.atsa.com/pdfs/Report-TFCSBP.pdf

Crisci, G., Lay, M., & Lowenstein, L. (1998). *Paper dolls and paper airplanes: Therapeutic exercises for sexually traumatized children*. St. Paul, MN: Jist.

Daleiden, E., Kaufman, K., Hilliker, D., & O'Neil, J. (1998). The sexual histories and fantasies of youthful males: A comparison of sexual offending, nonsexual offending, and non-offending groups. *Sexual Abuse: Journal of Research and Treatment, 10*, 195–209.

Ewell, B. (2012, November). *Responding to sexual behavior problems in children twelve and under*. PowerPoint presentation at the New York State coalition for Children's Mental Health Services, Office of Mental Health, Staff Development Training Forum, Saratoga Springs, NY.

Friedrich, W. N. (2007). *Children with sexual behavior problems: Family-based attachment-focused therapy*. New York, NY: Norton.

Garza Louis, D. (2009). *The Responsibility Game*. Austin, TX: Rio Grande Counseling Center.

Gil, E., & Johnson, T. (1992). *Sexualized children: Assessment and treatment of sexualized children and children who molest*. Rockville, MD: Launch Press.

Gil, E., & Shaw, J. (2014). *Working with children with sexual behavior problems*. New York, NY: Guilford Press.

Goodyear-Brown, P. (Ed.). (2011). *Handbook of child sexual abuse: Identification, assessment, and treatment*. Hoboken, NJ: Wiley. http://dx.doi.org/10.1002/9781118094822

Grant, R. K., & Lundeberg, L. H. (2009). *Interventions for children with sexual behavior problems: Research, theory, and treatment*. Kingston, NJ: Civic Research Institute.

Gray, A., Busconi, A., Houchens, P., & Pithers, W. (1997). Children with sexual behavior problems and their caregivers: Demographics, functioning, and clinical patterns. *Sexual Abuse: Journal of Research and Treatment, 9*, 267–290.

Johnson, T. C. (2009a). *Space Invaders: A game about boundaries*. Pasadena, CA: Author.

Johnson, T. C. (2009b). *Understanding children's sexual behaviors: What's natural and healthy*. Pasadena, CA: Institute on Violence Abuse and Trauma.

Kahn, T. (2007). *Roadmaps to recovery*. Brandon, VT: Safer Society Press.

Kellogg, N. (2010). Sexual behaviors in children: Evaluation and management. *American Family Physician, 82*, 1233–1238.

Letourneau, E. J., Chapman, J. E., & Schoenwald, S. K. (2008). Treatment outcome and criminal offending by youth with sexual behavior problems. *Child Maltreatment, 13*, 133–144. http://dx.doi.org/10.1177/1077559507306717

Macfarlane, K., & Cunningham, C. (2003). *Steps to healthy touching*. St. Paul, MN: Jist Works.

National Center on Sexual Behavior of Youth. (2003, July). *NCSBY fact sheet*. Oklahoma City, OK: Author.

Pithers, W., Gray, A., Busconi, A., & Houchens, P. (1998). Children with sexual behavior problems: Identification of five distinct child types and related treatment considerations. *Child Maltreatment, 3*, 384–406. http://dx.doi.org/10.1177/1077559598003004010

Silovsky, J. F., & Niec, L. (2002). Characteristics of young children with sexual behavior problems: A pilot study. *Child Maltreatment, 7*, 187 197. http://dx.doi.org/10.1177/1077559502007003002

St. Amand, A., Bard, D. E., & Silovsky, J. F. (2008). Meta-analysis of treatment for child sexual behavior problems: Practice elements and outcomes. *Child Maltreatment, 13*, 145–166. http://dx.doi.org/10.1177/1077559508315353

Widdifield, J. (2013, July). *Problematic sexual behavior in children: Current findings and implications for practice*. PowerPoint presentation at the 2013 Florida Krimes Against Kids Conference, Lake Buena Vista, FL. Retrieved from http://ebookbrowsee.net/problematic-sexual-behavior-in-children-handouts-pdf-d506156438

6

ENJOYING THERAPLAY WITH SCHOOL-AGE CHILDREN

DAVID L. MYROW

Theraplay is an approach to play therapy based on attachment theory. It is designed to help children improve their sense of self, relationships with others, and capacity to get needs met constructively. The Theraplay therapist starts with an assessment of the child and, when possible, of the child interacting with the parents. Particular attention is given to the child's emotional developmental age and whether behaviors or problems reflect unresolved concerns from earlier developmental stages. Because Theraplay activities resemble games typically played by school-age children, these children find them attractive and fun. There is a high probability that client and therapist will enjoy some hearty laughs together in a Theraplay session.

The Theraplay therapist endeavors, through attunement, genuineness, and presence, to establish a close relationship with the child. Using emotional and physical connection, the therapist attempts to make eye contact and physical contact through most of each session. It is a connection informed by that of a parent with a young child and uses that kind of intimacy

http://dx.doi.org/10.1037/14776-007
Play Therapy in Middle Childhood, A. A. Drewes and C. E. Schaefer (Editors)

to quickly build a working alliance and to get engaged at a more primal level than can be accomplished with strictly verbal communication. This view is supported by the latest thinking in neurobiological research (Siegel, 2012), in which a physical relationship is considered central for the development of regulation of affect and behavior. Physical play can be seen as central to increasing capacity for self-regulation and decreasing out-of-control aggression (DeBenedet & Cohen, 2010).

This chapter focuses on the large group of children who present with depression, overactivity, anxiety, poor self-confidence, attachment issues, or low self-esteem, but Theraplay can also help children with other problems. It can be useful as part of the treatment plan—along with projective play techniques and cognitive–behavioral strategies—for children who are experiencing divorce or other situational problems. It can also play an important role in treating school-age children who have experienced serious trauma, perhaps because of its capacity to help these children accept nurture and increase self-valuation. For children on the autism spectrum, Theraplay can be the core approach (Bundy-Myrow, 2012). Theraplay also has applications for most ages, from families preparing to adopt a child (Booth & Jernberg, 2010) to teenagers (Booth & Jernberg, 2010; Myrow, 2007, 2013) and senior citizens (Kyung, 2010). This chapter shows how mental health and educational professionals can use Theraplay with a very large group of typical school-age children.

DEVELOPMENTAL ISSUES

Theraplay assumes that early experience profoundly influences a child's sense of self, capacity to relate to others, and development of resources to meet his or her needs. Ann Jernberg, who pioneered the development of Theraplay, assumed that current behavior depends on a child's emotional stage of development, which is shaped by parent–child interaction and its implications for perceptions of self and others. This view is supported by Bowlby's (1988) work on attachment. Parent–child interaction in the first years of life sets the stage for children's view of themselves and others and for development of coping skills, including self-regulation of behavior and affect. In short, it is assumed that

- the primary motivating force in human behavior is the drive toward relatedness;
- in the course of playful, responsive parenting, a child develops a clear sense of self, feelings of self-worth, and the capacity to empathize with other people;

- for a child to develop self-regulation of affect and behavior, he or she needs to have experiences of coregulation with a caregiver who is well regulated and sensitive to the child's needs; and
- when the relationship is attuned and responsive and the child is able to use the parent's efforts, the child develops inner working models (i.e., expectations and beliefs) about himself or herself and other people as trustworthy, loving, and competent, and this development supports a desire to interact with the world around him or her and provides the child the foundation to be able to get his or her needs met constructively (Bundy-Myrow & Booth, 2009).

Theraplay therapists assume that unresolved issues from the child's earlier years often play an important role in current behavior. A child may be moving along physically and intellectually on schedule but be emotionally stuck at an earlier developmental point. In the school or the clinic, a child's apparent presentation may not reveal the underlying issues. Two of Theraplay therapists' special contributions are (a) systematically assessing the parent–child dynamics and (b) finding ways to address issues left over from earlier stages, including preverbal times—for example, issues regarding self-esteem, self-worth, and beliefs about others. An 8-year-old who is endlessly oppositional may have problems harkening back to the 1½- to 3-year-old period, when the developmental challenge was resolving the wish for autonomy in the face of needing parents' help. A 10-year-old who falls apart when losing at a game might have not finished the work of a 5-year-old in the struggle to feel able to compete.

Children need help with calming anxiety or discomfort, being emotionally engaged, accepting nurture, and meeting challenges in different ways at different developmental stages. If these needs are met attentively, children become able to self-regulate affect and behavior and to initiate constructively to get their needs met.

THEORY AND RATIONALE

The approach that eventually came to be called Theraplay emerged from Ann Jernberg's work in the late 1960s with Head Start 4-year-olds. Psychologist Ted Hurst had the task of providing psychological services to the first Head Start classrooms in Chicago. It soon became apparent that there were many children with problems severe enough to require intervention. Most common were children who disrupted the class with acting out behavior and children so withdrawn as to be nearly impossible to engage. Yet mental health services were scarce.

In search of interventions that could work quickly and be cost-effective, Hurst turned to Jernberg, who chose to move from the tendency to pathologize children toward a focus on healthy development. She was influenced by Bowlby (1988) and by her own mother's clever work on infant development (Marschak, 1980). Jernberg also looked to the family therapy movement and was influenced by strategic approaches (Haley, 1973). The focus was on how to change children's view of themselves on the way to changing their behavior.

Jernberg's efforts started with therapists treating children individually, often in a corner of a busy Head Start classroom. Therapists would see a child once or twice a week, typically for 30 minutes at a time, averaging about 15 sessions per child. As Jernberg developed the Theraplay model, she moved to include parents when possible in the treatment process, first by observing the therapist working with the child and then by joining the child in the playroom.

To assess the parent–child relationship, Jernberg adapted her mother's research instrument, the Marschak Interaction Method (MIM), for clinical use (Jernberg, 1979). For example, the MIM analysis might reveal that an acting out, aggressive 9-year-old may actually be desperately in need of more nurturing from the parent. A 10-year-old who tries to control interactions may need clearer structure and nurture from the parent and to experience the adult as being safely in charge. A 7-year-old depressed child who seldom initiates may need to be challenged by the parent to accomplish things on his or her own. In all of these cases, the children did not experience what they needed from parents at some point in their development. In some cases, situational variables (e.g., a parent who is called to active military duty, has a physical or mental illness, or needs to be away to support the family financially) have interfered. Or there might be a mismatch between a child's physical limitations, temperament, or tempo and the adult's. The MIM helps clarify the issues to allow the Theraplay therapist to help children learn better ways to interact with their world and, when possible, to help their parents understand and meet their children's needs.

Given that behavior depends on a child's emotional stage of development, shaped by parent–child interaction and its implications for perceptions of self and others, the challenge was how to devise interventions that would meet the child at the stuck stage and be comfortable for the older child. Jernberg observed healthy parent–child interactions and devised therapeutic interventions that mimicked them. She prescribed which interactions to use on the basis of the child's emotional developmental needs, adapting familiar parent–child games to include aspects that spoke to the needs of the younger child inside.

THERAPLAY PROCESS

The Theraplay process begins with an intake interview with only the parents (or primary caregivers). In addition to gathering the history of the concerns and of the child's physical and social development, special emphasis is placed on finding out about the caregiving and programming experience. An important goal is to understand the history of the child's attachment relationships. After the initial interview, the adults and child are observed together in the MIM analysis.

Marschak Interaction Method Analysis

The MIM is a behavioral projective assessment technique. Most often, the protocol is as follows: A parent and child sit next to each other on the same side of a small table. It is explained that the therapist will be observing through a one-way window and making a video of the session. The adult is given a stack of instruction cards and supplies. The therapist instructs the parent to read the cards aloud and then for the two to engage in the activities.

What ensues reveals the dynamics and patterns in the relationship. Consider an activity often used with school-age children and their fathers: The card reads, "Adult and child put hats on each other." Does the child grab the card and read it? Do the child and father make eye contact? Do they admire how each other looks in the hats? Does the dad choose a hat for the child that is relevant to the child's life, such as a baseball hat for a Little Leaguer? Does the child put the frilly ladies' hat on the dad? And so on. Different MIM tasks are designed to bring out various qualities of the child–parent relationship.

After the MIM results are completed and analyzed, the therapist shows segments of the videos to the parents to help them understand what happens in their interactions. Sometimes it offers an opportunity to reframe behavior: What the parents interpreted as "bad" or disobedient behavior might better be understood as an attempt to predict situations. "Hyperactive" moves might be seen as coming from anxiety. When the therapist and parents see these things together, it helps them develop a working alliance and also to devise treatment goals and methods.

The reliability and validity of the MIM have support in the research literature (Bojanowski & Ammen, 2011; Hitchcock, Ammen, O'Connor, & Backman, 2008; Martin, Snow, & Sullivan, 2008). Interrater reliability between trained observers is very high.

In addition to developing the MIM as a clinical instrument, one of Jernberg's other masterful contributions was her development of a model for the dimensions of parenting. This elegant design organizes what a child needs from a parent in a way that translates easily into clinical practice. Jernberg postulated that the child's needs for parenting and, consequently, the parents' responsibilities may be seen in the four dimensions of structure, engagement, nurture, and challenge. Booth and other Theraplay practitioners have expanded on this methodology (Booth & Jernberg, 2010; Jernberg & Booth, 1999).

Structure

The parent builds a holding environment and takes charge of defining physical boundaries and setting limits. For a newborn, this activity involves schedules, rhythms, and routines for feeding, sleeping, and diaper changing. Soon the parent teaches the child about himself or herself—for example, "These are your ears." Structuring takes different forms at the various developmental stages. For the school-age child, it includes getting homework done and setting norms of behavior with peers. For the teenager, there might be curfews and help organizing the search for college or a job.

Engagement

The parent connects emotionally with the child. There is a sense of immediacy and intimacy. Accurate affective attunement is essential. In interaction with the infant, engagement is seen in mirroring behavior that is in synchrony with affective volume and tone. As children develop, attending to their emotional states and teaching the words for them helps children know themselves and feel known. For a child who avoids closeness (e.g., a parentified, obsessive–compulsive child), sometimes little surprises can help her or him let go and have fun. An anxious 7-year-old might be delighted to find that he or she can jump farther and farther distances from a tabletop into the arms of an enthusiastic parent, who ends the game by swinging the child around in a circle and then gazing into his or her eyes.

Nurture

The parent protects and comforts, feeds, and clothes the child. Warm physical touch supports the process of self-regulating. When a child scrapes a knee playing ball, a parent checks it out, places a bandage, and sends him or her back to play (assuming no stitches are needed!). A grandparent makes treats for after-school snacks.

Challenge

Parents notice their children's budding capacities and provide situations to help them develop. Five-year-olds are taught to tie their own shoelaces. School-age children are given opportunities to help around the house and offered opportunities to try activities. By accomplishing just-enough challenges, children start to feel competent and develop self-confidence.

Thinking about the needs of children in interaction with their parents in this way helps the therapist make sense of what children need to move toward psychological health. It helps the therapist work with parents and can be used to teach parents about their child.

In a mental health setting, the usual Theraplay protocol consists of five steps:

1. intake meeting with parents only to gather history and develop an assessment plan;
2. MIM analysis with each parent;
3. feedback meeting with parents to review findings and develop treatment goals and plan;
4. individual Theraplay sessions in which the child is seen for the first 25 minutes, then parents view a video of that session while the child waits in the playroom; and
5. Family Theraplay sessions in which the therapist sees the child for the first half and includes the parents in the second.

There are variations on this protocol for complex cases. For example, sometimes the parents are included in sessions from the beginning.

In work with school-age children, the therapist may depart from the Theraplay protocol and add an individual session with the child after the MIM is completed and before the review session with the parents. At this meeting, the therapist may administer projective drawings and interview the child. Seeing the child individually allows a look at the child's perception of the world directly, validates the child as an individual, and gives a peek at the child intrapersonally.

In an educational setting, it is not always possible to include parents directly in the treatment process. A counselor or special education teacher trained in Theraplay can still use the approach effectively. In addition, group Theraplay (Rubin & Tregay, 1989), with its fun and engaging emphasis on development of prosocial behavior, offers teachers and counselors effective strategies for increasing children's cooperation, respect, and self-esteem.

The more recent development of Sunshine Circles (Schieffer, 2013), intended to be part of the general education curriculum, is yet another application of Theraplay with goals such as managing bullying and developing constructive interpersonal skills. Even when a relatively healthy child is able to verbalize concerns (e.g., in the midst of parental divorce or when experiencing bullying at school), Theraplay can be part of the treatment by helping to quickly form a therapeutic alliance followed by verbal strategies for problem solving.

CASE STUDY INCLUDING CAREGIVER INVOLVEMENT

At the intake meeting, the parents of Derek, an 8-year-old boy, stated that he was struggling in his public school and at his church's religion class. His teacher reported that Derek would "shut down" on tasks at the slightest frustration. He would either complain loudly or fold his arms on his desk and rest his head on them, refusing to do anything. His perturbations became increasingly problematic to the point of disrupting classroom activities.

At home, Derek's parents said that he seldom played sports and had no best friend. Derek was the younger of two children, with a 10-year-old brother. His father reported feeling that he had trouble connecting with Derek, largely because his son did not like the usual "guy things." The father liked football, soccer, and woodworking. The older brother shared these interests, but Derek gave up early on when he was introduced to them. Derek's brother was seen as successful in school and with friends. Derek and his parents had battles over doing homework, from which his parents tended to withdraw.

The father's parents were from the Old Country and had immigrated to the United States when Derek's father was 10 years old. This family history turned out to be pivotal as therapy progressed and illustrates how Theraplay can address the whole family system.

The therapist, Dr. M, first administered the MIM with Derek's mother. Derek and his mother both presented with constricted affect. For both, mood seemed depressed, shy, and anxious. Derek soon started taking over the session, grabbing the instruction cards and reading them. When they played Thumb Wrestling, Derek started off each of the three rounds, speaking softly but nevertheless in charge, with his mother going along.

With his father, Derek frequently moved toward him physically, and they made positive contact often. Derek's father struggled to read and understand the instruction cards. On some occasions, Derek tried to help his father (not always very successfully) by reading aloud the questions or trying to explain the directions. Derek's father could be somewhat judgmental and critical. When Derek read a card instructing him to "Close your eyes and tell me everything that is in the room," he struggled at first, seeming unsure about what to do. Derek seemed stuck and started to shut down (this behavior was strikingly similar to the situations described by the teacher). Eventually, his father gave a few prompts, and Derek mentioned a few items in the room. Then his father pointed to the many items that Derek missed. When playing Bean Blow, the instructions were for the adult to place three beans in the center of the table and then for each to take a straw and try to blow the beans to the opponent's side. At one point, Derek's father accused him unfairly of cheating. When the two were to comb each other's hair, Derek said, "Ow!" several times, but his father dismissed his complaint as being overly sensitive. Derek was much gentler combing his father's hair.

After Derek and his parents completed the MIM, Dr. M interviewed Derek individually. Please note that this is not a Theraplay procedure; rather, it is an example of how each Theraplay therapist brings his or her own resources to bear in the work. Dr. M believed that the MIM provides a uniquely valuable opportunity to understand the interpersonal dynamics between a child and a parent. But because most school-age children can express themselves verbally, at least to some extent, Dr. M also believed it was valuable to talk with Derek about his life.

The individual session with Derek was very informative, but not in the expected way. Typically, children complete the projective drawings expeditiously and then answer questions about school, friends, dreams, and so forth. In Derek's case, however, he started to cry and wanted to quit in the middle of the Draw-A-Person test. When a variety of interventions failed to calm him, Dr. M invited Derek's mother to sit in the corner of the room. Derek managed to complete the tasks—although still crying intermittently—while his mother sat quietly in the corner. The crying seemed to be triggered when he was not sure how to respond to the questions.

Dr. M also spoke with Derek's teacher and the school psychologist. They had set up a behavior modification plan, but it was unsuccessful. Any situation that seemed difficult led to his withdrawing or obstinately refusing to participate. The school psychologist reported that Derek's teacher was extremely frustrated and bewildered over the situation.

Assessment Review With the Parents

Dr. M reviewed the projective drawings and showed the MIM results, referring back to the initial presenting concerns. He focused on parts of the MIM videos that illustrated the following dynamics: Derek and his father both wanted more relationship with each other. Yet his father tended to dismiss Derek's nurturing needs. Derek's mother's passive attitude encouraged Derek to take over and assume the authoritative role. When she did take charge, things went more smoothly. Derek had little self-confidence to try new things or attempt a task. He showed little capacity to manage his anxiety or frustration. In addition, on the basis of Derek's difficulties in understanding some of the MIM instructions, his similar difficulties when directions and requests were made in school, and his behavior during the individual session, Dr. M asked the parents to request a school psychological evaluation to rule out learning issues or related concerns.

In the process of looking at the drawings and MIM results with Derek's parents, Dr. M sometimes reframed the way the parents were constructing the concerns. For example, what was seen as oppositional was now seen as driven by anxiety. Derek's parents seemed relieved to find new ways to understand their child's problems. Together, Dr. M and Derek's parents established the following treatment goals:

- Derek will have more self-confidence in trying new things (including activities, foods, and school tasks).
- Derek will manifest less anxiety and have an increased capacity to manage frustration. He will persevere more on tasks.
- Derek's parents will provide more consistent organization and structure for Derek at home.
- Derek and his father will find more ways that they can share closeness and have fun.
- Derek will be more cooperative in school and at home.

Regarding methods, in addition to the school psychological evaluation and support of the teacher's efforts, the family was to begin a course of Theraplay, starting with individual Theraplay and then moving to family sessions.

First Individual Theraplay Session With Derek

Dr. M met Derek and his parents in the waiting room. The parents reported that the school psychologist had evaluated Derek and found his intellectual abilities to be average or higher in every area. As planned, individual Theraplay began.

Dr. M took Derek's hand, and they walked to the playroom. The room had soft carpeting and pictures by children on the walls but no toys. Dr. M moved Derek to a large pillow and sat on one himself, both cross-legged, with knees touching. Dr. M explained the rules of the playroom as follows: "1. No one gets hurt." (Dr. M gently touched Derek's chest and then his own.) "2. Everyone has as much fun as possible. That's all." A big smile crept slowly onto Derek's face. Dr. M then reviewed the treatment goals that had been developed with the parents in terms that made sense to an 8-year-old: "Feel safe trying new things. Follow clear directions from adults. When I feel angry or scared, talk out my feelings instead of throwing a tantrum or shutting down. Have more fun with Mom and Dad."

Dr. M then did a check-in. He described Derek's eyes (light blue in the middle with darker blue around the edges). He counted his fingers using a trick invented by an early Theraplay therapist, Terrence Kohler: "Should be 10 . . . 10, 9, 8, 7, 6 on the left . . . 1, 2, 3, 4, 5 on the right. . . . Hmm, 5 plus 6 equals 11!" When Derek protested, Dr. M agreed that he might count differently. He then asked Derek to stick out his tongue to see if he could touch his nose, then his chin. The therapist rolled up Derek's sleeves, showed him how to "make a muscle" by turning his fist to face his ear so that his biceps got bigger, and said, "Wow, those are big muscles! Look how hard they are, too!"

By giving Derek real, concrete descriptions of himself and examples of his strengths, the therapist helped Derek build a positive sense of self. Physical contact engages the child right away. Surprise adds engagement and makes things fun.

Dr. M then lined up three big pillows together on the floor. He had Derek lay on his stomach on one of the pillows and placed himself on the third pillow facing Derek. They made fences with their outstretched hands across the middle pillow. Dr. M placed a cotton ball in the center of the middle pillow and said, "When I say 'go,' you try to blow the cotton ball over to my goal line, and I'll try to get it to yours. First one to win 10 goals wins the game. Ready, set, go!" Dr. M made sure Derek won the first two rounds. Twice Derek jumped the gun on the start, and Dr. M said, "Uh-oh, have to start over." There were a lot of laughs. Dr. M asked for a high five to congratulate the winner. In this interaction, the therapist stayed in charge, but there were no reprimands for making a mistake. Derek realized he could succeed at something totally new. He could lose a bit and survive. He was practicing self-regulation of behavior and frustration. He and another male adult could have fun together.

Next, Dr. M had Derek stand facing him and said, "We're going to play I Say, You Say. I'm going to say and do something, and *when I'm done*, you copy me exactly." Dr. M said, "Boo!" loudly and feigned falling backward a step. Derek quietly mimicked this. Dr. M, standing tall like a soldier, did an about-face and said, "Around!" Derek at first balked, then copied this quietly. Dr. M led Derek through seven more of these imitations, the boy eventually laughing. Dr. M ended the activity in three steps: (a) Pointing to himself, he said, "I," and Derek pointed to himself and said, "I." (b) Taking a step forward, Dr. M said, "like," and Derek said, "like," and stepped forward; the two were at this point 2 feet apart. (c) Dr. M continued, "you" while throwing up his arms; Derek threw up his arms and said, "you." Then, sensing that Derek could manage this, as Derek's arms were in the air, Dr. M reached over, gave Derek a gentle hug, and said, "I like you, too!" A huge smile sprang to Derek's face.

This was a boy who tended to fold and pull in when new tasks were introduced. He also tended to speak quietly and had restrained affect (except when having a tantrum). This activity encouraged him to be silly and loud in an appropriate way. He had to follow directions. Although a therapist would typically be cautious about giving a hug in an early session, Dr. M sensed from the early responses—and based on the MIM assessment of wish for closeness with his father—that he could take a chance on showing a little affection. The hunch was affirmed by Derek's response.

After the exuberant game of I Say, You Say, Dr. M had the two of them sit again on the pillows. He introduced the Staring Contest. Dr. M provided structure by having them sit cross-legged, touching knees; by placing his hands on Derek's shoulders and Derek putting his hands on Dr. M's shoulders; and by clearly stating the rules: When Dr. M gave the signal to start, each was to try to keep his eyes open longest. "The last guy to blink wins!"

A Theraplay therapist manages the ebb and flow of the session by varying the tempo, the intensity, and the types of activities. The Staring Contest was quiet and more intimate than the previous game. The physical arrangement—with Dr. M's hand and arms outside and on Derek's shoulders—provided a metaphorical holding environment. It gave the message "I am providing a secure, safe, and nurturing place for you." This game also gave Derek another opportunity to succeed at something new and to have fun doing it.

Moving again to a more active game, Dr. M had Derek sit, facing the therapist, on a large pillow that had handles attached. Dr. M showed Derek how to hold on to the outside of the loop handles. "When you look at me right in the eye, the pillow will go. When you look away, it will stop." As Derek looked, Dr. M started pulling the pillow across the carpeted floor. Dr. M helped Derek stay on the pillow as they made slow circles and figure eights around the floor. Derek smiled sheepishly at first, as if surprised that he could do this. At the end, Derek stood up and had a wide grin on his face. Dr. M spoke for him: "Wow! Your first time at this and you were really good at it! Great!"

This activity provided another opportunity to succeed at something new. In the course of the session, the challenges increased incrementally, and this one was the most difficult. The sensation of sliding around on the floor was scary but intriguing—somewhat like being on a roller-coaster. Because Derek could control it by how much eye contact he gave, he could feel in charge. He had to trust his therapist to take good care of him. The whole event was fun and exciting—and he could do it!

Dr. M finished this first session with a game of Guess the Goodies. Seated facing each other again on the pillows, he brought out an envelope with Derek's name printed on it. "Inside this envelope, I have some delicious goodies. Your job is to close your eyes and open your mouth. I'll put in a delicious treat, and you can open your eyes and try to guess what it is." Dr. M put in a chocolate candy, then a little pretzel, a cracker, a miniature cookie, a grape, and other treats. Before Dr. M ended the activity, he ran through the list of activities they had enjoyed together during the session. "Which one did you like best?" Derek said, "I liked all of them!"

By ending the session with a food game—typical of Theraplay sessions—Dr. M was able to end the session with nurturing and closeness. Guess the Goodies also builds trust, as Derek had to close his eyes and assume that something nice would be given to him.

Derek was seen for five more individual meetings. After each session, Derek's mother and father viewed videos of the time with Derek. The therapist connected the interactions in the session with what was going on at home. He focused on how to help Derek manage frustrating situations, how his father could be more persistent in trying to engage his son in activities together, and how his mother could be more authoritative. Dr. M sometimes role-played with the parents the games that he had played with Derek and suggested that they practice at home.

Later in Treatment: A Session With Derek and His Father

The individual sessions took place primarily during the summer, during which time Derek made many gains. He started playing more with friends in the neighborhood and was invited to their homes. During the summer break, Derek made gains in self-confidence and was more optimistic. When school resumed, his parents reported that Derek had been cooperating in school and getting homework done. He looked forward to going to school.

At this point, Derek was seen with his father for part of the next Theraplay session. Dr. M met with Derek's father first to check on progress and to prepare him for when Derek would join the session. Dr. M then walked Derek's father through the activities that he would be doing with Derek later in the session. The goal was to prepare for any resistance that Derek might present and to build Dad's confidence.

Something quite interesting happened as Dr. M started this preparation. Dad revealed that he had been working quite hard on this whole process. He remembered that when he came to the United States as a 10-year-old boy, he had felt quite inferior. His English was very poor. He struggled in school. Like his son, he was the youngest in his family and was dwarfed in many ways by his older siblings. Dad had realized that his tendency to criticize his son came out of his own self-doubts and feelings of inferiority. As he had become more mindful of his own history, he had become more open to his son's reality. He had taken more interest in Derek's activities. Dr. M gave Dad a lot of support for his work and congratulations on how nicely things had been developing with his son. This kind of experience—the parent's integration of his or her own history—is just the sort of thing that Siegel and Hartzell (2003) identified as the key to becoming an effective parent.

As planned, Dr. M then saw Derek alone briefly to touch base and also to prepare for his father joining them. After an opening activity, Dr. M departed briefly from the Theraplay protocol, talking with Derek about how things were going. Now much more outgoing, Derek said that he liked school a lot. He volunteered that in gym class that day, he was able to do hula hoops, play basketball, and jump rope. "I can do it fast!" Derek volunteered enthusiastically that he and his father had gone to the family's cabin and that they had built a tree fort together.

Dr. M prepared Derek for Dad to come into the playroom. Derek would be Jack in a jack-in-the-box of pillows. In a corner of the playroom, the two built a box of pillows with Derek inside. Dr. M arranged that Derek would jump out when Dr. M said a secret word, which Derek chose. On cue, Derek was to jump out and go over to give Dad a big hug.

When Dad was brought into the playroom, the two men hunted around the room for Derek and on cue, the boy jumped out and went right over to Dad. They gave each other a big hug. This was followed with a check-in, during which it was discovered that the color of Derek's eyes was much like that of his father's. When his father, using his fingers as a caliper, measured the biceps on Derek's arms and proudly remarked on their large size, Derek beamed. With this activity, Dad was shown how to "claim"—to validate and value—his son. The boy accepted this specific and personal information joyfully. They got to know and appreciate each other more.

The next activity was Crawling Into Arms. Derek was on his hands and knees in the far corner of the room. His father stood in the opposite corner, his outstretched hands forming a circle in front of him. Derek's challenge was to crawl over to Dad and stand up inside of the circle. But Derek had to wait for Dad's signals to crawl. If Dad winked one eye, that meant *go*. Blinking both eyes meant *stop*. When Derek arrived in his father's arms, Dad would give him a big hug. Then Dad would give Derek winks and blinks for him to crawl backward to the corner of the room. This process was repeated several times, with Derek's father making the circle smaller each time. Dr. M noted, "It will be pretty hard to get that big head, with so many brains in it, and those big shoulders, into that little circle." Just as Dr. M had planned with Dad, for the last round, Dad held Derek in his arms and stood up to give Derek a big swing around. Derek's smile was almost as big as the circle the two made.

In this activity, Derek's father was shown how to be more authoritative, to take charge in a caring and playful way. Derek had to follow the adult's rules. In return, he received affection and nurture. The activity required the child to approach the parent and the parent to accept him. The encircled arms provided, symbolically, a secure base.

The session was concluded with a Candy Drop. Dad sat on the floor, and Derek stood in front of his father's legs. One at a time, Dr. M placed a goody on top of Derek's head. Derek had to watch Dad's eyes, so that when Dad winked, Derek would tilt his head forward and try to land the snack into his father's outstretched hands. When he did, his father would look into Derek's eyes and feed it to him. On the few occasions in which Derek was unsuccessful, he was comfortable trying again. For the last snack, Dr. M placed two chocolate drops on Derek's head. Derek was able to get them into his father's hands simultaneously. The session ended as they each unwrapped a drop and fed it to the other—and Dad spontaneously gave his son a huge hug.

Derek and his father now could play together and have fun. Dad could take charge in a firm but playful way. Derek could accept his role as a child. He could manage frustration and persevere with a task. He welcomed new experiences with confidence. His affect was more spontaneous and cheerful.

RESEARCH SUPPORTING THERAPLAY

Clinical reports and qualitative research over a 50-year period have documented the use of Theraplay with diverse populations, from prenatal preparation for parents to senior citizens (Booth & Jernberg, 2010). Most recently, quantitative evidence of the effectiveness of Theraplay has included children presenting with depression, attachment disorders, autism, speech and language disorders, overactivity, social anxiety, and aggression (Booth & Jernberg, 2010; Wettig, Coleman, & Geider, 2011).

Early qualitative research occurred during Theraplay's years in Head Start psychological services. Outcome interviews of 23 teachers regarding the progress of 41 children found improvement in social relationships with adults (87%) and peers (73%), in overall behavior (87%), and in pretest–posttest predictions of success in kindergarten for the upcoming year (Myrow, 2000). During the early years, Jernberg and Hurst also produced two movies documenting change in functioning as a result of early Theraplay treatment. *Here I Am* (Worthington Hurst and Associates, 1969) and *There He Goes* (Worthington Hurst and Associates, 1975) showed how powerful brief individual Theraplay treatment could be with profoundly withdrawn and disruptively overactive children. Each movie included a 3-year follow-up and interview illustrating the longevity of the effects (Myrow, 2000).

The most extensive experimental Theraplay study was conducted in Germany and Austria (Wettig, Franke, & Fjordbak, 2006). Children dually diagnosed with language disorder and a wide variety of other presenting problems were studied. A representative section of this enormous project showed how family Theraplay was used to treat dually diagnosed children with language disorder and shyness or social anxiety (Wettig et al., 2011). This well-controlled, two-part study first addressed 22 children ranging in age from

2 years, 6 months, to 6 years, 11 months, at a single institution by one therapist. The second study improved generalizability by looking at nine qualitatively different sites (e.g., a preschool in a poor neighborhood, a private practice clinic) and multiple therapists, with a pool of 167 children. Results indicated statistically significant improvements in assertiveness, self-confidence, and trust; improved expressive and receptive language skills; and maintenance of gains at 2-year follow-up. The results were consistent across the nine sites. Following treatment, social behavior tended to be within normal limits, typical of nonclinical peers. Receptive and expressive language skills improved as part of the Theraplay experience. In addition, Theraplay required a relatively brief treatment phase of an average of 18 sessions.

Theraplay has received evidence-based status from two states. California noted that Theraplay is "well-supported by research," and in Washington it was rated as a "promising practice" by the Washington State Inventory of Evidence-Based, Research-Based, and Promising Practices (see http://www.theraplay.org for details).

TOWARD THE FUTURE: THERAPLAY DOWN THE ROAD

Kenney-Noziska, Schaefer, and Homeyer (2012) made a strong argument for taking a principled approach in what methods to use with a child according to the child's situation and needs. The Theraplay therapist chooses interventions based on the child's needs. As with other approaches, research on effectiveness with various children and concerns must continue. One common thread probably will be what Crenshaw and Kenney-Noziska (2014) called the essential quality of "presence." Theraplay fills this need: It cannot be practiced without presence! It has a principled origin that is based on attachment theory, which has been substantiated by recent developments in neurobiological science.

This foundation also gives Theraplay practice room to grow with continuing developments in the field. For example, as attention-deficit/hyperactivity disorder has most recently come to be seen as a regulatory disorder with potential influence in a child's early history, the emphasis in Theraplay on experiences that reach into preverbally established patterns offers promise to change behavior that has resisted more behaviorally based approaches. For children with complex concerns—for example, those who have experienced trauma and abuse—Theraplay can play a role, along with other interventions (Gil & Shaw, 2013; Gomez & Jernberg, 2013). Work needs to continue on the amalgamation of these approaches. Sunshine Groups and group Theraplay need to be used and studied with typical and special needs students.

One of the challenges for Theraplay therapists is gaining acceptance of the physical closeness that is inherent in the approach. There are many strategies to protect both clients and therapists. These strategies include engaging in skillful relationship building with parents, making videos of sessions, and including two or more adults in sessions. Most of all, professionals using Theraplay need to have thorough, supervised training and certification. Training includes strategies for teaching administrators and colleagues about Theraplay and its appropriate uses.

With its roots in developmental psychology and attachment theory, and with accumulating evidence from neurobiology, Theraplay gives a new therapist a strong position from which to grow. Theraplay has found its way around the world and is practiced in 40 countries, including the United States, Canada, Finland, Ireland, the United Kingdom, Turkey, and South Korea. For Theraplay to be more widely appreciated in the United States, it needs to find its way into academia. The possibilities for linking with research on human development, neurobiology, counseling, education, and clinical and social psychology are so remarkable that it seems inevitable. Using physical, emotionally present, attuned fun as a way to help children and their parents become closer and become themselves is what Theraplay is all about.

REFERENCES

Bojanowski, J. J., & Ammen, S. (2011). Discriminating between pre- versus post-Theraplay treatment Marschak Interaction Methods using the Marschak Interaction Method rating system. *International Journal of Play Therapy, 20*, 1–11. http://dx.doi.org/10.1037/a0022668

Booth, P., & Jernberg, A. (2010). *Theraplay: Helping parents and children build better relationships through attachment-based play* (3rd ed.). San Francisco, CA: Jossey-Bass.

Bowlby, J. (1988). *A secure base*. London, England: Routledge.

Bundy-Myrow, S. (2012). Family Theraplay: Connecting with children on the autism spectrum. In L. Gallo-Lopez & L. C. Rubin (Eds.), *Play-based interventions for children and adolescents with autism spectrum disorders* (pp. 73–96). New York, NY: Routledge.

Bundy-Myrow, S., & Booth, P. B. (2009). Theraplay: Supporting attachment relationships. In K. J. O'Connor & L. D. Braverman (Eds.), *Play therapy theory and practice: Comparing theories and techniques* (2nd ed., pp. 315–336). Hoboken, NJ: Wiley.

Crenshaw, D. A., & Kenney-Noziska, S. G. (2014). Therapeutic presence in play therapy. *International Journal of Play Therapy, 23*, 31–43. http://dx.doi.org/10.1037/a0035480

DeBenedet, A. T., & Cohen, L. (2010). *The art of roughhousing*. Philadelphia, PA: Quirk Books.

Gil, E., & Shaw, J. (2013). *Working with children with sexual behavior problems*. New York, NY: Guilford Press.

Gomez, A. M., & Jernberg, E. (2013). Using EMDR therapy and Theraplay. In A. M. Gomez (Ed.), *EMDR therapy and adjunct approaches with children* (pp. 273–297). New York, NY: Springer.

Haley, J. (1973). *Uncommon therapy: The psychiatric techniques of Milton H. Erickson, M.D.* New York, NY: Norton.

Hitchcock, D. L., Ammen, S., O'Connor, K., & Backman, T. (2008). Validating the Marschak Interaction Method rating system with adolescent mother–child dyads. *International Journal of Play Therapy, 17*, 24–38. http://dx.doi.org/10.1037/1555-6824.17.1.24

Jernberg, A. (1979). *Theraplay*. San Francisco, CA: Jossey-Bass.

Jernberg, A., & Booth, P. (1999). *Theraplay: Helping parents and children build better relationships through attachment-based play*. San Francisco, CA: Jossey-Bass.

Kenney-Noziska, S. G., Schaefer, C. E., & Homeyer, L. E. (2012). Beyond directive or nondirective: Moving the conversation forward. *International Journal of Play Therapy, 21*, 244–252. http://dx.doi.org/10.1037/a0028910

Kyung, K. Y. (2010). The effect of group Theraplay on elderly women living alone. *Korean Journal of Play Therapy, 13*, 153–169.

Marschak, M. (1980). *Parent–child interaction and youth rebellion*. New York, NY: Gardner Press.

Martin, E. E., Snow, M. S., & Sullivan, K. (2008). Patterns of relating between mothers and preschool-aged children using the Marschak Interaction Method rating system. *Early Child Development and Care, 178*, 305–314. http://dx.doi.org/10.1080/03004430600789290

Myrow, D. L. (2000). Theraplay: The early years. In E. Munns (Ed.), *Theraplay: Innovations in attachment-enhancing play therapy* (pp. 3–8). Northvale, NJ: Jason Aronson.

Myrow, D. L. (2007, Summer). Men in Theraplay: Heavy lifters. *Theraplay Institute Newsletter*. Retrieved from http://www.theraplay.org/index.php/articles-about-theraplay/77-general-articles-about-theraplay/49-article-men-in-theraplay-heavy-lifters

Myrow, D. L. (2013, Winter). Theraplay activities for older children and young teens. Chicago, IL: *Theraplay Institute Newsletter*, pp. 12–15.

Rubin, P., & Tregay, J. (1989). *Play with them—Theraplay groups in the classroom*. Springfield, IL: Charles C Thomas.

Schieffer, K. (2013). *Sunshine Circles teacher resource manual and DVD*. Chicago, IL: Theraplay Institute.

Siegel, D. J. (2012). *The developing mind: How relationships and the brain interact to shape who we are* (2nd ed.). New York, NY: Guilford Press.

Siegel, D. J., & Hartzell, M. (2003). *Parenting from the inside out*. New York, NY: Putnam Press.

Wettig, H. H. G., Coleman, A. R., & Geider, F. G. (2011). Evaluating the effectiveness of Theraplay in treating shy, socially withdrawn children. *International Journal of Play Therapy*, *20*, 26–37. http://dx.doi.org/10.1037/a0022666

Wettig, H. H. G., Franke, U., & Fjordbak, B. S. (2006). Evaluating the effectiveness of Theraplay. In C. E. Schaefer & H. G. Kaduson (Eds.), *Contemporary play therapy: Theory, research, and practice* (pp. 103–135). New York, NY: Guilford Press.

Worthington Hurst and Associates (Producer). (1969). *Here I am* [Motion picture]. United States: Theraplay Institute.

Worthington Hurst and Associates (Producer). (1975). *There he goes* [Motion picture]. United States: Theraplay Institute.

7

USING PUPPETS WITH AGGRESSIVE CHILDREN TO EXTERNALIZE THE PROBLEM IN NARRATIVE THERAPY

JEFFREY T. GUTERMAN AND CLAYTON V. MARTIN

In the past three decades, an increasing number of narrative models have emerged in the field of psychotherapy. The pioneering narrative therapy model was developed by Michael White (1989, 1995, 2000, 2007, 2011) and his colleagues (e.g., Denborough, 2014; Madigan, 2010; Monk, Winslade, Crocket, & Epston, 1996; White & Epston, 1990, 1992) at the Dulwich Therapy Centre in Australia. The narrative approach views clients' problems as restraining narratives or dominant stories that are influenced by their culture (Denborough, 2014; White & Epston, 1990). In narrative therapy, clients are helped to replace problem-maintaining dominant stories with preferred narratives about their lives (Denborough, 2014; White, 2000; White & Epston, 1990, 1992).

http://dx.doi.org/10.1037/14776-008
Play Therapy in Middle Childhood, A. A. Drewes and C. E. Schaefer (Editors)

One of the main principles in narrative therapy is externalizing the problem (Denborough, 2014; White, 1989; White & Epston, 1990). White and Epston (1990) suggested that *externalizing the problem* refers to "an approach . . . that encourages a person to objectify and, at times, to personify the problems that they experience as oppressive" (p. 38). In contrast to *externalizing disorders*, which refers to a pattern of acting out behaviors (Cosgrove et al., 2011), *externalization* in narrative therapy is a process aimed at helping clients see themselves as separate from their problems (White & Epston, 1990). Through externalization, clients are encouraged to understand that they are not the problem; the problem is the problem (White, 2000; White & Epston, 1990). The principle of externalization has been applied to various clinical problems and clients. For example, Matos, Santos, Gonçalves, and Martins (2009) used externalization to assist female victims of interpersonal violence.

In this chapter, we present a clinical application for using puppets with aggressive children to externalize the problem in narrative therapy. Lund, Zimmerman, and Haddock (2002) found that in 17% of family therapy cases, puppets or dolls were used to engage children in treatment. Puppets have been used for various clinical purposes, such as assessment (Ringoot et al., 2013), enhancement of communication (Karakurt, 2012), and problem solving (Kim, 1993). Puppets have also been used within different clinical theories, including cognitive–behavioral therapy (Knell & Dasari, 2012), gestalt play therapy (Blom, 2006), and psychodynamic treatment (Bromfield, 2007).

White (1989) developed the principle of externalizing the problem with young children to engage their imaginations. Freeman, Epston, and Lobovits (1997) used puppets as "cotherapists" in narrative therapy. Butler, Guterman, and Rudes (2009) presented a clinical application for using puppets with children in narrative therapy to externalize the problem. Building on the narrative therapy applications set forth by Freeman et al., Butler et al., and others (Ayland & West, 2006; O'Connor, Meakes, Pickering, & Schuman, 1997; Sheehan, 1997), we have developed a narrative therapy approach for using puppets to externalize the problem with aggressive children.

In this chapter, we present the theory and rationale of the narrative therapy approach used in our clinical application. Next, developmental issues are addressed pertaining to the use of narrative therapy with children. Then, play intervention procedures for the clinical application are described. Empirical support is provided for the clinical application. A case illustration is presented to illustrate the application. Finally, conclusions and future directions are considered for using puppets with children in narrative therapy.

THEORY AND RATIONALE[1]

Narrative therapy's theory of problems and change is informed by postmodernism, an intellectual movement developed in various disciplines that rejects modernist conceptions of objectivity (Lyotard, 1984). In particular, the theory of narrative therapy has been influenced by two factions of postmodernism: deconstructionism (Derrida, 1967, 1996) and poststructuralism (Foucault, 1987, 1988).

Deconstructionism is a postmodern literary theory developed by Derrida (1967) that challenges modernist conceptions of rationality, reason, and truth. Derrida developed deconstructionism as a critique of structuralism, a modernist literary theory that holds that it is possible to understand the true intention of an author's word usages through the interrelations among them. According to Derrida, an author's true intention or meaning can never be discovered because any attempt to do so is always an endless, circular process. In other words, any word has no meaning until its definition is read, then the definitions of the words within its definition, and so on.

Deconstructionism holds that language is a system of differences whereby each word is distinct from other words. Any given word is to be understood as a *binary*, or division into two words. To differentiate a word, it is necessary to distinguish between the word and what is "not the word." For example, the meaning of the word *problem* depends on distinguishing problem from what is "nonproblem," or solution. The meaning of a word is dependent, then, on drawing a distinction between the presence of the chosen word (in the example, *problem*) and the absence of the contrasted word (*solution*). In everyday language, to make sense, one speaks of presences, which are privileged, against absences, which are suppressed. Without the binary distinctions, the presences would not make sense. The word *problem* makes sense only when contrasted with the word *solution*, and conversely *solution* becomes sensible only when contrasted with *problem*.

From a deconstructionist perspective, there is no ultimate justification for so-called rational statements. Any rational statement is empty because words depend on other words for meaning, and all words defer meaning. Returning to the previous example, to speak about the word *problem*, it is necessary to contrast this term with *solution*. In an effort to clarify meaning, people defer to other terms. To clarify the meaning of other terms, they defer to other terms, and so on. The result is an endless loop that is devoid of any

[1]This section is adapted from *Mastering the Art of Solution-Focused Counseling* (2nd ed., pp. 21–23), by J. T. Guterman, 2013, Alexandria, VA: American Counseling Association. Adapted with permission.

definitive meaning. In effect, the term *problem* is undecidable (cf. Collins & Selina, 2005).

Deconstructionism therefore challenges privileged discourses that dominate suppressed and less powerful discourses (Gergen, 2009; Rolfe, 2005). Dominant groups tend to maintain privileged views, whereas disenfranchised others are relegated to the suppressed sides of binary distinctions. Societies are replete with examples of privileged discourses. In Western societies, masculinity tends to be associated with rationality and leadership, whereas femininity is commonly related to emotionality and dependence (Gergen, 2009). In contrast, women who assume leadership roles and men who openly express emotions deviate from some cultural norms. Deconstructionists understand these and other binaries as oppressive and seek to blur such distinctions. Along similar lines, proponents of narrative therapy hold that pathologizing clinical models consist of privileged discourses that often serve to oppress clients (e.g., Combs & Freedman, 2012; Monk et al., 1996; White & Epston, 1990).

Poststructuralism holds that knowledge is constitutive (Foucault, 1987; Madigan, 2010). According to Foucault (1987, 1988), powerful institutions hold privileged knowledge that, in turn, becomes a dominant story in a given culture. Individuals then internalize thoughts and actions that are products of normalizing ideas informed by dominant stories that are embedded in cultural, political, and social contexts. Narrative therapy conceptualizes clinical problems as constraining stories that significantly shape one's history (White & Epston, 1990). These constraining narratives are considered dominant stories and are experienced as oppressive for the lives, identities, and relationships of individuals (Foucault, 1987; White & Epston, 1990).

The binary distinction of deconstructionism serves as a foundation for the theory of problem formation and change in narrative therapy. Narrative therapy holds that a problem-maintaining dominant story persists because preferred stories remain hidden or suppressed. In narrative therapy, *unique outcome* refers to any thought, behavior, feeling, or event that contradicts the dominant story (Denborough, 2014; Madigan, 2010; White, 1995; White & Epston, 1990). For example, when working with aggressive children, the therapist may ask about times when they were able to effectively channel their anger. Such instances, even small ones, are considered unique outcomes. The change process in narrative therapy involves helping children identify and amplify unique outcomes and thereby decrease or eliminate the problem (White & Epston, 1990). From a deconstructionist perspective, this means that the unique outcomes are highlighted and privileged rather than hidden from view. Whereas the problem was once the dominant discourse and the unique outcomes were subjugated, an inverse process has now occurred.

The change process in narrative therapy involves helping children challenge dominant stories and create more empowering narratives about their lives (Denborough, 2014; White, 2000; White & Epston, 1990). This process involves externalizing the problem. In narrative therapy, externalizing the problem involves creating a linguistic separation between the client and the problem (White & Epston, 1990). We suggest that puppets are an effective tool to help aggressive children externalize the problem within a narrative therapy approach for two reasons. First, using puppets serves to objectify the problem. Second, the application begins to create distance between the problem and the child, which is a first step in the process of externalizing the problem (White & Epston, 1990).

DEVELOPMENTAL ISSUES AND SETTINGS

An increasing literature has found narrative therapy to be an effective treatment approach for the unique developmental issues of children (de Faoite, 2011; Freeman et al., 1997; Looyeh, Kamali, Ghasemi, & Tonawanik, 2014; Lundby, 2014). In particular, narrative therapy uses the child's subjective language to define problems and goals and to organize the change process (Denborough, 2014; Lundby, 2014; White & Epston, 1990, 1992). Metaphors, idioms, and the precise words used by the child are incorporated within the therapeutic conversation (White & Epston, 1992). As a result, treatment is tailored to the child's current stage of development and worldview. For example, Lundby (2014) organized narrative therapy around a term introduced by an 11-year-old Norwegian boy referred for aggressive behavior at school. The term *terga*, which roughly translates to "short fuse," established a basis for defining the presenting problem and goal in a manner that was congruent with the child's worldview and served as an organizing metaphor during the change process (Lundby, 2014).

Narrative therapy also emphasizes the role of storytelling with children (e.g., Cattanach, 2009; Freeman et al., 1997; Madigan, 2010; White & Epston, 1990). Through stories, fables, and nursery rhymes, children construct realities, including ideas about right and wrong, cause-and-effect relationships, and the human condition. Looyeh et al. (2014) developed an exercise for school-age children using fairy tales as metaphors aimed at reducing symptoms of social phobia. In this exercise, therapists read fairy tales in which a character has social phobia symptoms. The fairy tales end with the characters feeling positive about identifying effective solutions. The children are then encouraged to identify unique outcomes to their own problem.

The externalization process in narrative therapy is often well suited for children because it highlights the role of imagination and creativity (White, 1989). Externalization is aimed at creating space between clients and problems (Denborough, 2014; Looyeh et al., 2014; White, 1989; White & Epston,

1990). Children are typically familiar with characters depicted in popular cartoons, movies, and other media. The various emotions and behaviors expressed by such characters provide a frame of reference that makes externalization a natural process for many children:

> A young person can develop the sense of being the protagonist in a story of change and hope, while the problem is considered an antagonist. Against the child's qualities of courage, determination, and ingenuity, for example, the externalized problem is vilified in terms of its "unfair" effects. Not surprisingly, the child, sensing an injustice, is highly motivated to test his [or her] mettle and challenge his [or her] relationship with this problem. (Freeman et al., 1997, pp. 51–52)

Narrative approaches have been used in various clinical settings for children, including outpatient facilities, schools, and hospitals. Narrative therapy has also been used with children in individual, family, and group modalities. We have found narrative therapy with children to be particularly effective in individual and family work because treatment can more easily be tailored to the unique aspects of each case. In some situations it may be contraindicated to use puppets with children to externalize the problem in narrative therapy. The therapist might conclude following assessment that narrative therapy may be more effective without the use of puppets. Some children might be fearful, distracted, or not amenable to using a puppet for such purposes.

PLAY INTERVENTION PROCEDURES

We use puppets in our work with children at various stages in narrative therapy in an effort to externalize the problem. The narrative therapy approach we follow typically has five stages (cf. Butler et al., 2009; Denborough, 2014; White, 2007; White & Epston, 1990), although they are meant to serve only as a guide. Because each child is unique, the stages do not account for situations that are distinctive to each case. The stages are meant to be used during the initial and subsequent sessions. Nevertheless, the recursive nature of narrative therapy's clinical stages makes them applicable to all sessions. Despite the approach's recursive aspects, the process is explicated here in terms of discrete stages, although they are not meant to be understood as having clear boundaries. The stages are (a) defining the problem, (b) mapping the influences of the problem, (c) evaluating and justifying the effects of the problem, (d) identifying unique outcomes, and (e) restorying.

When defining the problem, the therapist attempts to obtain a description of the problem from the child. During this stage, it is important to identify the words that most closely approximate the child's experience of the problem. This identification allows children to achieve a near experience of the problem and serves to privilege their descriptions (Denborough, 2014; White, 2007; White & Epston, 1990). Children are also often encouraged to put a name to the problem (White & Epston, 1990). For example, White and Epston (1990) described the case of a 6-year-old boy presenting with encopresis. During family therapy, the boy and his parents defined the problem as frequent soiling and described a pattern of the "accidents" sneaking up on the family and taking on a life of its own. It is critical for the name to be related to the words used by the child. In this case, it was fitting for the boy to name the problem as *sneaky poo*. Naming the problem is often a first step during the process of externalization. Doing so creates a linguistic separation between the problem and the child. In some cases, defining the problem is difficult and for various reasons is not achieved during the first stage, or even during the first session. If children are unable to define the problem, it is sometimes preferable to proceed to the next stage, mapping the influences of the problem.

Mapping the influences of the problem is a questioning process aimed at helping children identify and increase their experience of the problem's influences and thereby helps to externalize the problem (White, 2004; White & Epston, 1990). When mapping the influences, therapists ask how the problem has affected various domains of the child's life, including daily functioning, work, and relationships. An example of such questioning might be, "How is the problem affecting the view you have of yourself?" By identifying ways a problem has affected their lives across different domains, children are encouraged to view themselves as separate from the problem. Another purpose of mapping the influences is to increase a sense of agency by recognizing opportunities for identifying unique outcomes during the clinical process. After the child has mapped various influences, the therapist can go back to these influences and inquire about unique outcomes (described later in this section).

The next stage, evaluating and justifying the effects of the problem, invites children to consider their position in relation to the problem—good or bad, helpful or unhelpful—in an effort to elicit a clear evaluation of the presenting issue. This line of questioning can be new and unexpected for children because often other people (e.g., family members, friends, teachers) already hold positions regarding the problem. If the child evaluates the problem as negative, then the therapist seeks a justification through various questions. For example, the therapist might ask children to articulate how the negative effects of the problem are at odds with their goals and intentions. If the child does not evaluate the effects of the problem as negative, it might be necessary to consider whether the "problem" is indeed a problem for the child. In some cases, it might be helpful to return to previous stages and redefine the problem or map its influences.

The next stage in narrative therapy is identifying unique outcomes. Therapists use interventive questions to help children identify unique outcomes—for example, "How were you able to not let the problem influence you at this time?" or "What did you do to overcome the problem in this situation?" The influences identified during the mapping process can be used during this stage as a basis for identifying unique outcomes. For example, if a child reported an influence related to anxiety about school issues, the therapist might ask a series of questions to identify unique outcomes related to the worry in this domain.

After identifying unique outcomes, children are helped to ascribe meaning to these events through the next stage, restorying, a therapeutic process designed to help create a sense of self-efficacy, empowerment, and hope (Monk et al., 1996; White, 2000; White & Epston, 1990). Restorying might involve the therapist asking the child, "What does this [i.e., the unique outcome] say about you and your ability to influence this problem?" or "What qualities does a person require to deal with this problem?"

EMPIRICAL SUPPORT

Numerous narrative therapy approaches have been set forth for working with children (e.g., McLuckie & Rowbotham, 2014; Wang & Lin, 2011; Young, 2008). In particular, research has investigated the use of narrative therapy with aggressive children and youth to externalize the problem (e.g., Ayland & West, 2006; Bennett, 2008; O'Connor et al., 1997; Sheehan, 1997). Clinical applications have also been developed for using puppets and toys with children in narrative therapy (Bennett, 2008; Butler et al., 2009; Freeman et al., 1997).

O'Connor et al. (1997) conducted ethnographic research on eight families' experiences of narrative therapy and discussed major themes in interviews, including externalizing the problem. Families presented to therapy for various problems, including aggressive behaviors of their children between 6 and 13 years of age. According to O'Connor et al., families found the narrative therapy to be effective. The results of the research by O'Connor et al. support the view that narrative therapy provides an effective context for empowering clients with personal agency as family members were able to take responsibility and credit for positive changes in their lives.

Ayland and West (2006) developed a narrative therapy approach for children and youth with intellectual difficulties and sexually abusive behavior. The intervention used by Ayland and West included helping clients to identify their strengths and understand the consequences of their actions and the impact on others of the abusive behavior. At the time of this writing, none of the clients completing the program were known to have sexually reoffended. The model set forth by Ayland and West affirms that narrative therapy is effective at helping children and youth identify and build on their effective coping skills.

Freeman et al. (1997) described using puppets as cotherapists in narrative therapy. According to Freeman et al., puppets can be used to support the therapist to facilitate conversation:

> Although the use of reflecting teams has increased, it is rarely practical to have human cotherapists on board for most of our sessions. Instead, we might invite members of the family or anyone else present at the session to pick up a puppet and form a reflecting team with it. Puppet reflecting teams can bring a range of voices into the room. Imagine a team consisting of a Wise Owl, a Snail, and a Wizard, or a King and a Queen, a Dragon, and a Frog! (p. 173)

Bennett (2008) combined narrative therapy with expressive therapeutic techniques, including using toys to externalize the problem. In a case involving a 10-year-old boy who presented to therapy for aggressive behavior at school, toy army figures were used to represent the child's "good" and "bad" sides and thereby help him work toward externalizing the problem.

Butler et al. (2009) developed a clinical application for using puppets with children in narrative therapy with the intention of externalizing the problem. A case example was described involving an 8-year-old boy named Eric with the problem of disruptive behavior and getting into fights with classmates. Eric was an only child residing with his mother. His father had moved out 1 year previously, and his parents' divorce became final 3 months prior to the referral. During the first session, the mother stated that teachers reported that when her son did not get his way, he got angry and erupted like a volcano. She said this pattern was similar at home.

During the first session, the therapist introduced a selection of puppets and asked Eric to choose one that most closely represented his anger. The child chose a large bug puppet. Butler et al. (2009) pointed out that through the use of the puppet, the child's anger "became a thing, an entity—in effect, an objectification of the problem—which, in turn, enacted the externalizing process" (p. 230). Butler et al. noted that using the puppet gave the child a voice to the problem, which assisted in the process of identifying unique outcomes and restorying. After eight sessions, the child's anger had dissipated and his coping and social skills had improved. A consensus was reached that the treatment was no longer needed but that therapy could be resumed if the need should arise. The case provided by Butler et al. suggests that using puppets in narrative therapy is an effective treatment for aggressive children.

CASE ILLUSTRATION INCLUDING CAREGIVER INVOLVEMENT

An 8-year-old girl, Jacqueline, was referred by her school for therapy because of aggressive behavior at school. Jacqueline was an only child and resided with her mother and father. Jacqueline's father had a history of alcohol abuse, and he was currently in an inpatient rehabilitation program at the time of her referral. Jacqueline came to the first session accompanied by her mother.

At the start of the first session, the therapist began the first stage of narrative therapy, defining the problem. Her mother reported that Jacqueline's most recent aggressive episode resulted in her throwing a chair in class and damaging a wall. Her mother also reported that Jacqueline had been defiant, disrespectful, and threatening toward her ever since she was a very young child, but that her behavior escalated whenever her father left the home because of their separating or his entering treatment. She described Jacqueline as an uncaring child who did not consider the consequences of her behavior. The mother also stated that when Jacqueline was expected to work in school or was told what to do by a peer, she often became verbally or physically aggressive. Jacqueline's mother explained that because of the escalation of her behavior at school, most children refused to speak to her except for times when they teased or insulted her. The mother added that at home, she often disengaged from communicating with Jacqueline when she manifested aggressive behavior: "I just let her rot in front of the TV and I go away; it's the only thing that keeps both of us from pulling our hair out."

After several unsuccessful attempts at eliciting participation from Jacqueline, the therapist moved to the next stage of narrative therapy, mapping the influences of the problem. The therapist considered that identifying the effects of the problem at this point might contribute to helping Jacqueline define the problem and begin understanding how it had impacted various aspects of her life. This stage was also designed to create a linguistic space between Jacqueline and the problem. The mother reported that Jacqueline's anger often got her in trouble at school and led to her being sent to suspension, which Jacqueline reportedly despised. The mother also described how Jacqueline's anger had contributed to frequent arguments between them that, in turn, had driven Jacqueline's mother to disengage from the relationship. At this point, Jacqueline nodded her head. The therapist then asked Jacqueline, "Do you think this sounds right, Jacqueline? Does anger take you away from people and put you into places that feel lonely and quiet? " Jacqueline replied, "Yes, sometimes." Jacqueline went on to describe several effects of the influences of the problem, stating that anger led her to lose privileges at home and school and to break toys and possessions that she enjoyed and made classmates scared to be around her.

The therapist summarized Jacqueline's understanding of the problem and suggested that it had led to various negative feelings and experiences. Upon hearing the therapist's summation, Jacqueline described the problem as an annoyance in her life that had interfered with things she enjoyed. Jacqueline stated, however, that the anger was not all bad: "It keeps people I don't like from bothering me or being mean to me. It shows them that I mean business!" The therapist confirmed with Jacqueline that her anger stood up for her sometimes in addition to getting her into trouble. This was a realization for Jacqueline that established a basis for evaluating and justifying the effects of the problem. Given this development, the therapist chose to introduce puppets as a clinical tool to continue working toward externalizing the problem.

The therapist displayed a selection of puppets while explaining that he frequently used them to help children with their problems. The therapist asked Jacqueline to choose a puppet that most closely represented her feelings toward anger. Jacqueline chose a rhinoceros puppet and stated, "This is it!" The therapist asked Jacqueline a series of questions regarding why she had chosen that particular puppet. Jacqueline stated that the rhino charges anything that hurts it or makes it upset, and it often ends up "stepping all over everything else while it's chasing down mean people." Jacqueline then moved the puppet toward her mother and stated, "He's going to charge!" Jacqueline moved the rhino closer and closer to her mother and the therapist. Jacqueline stopped only when her mother playfully raised her voice and stated, "Get your nose out of my business!" Both Jacqueline and her mother erupted in laughter, which Jacqueline's mother stated was a rare occurrence.

Through the use of the puppet, Jacqueline's anger became an objectification of the problem, which served to enact the externalizing process. Toward the end of the first session, the therapist asked Jacqueline and her mother if they would like to take the puppet home between sessions. The therapist suggested that it might be useful for Jacqueline and her mother to observe the rhino's annoying, shortsighted, and sometimes protective ways. In addition, the therapist suggested that Jacqueline be assigned to consult with her mother when she was able to control the puppet, and also when it got the better of her. Both Jacqueline and her mother agreed to the task.

At the start of the second session, the therapist followed up on the task. The mother, wearing a broad smile, said it had been a much better week. With puppet in hand, Jacqueline was attentive to her mother's descriptions of the good week. Following is a transcript of the conversation that transpired at this point in the session:

Therapist: May I ask the rhino how things have been this past week?

Jacqueline: *[Continuing with puppet in hand]* Sure. It's OK.

Therapist: OK.

Mother: It's alright.

Jacqueline: *[Speaking as the puppet]* People make me mad! They make me charge! They make me stamp on things!

Therapist: OK!

Jacqueline: But I couldn't stamp when I wanted to this time. Jacqueline said, "Keep your nose out of my business!" It hurt my feelings. *[Mother smiles.]*

Therapist: How are you feeling now?

Jacqueline: OK. But I'm gonna keep charging!

Therapist: You are?

Jacqueline: Yeah.

Therapist: What else can rhinos do when they're mad?

Jacqueline: Huh? I don't know. I just charge. It stops people.

Therapist: Maybe you can help stick up for Jacqueline without charging?

Jacqueline: How?

Therapist: Maybe Jacqueline and her mom can come up with some ideas for you this week.

As a result of this enactment, the puppet gave a voice to the problem. After Jacqueline spoke for the puppet, the therapist moved to the stage of identifying unique outcomes. The therapist asked Jacqueline, "Is the rhino always in charge?" An active discussion ensued about more ways in which Jacqueline had told the rhino to "keep your nose out of my business." Jacqueline identified an instance when the puppet did not lead her to lose control. Jacqueline recalled that during the week, a classmate called her a bad name at school and she did not respond in her usual way. The therapist asked Jacqueline, "How did you manage to not let that person get to you?" Jacqueline was not able to account for how she maintained control. The therapist, however, considered this event to be an opportunity to identify a unique outcome in relation to the problem. Jacqueline had not ascribed meaning to what had occurred in school, and the event was therefore not yet understood as a unique outcome. The puppet would be used to help Jacqueline attach meaning to the event and thereby identify it as a unique outcome.

With Jacqueline characterizing the rhino as the problem, the therapist asked a series of questions designed to make connections between the event of the classmate calling her a bad name and her good experience of it. For example, the therapist asked Jacqueline, "What did the rhino think about how you handled being called that name in class?" Jacqueline responded quickly, "He got mad at first, but when the boy left me alone, he settled down!" Toward the end of the session, Jacqueline came to see the event at school as a unique outcome.

During the next several weeks, Jacqueline identified additional unique outcomes related to the problem. Jacqueline continued to take the puppet home between sessions and reported being very successful at controlling it. She continued checking in with her mother on her progress with the puppet. Jacqueline came to one session with a bandage affixed to the rhino's horn and explained, "The rhino tried to charge at my teacher, but I would have lost the field trip if it did. So I grabbed it by its nose and it got hurt." What came out of that session was Jacqueline's caring and concern for the puppet despite her dislike for its charging and smashing behavior.

As the treatment progressed, the therapist helped Jacqueline ascribe meaning to the unique outcomes during the restorying stage. The therapist asked Jacqueline a series of questions, including "What is it like to be a Rhino Tamer?" and "What is it like to be a girl who can control her anger?" The child's focus shifted away from an emphasis on problem talk and more toward her goals, purposes, and intentions. For the first time, Jacqueline began to speak about her father, which, until this time, was a topic expressed only in negative ways. She also began to deal with her angry and sad feelings about her father's inconsistent presence in her life. Jacqueline's mother supported these developments through offering story lines of Jacqueline being a caring, rather than an uncaring, child. The mother's role in the therapy was understood as that of an outside witness. In narrative therapy, an *outside witness* is any significant person or figure who speaks with authority to the child's new, preferred narrative (White, 2007). The mother's responses were influential in the restorying process in several ways, including acknowledging Jacqueline's improvement, identifying additional unique outcomes, and ascribing new meanings to her daughter's actions.

After eight therapy sessions conducted across 3 months, Jacqueline's anger had greatly dissipated. Her coping skills were markedly improved, and she also developed better social skills. A consensus was reached between the therapist, Jacqueline, and her mother that treatment was no longer needed at this time. It was agreed that therapy could be resumed if the need should arise. At the end of the final session, the therapist asked Jacqueline if she would like to keep the puppet. Jacqueline accepted and said, "I think I have more tricks to teach him!"

CONCLUSION AND FUTURE DIRECTIONS

From our clinical experiences, we have found puppets to be an effective tool in narrative therapy when working with aggressive children as well as children with various problems. It is reaffirmed that it is not necessary to use puppets to externalize the problem. Moreover, the therapist might conclude following assessment that narrative therapy may be more effective and efficient without the use of puppets. Some children might not be amenable to using a puppet for externalizing the problem in narrative therapy.

We have typically used puppets only with young children in narrative therapy. In some cases, older children, adolescents, and adult clients might benefit from the use of puppets or other props for the purpose of externalizing the problem. Clients of all ages are routinely encouraged to objectify the problem in narrative therapy through various clinical methods, such as letter writing and naming the problem (Monk et al., 1996; White & Epston, 1990). When therapists conclude after assessment that it is appropriate, clients can be encouraged to select from objects, personal or otherwise, that serve as tools to enhance the externalizing process. For example, an adult client might identify a work of art that most closely represents the problem.

Finally, we wish to highlight the important role that imagination plays during therapy and, in particular, the externalization process in narrative therapy (White, 1989; White & Epston, 1992). In narrative therapy, it is largely the child's ability to imagine the puppet as the problem that serves to enhance the externalization process and contribute to change. Accordingly, we consider children's imaginations to be the most important resource in narrative therapy. Imagination is a resource that clients of all ages possess. As therapists, our imaginations also serve as important resources as we work with clients toward therapeutic ends.

REFERENCES

Ayland, L., & West, B. (2006). The Good Way model: A strengths-based approach for working with young people, especially those with intellectual difficulties, who have sexually abusive behavior. *Journal of Sexual Aggression, 12*, 189–201. http://dx.doi.org/10.1080/13552600600841680

Bennett, L. (2008). Narrative methods and children: Theoretical explanations and practice issues. *Journal of Child and Adolescent Psychiatric Nursing, 21*, 13–23. http://dx.doi.org/10.1111/j.1744-6171.2008.00125.x

Blom, R. (2006). *The handbook of gestalt play therapy*. London, England: Kingsley.

Bromfield, R. (2007). *Doing child and adolescent psychotherapy: Adapting psychodynamic treatment to contemporary practice* (2nd ed.). Hoboken, NJ: Wiley.

Butler, S., Guterman, J. T., & Rudes, J. (2009). Using puppets with children in narrative therapy to externalize the problem. *Journal of Mental Health Counseling, 31*, 225–233.

Cattanach, A. (2009). Narrative approaches: Helping children tell their stories. In A. A. Drewes (Ed.), *Blending play therapy with cognitive behavioral therapy:*

Evidence-based and other effective treatments and techniques (pp. 423–447). Hoboken, NJ: Wiley.

Collins, J., & Selina, H. (2005). *Introducing Derrida* (3rd ed.). Cambridge, England: Icon Books.

Combs, G., & Freedman, J. (2012). Narrative, poststructuralism, and social justice: Current practices in narrative therapy. *Counseling Psychologist*, *40*, 1033–1060. http://dx.doi.org/10.1177/0011000012460662

Cosgrove, V. E., Rhee, S. H., Gelhorn, H. L., Boeldt, D., Corley, R. C., Ehringer, M. A., . . . Hewitt, J. K. (2011). Structure and etiology of co-occurring internalizing and externalizing disorders in adolescents. *Journal of Abnormal Child Psychology*, *39*, 109–123. http://dx.doi.org/10.1007/s10802-010-9444-8

de Faoite, A. T. (2011). Narrative play therapy. In C. E. Schaefer (Ed.), *Foundations of play therapy* (2nd ed., pp. 329–347). Hoboken, NJ: Wiley.

Denborough, D. (2014). *Retelling the stories of our lives: Everyday narrative therapy to draw inspiration and transform experience*. New York, NY: Norton.

Derrida, J. (1967). *Of grammatology* (G. C. Spivak, Trans.). Baltimore, MD: Johns Hopkins University Press.

Derrida, J. (1996). As if I were dead: An interview with Jacques Derrida. In R. Robbins & J. Wolfreys (Eds.), *Applying: To Derrida* (pp. 212–227). London, England: Macmillan.

Foucault, M. (1987). *Power/knowledge: Selected interviews and writings, 1972–1977* (C. Gordon, Trans.). New York, NY: Pantheon Books.

Foucault, M. (1988). *Madness and civilization: A history of insanity in the age of reason, 1965* (R. Howard, Trans.). New York, NY: Vintage Books.

Freeman, J., Epston, D., & Lobovits, D. (1997). *Playful approaches to serious problems: Narrative therapy with children and their families*. New York, NY: Norton.

Gergen, K. J. (2009). *An invitation to social construction* (2nd ed.). Thousand Oaks, CA: Sage.

Karakurt, G. (2012). Puppet play with a Turkish family. *Journal of Family Psychotherapy*, *23*, 69–78. http://dx.doi.org/10.1080/08975353.2012.654092

Kim, H. K. (1993). The effects of problem solving interaction through a puppet show on a child's interpersonal problem solving skills. *Korean Journal of Child Studies*, *14*(2), 49–63.

Knell, S. M., & Dasari, M. (2012). Cognitive–behavioral play therapy. In S. W. Russ & L. N. Niec (Eds.), *Play in clinical practice: Evidence-based approaches* (pp. 236–263). New York, NY: Guilford Press.

Looyeh, M. Y., Kamali, K., Ghasemi, A., & Tonawanik, P. (2014). Treating social phobia in children through group narrative therapy. *Arts in Psychotherapy*, *41*, 16–20. http://dx.doi.org/10.1016/j.aip.2013.11.005

Lund, L. K., Zimmerman, T. S., & Haddock, S. A. (2002). The theory, structure, and techniques for the inclusion of children in family therapy: A literature review. *Journal of Marital and Family Therapy, 28*, 445–454. http://dx.doi.org/10.1111/j.1752-0606.2002.tb00369.x

Lundby, G. (2014). Creating different versions of life: Talking about problems with children and their parents. *Australian and New Zealand Journal of Family Therapy, 35*(1), 31–45.

Lyotard, J. (1984). *The postmodern condition: A report on knowledge* (B. Massumi, Trans.). Minneapolis: University of Minnesota Press.

Madigan, S. (2010). *Narrative therapy*. Washington, DC: American Psychological Association.

Matos, M., Santos, A., Gonçalves, M., & Martins, C. (2009). Innovative moments and change in narrative therapy. *Psychotherapy Research, 19*, 68–80. http://dx.doi.org/10.1080/10503300802430657

McLuckie, A., & Rowbotham, M. (2014). Narrative play therapy with families. In N. R. Bowers (Ed.), *Play therapy with families: A collaborative approach to healing* (pp. 113–146). Lanham, MD: Jason Aronson.

Monk, G., Winslade, J., Crocket, K., & Epston, D. (1996). *Narrative therapy in practice*. San Francisco, CA: Jossey-Bass.

O'Connor, T. S. J., Meakes, E., Pickering, M. R., & Schuman, M. (1997). On the right track: Client experience of narrative therapy. *Contemporary Family Therapy, 19*, 479–495. http://dx.doi.org/10.1023/A:1026126903912

Ringoot, A. P., Jansen, P. W., Steenweg-de Graaff, J., Measelle, J. R., van der Ende, J., Raat, H., . . . Tiemeier, H. (2013). Young children's self-reported emotional, behavioral, and peer problems: The Berkeley Puppet Interview. *Psychological Assessment, 25*, 1273–1285. http://dx.doi.org/10.1037/a0033976

Rolfe, G. (2005). The deconstructing angel: Nursing, reflection and evidence-based practice. *Nursing Inquiry, 12*, 78–86. http://dx.doi.org/10.1111/j.1440-1800.2005.00257.x

Sheehan, M. (1997). Adolescent violence: Strategies, outcomes and dilemmas in working with young people and their families. *Australian and New Zealand Journal of Family Therapy, 18*, 80–90. http://dx.doi.org/10.1002/j.1467-8438.1997.tb00274.x

Wang, S., & Lin, M. (2011). A case study of narrative therapy with children. *Archive of Guidance & Counseling, 33*, 39–62.

White, M. (1989). The externalizing of the problem and the re-authoring of lives and relationships. In M. White (Ed.), *Selected papers* (pp. 5–28). Adelaide, South Australia: Dulwich Centre.

White, M. (1995). *Re-authoring lives: Interview and essays*. Adelaide, South Australia: Dulwich Centre.

White, M. (2000). *Reflections on narrative practice*. Adelaide, South Australia: Dulwich Centre.

White, M. (2004). *Narrative practice and exotic lives: Resurrecting diversity in everyday life*. Adelaide, South Australia: Dulwich Centre.

White, M. (2007). *Maps of narrative practice*. New York, NY: Norton.

White, M. (2011). *Narrative practice: Continuing the conversations*. New York, NY: Norton.

White, M., & Epston, D. (1990). *Narrative means to therapeutic ends*. New York, NY: Norton.

White, M., & Epston, D. (1992). *Experience, contradiction, narrative, and imagination* (2nd ed.). Adelaide, South Australia: Dulwich Centre.

Young, K. (2008). Narrative practice at a walk-in therapy clinic: Developing children's worry wisdom. *Journal of Systemic Therapies, 27*(4), 54–74. http://dx.doi.org/10.1521/jsyt.2008.27.4.54

8

KIDS TOGETHER: A GROUP THERAPY PROGRAM FOR CHILDREN USING COGNITIVE–BEHAVIORAL PLAY THERAPY INTERVENTIONS

SUSAN HANSEN

This chapter provides an overview of a group therapy intervention for children, describing the program's evolution during its 17-year span and recent data that support the program's effectiveness. Despite the program's initial focus on treating children with attention-deficit/hyperactivity disorder (ADHD) symptoms, as further assessment occurred, the program developers identified a disproportionate percentage of youth impacted by histories of trauma, thereby requiring a more trauma-informed intervention. In recognition of this population shift, programmatic changes occurred to reflect more appropriate interventions. In line with this shift, directive play and nonverbal modalities were integrated to support growing awareness of the effectiveness of these modalities with child trauma survivors. Overall, trauma symptom reductions have been reported and treatment effectiveness has been identified with the use of play therapy for a host of childhood emotional and behavioral challenges (Bratton, Ray, Rhine, & Jones, 2005; Ray, 2006; Ray, Bratton, Rhine, & Jones, 2001; Reyes & Asbrand, 2005).

http://dx.doi.org/10.1037/14776-009
Play Therapy in Middle Childhood, A. A. Drewes and C. E. Schaefer (Editors)

PROGRAM OVERVIEW

The Kids Together group therapy intervention served hundreds of children during its 17-year history. From the program's inception through its final group session, its evolution was marked by a growing awareness of the population's needs and the power of group work in supporting skill development in youth challenged by a variety of psychiatric as well as family dynamics issues. The Kids Together group therapy program was a skills-building, process-oriented, group therapy intervention. This interagency, community-based program was designed to serve children and adolescents ages 5 to 18 years who were challenged by social, emotional, and behavioral difficulties making them eligible for a mental health diagnosis. The program involved three discrete, developmentally driven child and adolescent groups running concurrent with one another. Each of the three child and adolescent groups was cofacilitated and structured by the common, developmentally informed curriculum. Facilitators included both professional and paraprofessional staff who were trained and continuously professionally supervised within the model. In addition to the child and adolescent groups, a parent group also provided a skills-building component for guardians and parents of the youth attending Kids Together.

The structured, skills-building intervention focused on supporting shifts in internalizing behaviors such as self-esteem, anxiety, and mood symptoms with the premise that externalizing behavior change was then more likely to follow. Change, within the program, was initially observed to occur through enhanced emotional and behavioral regulation, which was then followed by the ability to use improved cognitive strategies focused on enhancing problem-solving and decision-making skills. Anecdotal experience indicated that once youth were able to regulate their emotional states, allowing them to be more grounded and less reactive, they were more successful at inserting the rational decision-making strategies more typically the focus of clinical group interventions.

Theoretically, this process-based, structured format integrated Shulman's (1992) mutual aid model with cognitive–behavioral group therapy (CBGT; Rose, 2004), play therapy, and other nonverbal modalities; the curriculum and topic-based approach allowed for the exchange of ideas related to varying areas of focus within a supportive, dynamic environment. The interactions occurred both within a verbal, talk therapy format and through nonverbal group activities in which members were able to explore issues within the metaphor and via more engaging nonverbal tasks.

The group experience allowed for sharing of ideas, mutual support of one another, and challenge of self-destructive or unhealthy choice making by other group members. This mutually supportive environment was the foundation that supported the learning of new skills as youth processed their challenges while rehearsing and integrating new behaviors in a reciprocal, interactive process. A sense of community and shared experience allowed group members to support, and also challenge, one another in ways that adults are not often able to successfully do with youth individually.

The focus on challenging and shifting cognitions while seeking to integrate new behavioral strategies was more viable within an environment of mutual aid. Behavioral change related to emotion regulation and higher order reasoning was more attainable when group members experienced a sense of commonality and collaboration. The strength-based approach was focused less on the assessed pathological symptoms leading to the referral for services, often a pivotal focus in more traditional deficit-oriented, medical model approaches, and more on the creation of a community-based, supportive setting designed to engage youth who were often resistant to engaging in more traditionally structured mental health clinical settings.

Kids Together maintained a process-based, here-and-now focus. Yalom (1985) described an illumination process that occurred when the group material was present focused rather than focused on past events, as the former allowed for greater self-reflection and reevaluation. A potential exists for providing a corrective experience for group members who have struggled with issues outside the group process, as they can use the group for support to yield understanding, insight, and greater perspective about themselves and their particular challenges. The context can be supportive despite discussion of challenging material and thereby result in a corrective, empowering experience.

Focusing on both verbal and nonverbal communication and group dynamics, including interpersonal attunement and relationship building between group members, provided for personal growth and individual change. Change occurred in the context of the group members' relationships as these interactions were pivotal elements in the change process. As safety was built, greater self-disclosure occurred and openness to feedback and support grew. Through these relationships, internalizing behavior problems had the greatest chance of shifting given that change is more likely when participants feel connected, grounded, and supported within their environment. As support grew, group participants began to display greater self-regulation.

POPULATION

The goal of increased self-regulation became a priority within the Kids Together program given the growing clarity about the group population. It was originally conceived of as a program designed to serve youth presenting with ADHD symptoms, yet once initial assessment began and the program was under way, it became clear that the clustering of symptoms was not most accurately encapsulated in an ADHD diagnosis. In fact, as the group intervention evolved and demographics were collected, it was determined that 80% of group participants lived in households earning less than $40,000 annually, and close to the same number were growing up in households that had experienced divorce.

In addition, upwards of 90% of group participants had a known history of childhood abuse and neglect, resulting in what came to be identified as profound emotional, behavioral, cognitive, and neurobiological implications related to their traumatic experiences (van der Kolk, 2005). Of the close to 90% of youth with trauma histories, almost all had experienced ongoing chronic interpersonal trauma. This ongoing exposure was certainly implicated in their complex symptom profiles. Bessel van der Kolk (2005) asserted that there are irrefutable long-term health implications for children exposed to stressful, abusive environments. He described limitations in neurobiological development, attachment systems, and affect management systems in children exposed to interpersonal violence and purported that the result is a profound challenge in self-regulation, behavioral management, and rational, thoughtful decision making.

As the program evolved, an evolution toward greater trauma-informed programming occurred as a diagnostic reconceptualization of the clustering of symptoms for referred youth occurred. The overwhelming majority of children referred to the program presented as emotionally and behaviorally dysregulated, impulsive, and emotionally labile. Given their histories of abuse and neglect, children often experienced disorganized attachment, resulting in a myriad of behavioral consequences. These consequences often included poor stress management skills and a variety of externalizing behavior problems including aggressive, acting out behaviors (van IJzendoorn, Schuengel, & Bakermans-Kranenburg, 1999).

Abuse and maltreatment were identified as risk factors for insecure attachment given statistics demonstrating that upwards of 80% of children demonstrate insecure attachment when exposed to maltreatment (Cook et al., 2005). Cook and colleagues (2005) reported that complex trauma often results in children who struggle with "loss of core capacities for self-regulation and interpersonal connectedness" (p. 390). These limitations were directly targeted in the Kids Together intervention given its here-and-now, social learning, mutual aid model with emphasis given to skill building and improved overall emotional and behavioral functioning based on current research on the effects of trauma on the child's brain.

Given existing research, it has become increasingly clear that chronic deprivation, abuse, and neglect impact a child's developing brain. Neurophysiology, structural functioning, and the overall anatomy of the brain are impacted by early trauma (Siegel, 1999; Stien & Kendall, 2004; van der Kolk, 2005). The brain develops in a stepwise, orderly fashion with the brain stem and limbic system developing sequentially as they pave the way for the development of the cortex and neocortex (Stien & Kendall, 2004). Each brain region performs discrete tasks while also working in concert with the others to provide for overall integrated functioning.

During typical brain development, the cortex manages the impulses and reactivity system signaling a need to defend and protect oneself (Stien & Kendall, 2004). The brain stem helps to regulate basic cardiovascular functions, whereas the limbic system supports the monitoring of incoming stimuli, the appraisal of experience, memory processing, and the transfer of information between the two hemispheres; the brain stem is also involved in activating bodily reactions. These brain functions develop prior to the maturation of the cortex and neocortex, which form the seat of planning, conscious thinking, and rational decision making. The cortex plays a role in inhibiting reactivity and serves a modulating function (Stien & Kendall, 2004).

Contemporary research has demonstrated that when ongoing, chronic deprivation and trauma occur early in life, there are deficiencies in interpersonal, attachment-based experiences leading to cortical understimulation while at the same time providing experiences leading to overstimulation of the limbic system, thereby resulting in behavioral dysregulation (Morse & Wiley, 1997). The result is a child who struggles to modulate present-day emotional experience and to attune to and be appropriately responsive to his or her environment.

Reactivity, along with emotional and behavioral dysregulation, was consistently the reason for referral to Kids Together. As the program evolved, a shift away from more behavioral diagnostic terminology and toward a greater trauma-informed understanding supported the staff in differentiating between what appeared to be oppositional, antisocial-type behavior and a more trauma-reactive, skill-deficit-related symptom profile. As the staff began to use their therapeutic relationships with the group members within the here-and-now therapeutic framework, group members began to demonstrate greater skill at grounding and reconstituting. Triggering events within the group allowed for potentially corrective experiences in which group members began to attune to one another and support the modulation of reactive behavior. Insertion of more cognitive-oriented, logical intervention could then follow.

Group intervention has the power to provide grounding experiences when children have not been provided with solid, stable attachment figures early in life. Early attachment supports regulatory skills within children. Attachment theory (Bowlby, 1982) has served as the foundation for conceptualizing the influence of relationships on early childhood development. Bowlby (1982) espoused that early attachment relationships set the stage for a child to develop physiological regulatory capacities by means of a behavioral control system. In this coregulatory process, the child seeks proximity to the attachment figure to help regulate his or her emotional reactivity, particularly during times of stress or fear. When this coregulation support is not available because of absent attachment figures, children develop little ability to attune to themselves or others, to regulate their emotions, and to problem solve and rationally make decisions.

RATIONALE FOR PLAY AND NONVERBAL MODALITIES

Given the impact of early, chronic trauma on a child's ability to self-regulate, connect with others, and use cognitive, logical decision-making skills, play therapy and other nonverbal modalities have the potential to be effective interventions. Focused, directed play and expressive therapies supported the building of cognitive skills and subsequent behavioral shifts. Kids Together used a variety of play and other nonverbal modalities given the staff's growing awareness of the potential impact of these forms of treatment on children who have experienced trauma.

The use of play therapy, expressive mediums, and nonverbal modalities overall can support the accessing and processing of traumatic material as well as other stimulating and emotionally laden material. When material is accessed via play therapy, it can allow for modulation of the emotional content and a fuller overall integration of the experience. Once challenging material is accessed via nonverbal mediums such as play and art, there is greater potential for more rational, skills-building work to occur. The nonverbal processing of material allows for emotionally charged material to be accessed and integrated in a manner that might more typically be defended against within the verbal therapy process. When asked direct questions, youth may be likely to avoid some topics, but when accessed within the metaphor of play and nonverbal modalities, that same material can often be processed with much less physiological overarousal.

Play naturally engages the right hemisphere because of its use of metaphor and symbolism, and once processed, emotional material can be integrated with less discomfort via the more traditional left-hemispheric, talk therapy formats as the material no longer appears to have the same emotionally laden intensity associated with it. So it was not unusual to ask group members to engage in drawing, collage making, or any number of nonverbal activities for particular topics or when emotionally charged material was processed within the group.

EMPIRICAL PROGRAM SUPPORT

Three separate studies have yielded results supporting the demonstrated effectiveness of the Kids Together group therapy intervention. The first study collected pre–post data using the Child Behavior Checklist for ages 6 to 18 (CBCL; Achenbach & Rescorla, 2001, 2007) from a small sample of group participants between 1997 and 1998. Analysis of this data set demonstrated a significant reduction in internalizing symptoms and total behavior problems for participants who attended Kids Together (Hansen, Meissler, & Ovens, 2000).

The CBCL is a self-administered questionnaire that was completed by the youths' parent or guardian on referral and at completion of their initial Kids Together intervention. There are 120 discrete CBCL items that load onto eight syndrome scales, and these syndrome scales form three groupings: Internalizing, Externalizing, and Total Problems (Achenbach & Rescorla, 2001). Internalizing syndrome behaviors are characterized by overcontrol of emotions, such as withdrawal and sense of worthlessness, whereas Externalizing syndrome behaviors are typically characterized by undercontrol of emotions, including rule breaking and challenges with interpersonal relationships (Achenbach & Edelbrock, 1978).

The second study was a pilot study using CBCL pre–post data from 117 participants who participated in Kids Together from September 2001 to May 2011. Results from this second pilot study indicated that there were significant reductions in Internalizing behavior problems after participation in the Kids Together intervention (Hansen, 2013).

In the third study, the sample of 117 from the second study was increased to include group participants from an additional 6 years of the program, yielding a sample of 220. Statistically significant results were obtained in all three domains, indicating significant improvement in Internalizing, Externalizing, and Total Problem behaviors for group participants subsequent to intervention (Hansen, 2013). So children who participated in the Kids Together group therapy intervention demonstrated reduction in both internalizing, overcontrol symptoms and externalizing, undercontrol symptoms postintervention.

PROGRAM FORMAT

The format of each Kids Together group therapy session included five components:

1. Group opening: topic-related question and module discussion
2. Therapeutic activities: verbal and nonverbal activities

3. Therapeutic social skills games: experiential and cooperative games
4. Recreational activity: physical activities to reinforce skills learned earlier in the group session
5. Group closing: cooldown and relaxation to support the transition from the group back to the community and home environments.

The group opening in Component 1 involved discussion of a topic-related question pertaining to the group module for that particular session. All group members were asked to provide their thoughts about or an answer to the question posed in the group opening. This discussion was designed to engage each member in the group process. This investment in the group served a dual role of being an icebreaker and providing the group members and facilitators with information that could then be used to inform other activities. The group members invested some of themselves into the group discussion, thereby often decreasing their level of apprehension about participating in the larger group discussion and process. A desensitizing effect was therefore often experienced.

As the group evolved, self-disclosure increased, even within the group opening. The topic-related question framed the initial portion of the group; however, the discussions were general enough that group members could share more about themselves as they grew more engaged in the group. The more openly group members shared, the more invested they became in the group process overall, both as active participants and as emotional supports for others in the group.

Discussion of the topic-related question as part of Component 1 led to the session module. The group facilitator skillfully shifted the topic-related question discussion toward the session module. For example, if the group module topic was anger management and impulse control, a didactic discussion about the stages of anger might have occurred, and examples from conflicts discussed earlier might have been referred to as real-life examples to help group members deconstruct their triggers and the precursors to externalizing reactivity. Participants' own examples were more profound then facilitator-described events. Experience within the program supported the notion that didactic presentation of material was more effective once group members were engaged and attuned with one another via their own personal sharing process.

Therapeutic verbal and nonverbal activities, Component 2, were then provided on the basis of the module and group members' developmental stage. The activities reinforced elements of the group module and provided for a practical, in vivo reinforcement of the topic and discussion. The activities were designed to reinforce the verbal discussions and to support integration of material learned. Nonverbal activities were often used to integrate the material and process material more fully. Activities ranged from verbal role-plays and debates to play therapy and expressive arts activities, including drawing activities and the use of mediums such as clay, miniatures, and collages. Group members became more competent in integrating and generalizing concepts and skills when they were able to practice what they were learning.

The group members were then jointly engaged in experiential, cooperative therapeutic games, Component 3, and then in recreational activity, Component 4, in which they could use the community-based setting to swim, play basketball, participate in yoga, and do other activities. With the support of staff, they learned to negotiate challenges among one other and worked to gain skill in regulating their responses to one another. A group closing, Component 5, then provided a final opportunity to develop skills in relaxation and allow for full integration of the group experience with a review of learned skills.

Exhibit 8.1 lists example modules used in the program. Each topic provided a clear structure and was developmentally informed, providing options, within each component, designed for the distinct developmental needs of each of the three youth groups. Exhibits 8.2 and 8.3 show sample session formats for two of the modules, empathy and problem solving. In Exhibits 8.2 and 8.3, because Components 1 and 2 are specific to Kids Together, these components have a more extensive description than Components 3, 4, and 5.

EXHIBIT 8.1
Sample Program Modules for a 15-Week Session

1. Group opening and group building: Introduction
2. Communication: Part I—Nonverbal, expressive arts
3. Communication: Part II—Verbal forms of communication
4. Feelings: Overview of feelings identification
5. Empathy: Tolerance of differences and diversity
6. Self-esteem and self-image: Part I, External—How do you present to others?
7. Self-esteem and self-image: Part II, Internal—How do you see or feel about yourself?
8. Responsibility and accountability
9. Problem solving and solution building
10. Anger management and impulse control
11. Conflict resolution: Interpersonal conflict with peers and authority figures
12. Trust
13. Relaxation and stress reduction
14. Integration: Review of group experience and learned material
15. Termination

EXHIBIT 8.2
Sample Session Format for the Empathy Module

Component 1. Group opening: Topic-related question and module discussion
- What is empathy?
- How can you tell how someone else is feeling?
- How do other people's situations or feelings affect you?
- What makes people similar to and different from you?

Component 2. Therapeutic activities: Verbal and nonverbal activities

1. They Are All Different activity: Facilitators provide group members with drawing supplies. Group members are asked to spread out throughout the room so that they are unable to see what the other group members are drawing. The facilitators then instruct the group members to draw a scene such as a person walking down the street with a red hat and brown coat on or two children walking their dog on a leash. The instructions can involve drawing any scene as long as it is vague enough to accentuate how all group members create very different drawings of the same scene despite being given the same general instructions. Once group members have created their version of the instructed drawing, they are asked to show their drawing to the group.
   - How come all the drawings are different?
   - How come, if all group members were given the same information, they drew different drawings? Are any of the drawings better than the others, or are they just different?
   - How do the drawings compare to people?
   - How are people different? Does "different" mean better or worse?

The group can then be asked to jointly draw the same scene as a group using a large piece of newsprint, with each group member contributing to the creation and together developing a group version of the instructed drawing.

2. Diversity Mural activity: Group facilitators begin a discussion about diversity, difference, and prejudice (defined as judging others without facts). How do people differ from each other (e.g., in physical appearance, personality, religious beliefs, financial status, sexual orientation)? Is difference good or bad? Or is it a little bit of both? Once this discussion has occurred, facilitators provide the group members with art materials to create a group mural. Each member is supported to contribute to a mural that expresses a world of diversity.

Component 3. Therapeutic social skills games: Experiential and cooperative games

Component 4. Recreational activity: Physical activities to reinforce skills learned earlier in the group session

Component 5. Group closing: Cooldown and relaxation—breathing activities, visualization, and cooldown activities

DEVELOPMENTAL ISSUES

The developmental needs of the group participants were considered in developing the curriculum. The module illustrations and clinical case vignettes in this chapter provide examples of school-age child interventions. School-age children between ages 6 and 12 years typically participated in either the "younger" or "middle" group. These group participants could be categorized as falling within Erikson's (1950) industry versus inferiority psychosocial developmental stage, in which emerging competence in

EXHIBIT 8.3
Sample Session Format for the Problem Solving Module

Component 1. Group opening: Topic-related question and module discussion
- What is the difference between a problem and a solution?
- Do you or does someone else decide when there's a problem?
- If there is more than one problem, which do you deal with first?
- Is there a solution for every problem?

Component 2. Therapeutic activities: Verbal and nonverbal activities

1. Problem Sharing activity: Facilitators ask group members to draw an image of someone who is having a problem. The problem could be occurring at school, at home, or with peers. The image should convey what the problem is and who is involved in the problem. The drawings are then handed to the facilitators, and the facilitators shuffle the drawings as if they are a deck of cards and hand them back out to the group members one by one. Most group members do not receive their own drawing because they were shuffled. Each group member is asked to guess what the problem depicted in the story is about and then create a new drawing that includes a solution to the hypothesized problem; they then share the solution drawing with the group.
2. Draw the Problem activity: Facilitators provide paper and drawing materials to the group. Group members are asked to create a sketch of a problem scenario similar to a comic strip in that it includes what happened before, during, and after the occurrence of the problem. Each drawing is shared and reviewed using the following questions:
   - What might have changed the course of events?
   - Who might have helped solve the problem?
   - What might the group member have done before the problem occurred?
   - What happens now?

Component 3. Therapeutic social skills games: Experiential and cooperative games

Component 4. Recreational activity: Physical activities to reinforce skills learned earlier in the group session

Component 5. Group closing: Cooldown, and relaxation—breathing activities, visualization, and cooldown activities

intellectual, social, and physical skills makes group involvement appropriate given the importance of social interaction and effective task completion in advancing the development of self-confidence.

Piaget (1972) termed this stage the *concrete operational stage* of cognitive development. During this stage, Piaget hypothesized, children evolved from a more egocentric stage to one in which more logical thought was possible in the context of relational understanding. The thought process during this stage is inductive as children learn to use facts and details to draw conclusions to problem solve and strategize. Abstract thinking is not yet available, yet children begin to use information available to them to problem solve and strategize. The Kids Together group provided an arena to garner support from others to develop more enhanced skills for managing life's challenges as solutions were processed. In addition, the group provided a means to build greater empathy and understanding of other people's perspective as egocentric thought shifted.

CLINICAL CASE VIGNETTES

Exhibits 8.2 and 8.3 provide a brief introduction to the details of the concrete components of the session structure, but they do not provide a view into the process elements of the group dynamic. The vignettes in this section do not represent actual case examples in the sense of one individual but rather are amalgamations of the types of situations and scenarios that occurred over the course of the Kids Together program's existence. They also provide an overview of the Kids Together philosophy of intervention and its use of in-the-moment, coregulatory opportunities to help calm and ground group participants so that concrete skills building was possible.

Case Vignette 1: "I Don't Understand"

A 7-year-old boy was referred to the younger Kids Together group after experiencing several years of interpersonal violence within his home. He was reportedly an aggressive youth who struggled with interpersonal interactions and often resorted to violence and argumentative behavior at school and with peers. He had already been suspended from his second-grade class on multiple occasions, and his mother was requesting out-of-home placement for him. He had been referred to several other home-based and group-based interventions, but he had been asked to leave because of excessive externalizing, acting out behaviors.

He began the group late, after several weeks had already elapsed. He was somewhat reluctant to verbally participate but was not shy in his efforts to physically bully and threaten the other group members in subtle and not-so-subtle ways. During his first group session, while the group sat around a small table to discuss their past week and challenges they experienced, he kicked the other group members under the table, shoved their things out of the way, and made demeaning and derogatory comments about them. He did not respond to traditional limits or attempts at shaping behavior via reinforcers.

In the debriefing after the group, the facilitators asked for ideas and feedback from members of the staff as they expressed their frustration and shared regarding their countertransferential process. The facilitators felt disempowered and ineffective at terminating this group member's behavior. An idea was developed by the Kids Together team, and this plan was enacted during the next group session.

A very simple reinforcement system was set up in which group members were given a small basket to put in front of them where they sat at the group table. The facilitators did not provide much introduction; whenever any group member interacted in a nonviolent, helpful manner toward another group member (e.g., offering support, talking respectfully, giving positive feedback), that group member was given a penny in his or her basket. In spite of the lack of introduction about this intervention, most group members intuitively understood that "behaving nicely" was getting them pennies, yet this new group member became frustrated that he was not receiving any pennies, and he had little insight that his behavior was the reason he was not receiving pennies. After a couple of group sessions, he stood up and said, "I don't understand!" and talked about how unfair it was that he was not receiving any pennies. The cofacilitators asked the other group members to share their understanding about getting pennies, and a discussion ensued about respect, kindness, and support of one another without violence or aggression.

After this group session, the facilitators spoke with the group member, who continued to be noticeably agitated by the group's discussion. He shared that it was not fair that he was not getting pennies, and the facilitators asked him what he was doing differently from the other group members that made him not get pennies. He acknowledged that he was sometimes mean, and through his tears and emotion, he shared that in his home, this was how "we did things." He acknowledged that he was often yelled at and that his father was not only verbally abusive toward his mother but also would often hit her. Child protective services was currently engaged in an investigation, which is how he was referred to the program, so psychoeducation was provided to him about how kids who watch a parent being aggressive or hurtful to another parent sometimes then begin to be hurtful to other kids in their life. They explored how his body felt when he was agitated and the thoughts he had when that agitation grew. They discussed permission giving around being mean when he felt "bad inside," and they challenged these thoughts as they worked to shift his perceptions and schema by introducing the concept that "in Kids Together, we talk about our feelings and thoughts and practice new ways to calm ourselves and be patient and respectful to others."

Over the next few group sessions, this group member received more and more pennies as each respectful act received an immediate reinforcement and the process of behavioral shaping began. The insights learned about the behavioral links between his internal agitation, his cognitive misperceptions related to his justification for aggression, and his externalizing, acting out behavior were then shared with his parents and caregivers to help illuminate how a changing home environment could support more grounded, regulated behavior in their child. As each session progressed, regardless of the group topic, there were opportunities to use the group process to support this member's shifting behaviors as the topics of communication, anger management, self-esteem, and so forth could all emphasize components of this child's challenges.

Case Vignette 2: "Have to Get Out of Here"

During the recreational component of the program, group participants were able to interact with each other in more typical types of youth activities. Participating in a group therapy intervention can be another way of feeling ostracized from mainstream youth, but the recreational component of the program permitted both youth and facilitators to support engagement in conventional prosocial activities. Once the more traditional talk therapy portion of the group was concluded, group members were then engaged in joint recreational activities such as swimming, basketball, and yoga. The program philosophy was that once self-regulation skills developed, opportunities for youth to enact those skills in typical, organized activities would enable facilitators to support those learned skills. In other words, anger could be modulated as perceptions of unfairness arose, communication skills could be enhanced as rules were created for different activities, and impulsivity could be challenged when disagreements developed. In typical clinic settings, discussions about behavioral regulation are a focal point, but few programs allow for actual implementation of learned skills and support in enacting the new behaviors. Kids Together provided those opportunities.

One evening, during the course of the recreational component of that evening's group, a 12-year-old boy was playing basketball with several other group members. Suddenly, without apparent external cause, he ran out of the gym, down the hallway, and out the front door of the building, yelling, "I have to get out of here!" The facilitators were unable to stop him while he was still in the building but proceeded to follow him while he ran another two blocks down the street. He was unresponsive to verbal commands to stop, yet as the two facilitators drew closer to him, they began to "wonder" out loud what might have happened to trigger his need to get away. They normalized the desire to escape when one feels unsafe or unfairly treated in some way and began to offer support to help him return to the group and talk about what might have occurred.

He began to run more slowly and then came to a full stop as he began to tear up and softly cry. He struggled to articulate what occurred in the group but was clearly impacted by the choice of the facilitators to attune to the possible triggers and support greater self-regulation by virtue of the facilitators' intervention. Rather than threatening a consequence, the facilitators chose to use their therapeutic relationship with the group member to help him deescalate and reconstitute. Once the group member felt validated and understood, he was able to emotionally regulate and decrease his behavioral reactivity.

The group member later returned to the program. He was provided with drawing materials and asked to express his emotions by creating an image of how he was feeling. The drawing involved vibrant, obscure images that he created in what appeared to be a trancelike state. Shortly after completing the drawing, he verbally disclosed a history of physical abuse at a young age. The overstimulation of the gym, including the noise, lights, and the number of people, was physiologically triggering as it was reminiscent of how he had felt during the abusive experiences. After processing this connection, the cofacilitators provided developmentally appropriate psychoeducation about the impact of abuse and neglect on the developing brain and on physiology to help explain how his reactions were normal and then proceeded to work to develop coping skills, including emotion regulation skills, that the member could use during future group sessions.

CONCLUSION

Hundreds of similar youth were served by the Kids Together program over its 17-year history. The philosophy of acceptance, transparency, attunement, and true compassion were driving forces for engagement of youth who were often underserved because of their lack of full engagement in other services. Theories and therapeutic constructs provided guidance, but clinical wisdom, gut responses, and empathic attunement may have been even more important in the transformational experiences many youth reported after completing the program. The data indicate significant reductions in symptom presentation postintervention, but those numbers do not fully explain the anecdotal experience of watching youth who were disengaged from and disillusioned by life slowly transformed into productive, engaged Kids Together "citizens" who respected the program expectations and provided support for one another in ways often not experienced outside of the group. This program exemplified transformational process and taught all of the facilitators and administrators about how therapeutic engagement can have a long-lasting, profound impact. The use of play and other nonverbal modalities strengthened the integration of learned skills and supported not only engagement, but also more direct skills building via the modalities used.

REFERENCES

Achenbach, T. M., & Edelbrock, C. S. (1978). The classification of child psychopathology: A review and analysis of empirical efforts. *Psychological Bulletin*, 85, 1275–1301. http://dx.doi.org/10.1037/0033-2909.85.6.1275

Achenbach, T. M., & Rescorla, L. A. (2001). *Manual for the ASEBA school-age forms and profiles*. Burlington: University of Vermont, Research Center for Children, Youth, and Families.

Achenbach, T. M., & Rescorla, L. A. (2007). *Multicultural supplement to the manual for the ASEBA school-age forms and profiles*. Burlington: University of Vermont, Research Center for Children, Youth, and Families.

Bowlby, J. (1982). *Attachment*. New York, NY: Basic Books.

Bratton, S., Ray, D., Rhine, T., & Jones, L. (2005). The efficacy of play therapy with children: A meta-analytic review of treatment outcomes. *Professional Psychology: Research and Practice, 36*, 376–390. http://dx.doi.org/10.1037/0735-7028.36.4.376

Cook, A., Spinazzola, J., Ford, J., Lanktree, C., Blaustein, M., Cloitre, M., . . . van der Kolk, B. (2005). Complex trauma in children and adolescents. *Psychiatric Annals*, 35, 390–398.

Erikson, E. H. (1950). *Childhood and society*. New York, NY: Norton.

Hansen, S. (2013). *Kids Together child and adolescent group therapy program: Evaluating a therapeutic change process* (Doctoral dissertation). Retrieved from ETD Collection for Fordham University. (Order No. AAI3560671)

Hansen, S., Meissler, K., & Ovens, R. (2000). Kids Together: A group play therapy model for children with ADHD symptomalogy. *Journal of Child & Adolescent Group Therapy, 10*, 191–211. http://dx.doi.org/10.1023/A:1016631228545

Morse, R., & Wiley, M. S. (1997). *Ghosts from the nursery: Tracing the roots of violence*. New York, NY: Atlantic Monthly Press.

Piaget, J. (1972). *The psychology of the child*. New York, NY: Basic Books.

Ray, D. C. (2006). Evidence-based play therapy. In C. E. Schaefer & H. G. Kaduson (Eds.), *Contemporary play therapy: Theory, research, and practice* (pp. 136–160). New York, NY: Guilford Press.

Ray, D. C., Bratton, S., Rhine, T., & Jones, L. (2001). The effectiveness of play therapy: Responding to the critics. *International Journal of Play Therapy, 10*, 85–108. http://dx.doi.org/10.1037/h0089444

Reyes, C. J., & Asbrand, J. P. (2005). A longitudinal study assessing trauma symptoms in sexually abused children engaged in play therapy. *International Journal of Play Therapy, 14*, 25–47. http://dx.doi.org/10.1037/h0088901

Rose, S. D. (2004). Cognitive–behavioral group work. In C. D. Garvin, L. M. Gutierrez, & M. J. Galinsky (Eds.), *Handbook of social work with groups* (pp. 119–148). New York, NY: Guilford Press.

Shulman, L. (1992). *The skills of helping: Individuals, families, and groups*. Itasca, IL: F. E. Peacock.

Siegel, D. J. (1999). *The developing mind*. New York, NY: Guilford Press.

Stien, P. T., & Kendall, J. (2004). *Psychological trauma and the developing brain: Neurologically based interventions for troubled children*. New York, NY: Haworth Press.

van der Kolk, B. A. (2005). Developmental trauma disorder: Toward a rational diagnosis for children with complex trauma histories. *Psychiatric Annals*, *35*, 401–408.

van IJzendoorn, M. H., Schuengel, C., & Bakermans-Kranenburg, M. J. (1999). Disorganized attachment in early childhood: Meta-analysis of precursors, concomitants, and sequelae. *Development and Psychopathology*, *11*, 225–250. http://dx.doi.org/10.1017/S0954579499002035

Yalom, I. (1985). *The theory and practice of group psychotherapy* (4th ed.). New York, NY: Basic Books.

9

ADLERIAN PLAY THERAPY FOR CHILDREN WITH EXTERNALIZING BEHAVIORS

KRISTIN K. MEANY-WALEN AND TERRY KOTTMAN

Perhaps the most common reason for children being referred to counseling is externalizing behaviors (Abidin & Robinson, 2002), and the most common predictor of children's externalizing behavior is associated with abusive, inconsistent, or chaotic home environments (Price, Chiapa, & Walsh, 2013). *Externalizing behaviors* are behaviors that interfere with other people in a negative way (Achenbach & Rescorla, 2001). Children with externalizing behaviors might be disruptive to others, creating interpersonal problems between the child and other people in the child's life such as siblings, parents, peers, or teachers. Examples of such behaviors include breaking rules, swearing, having outbursts, displaying an inability or unwillingness to pay attention and focus, and acting aggressively toward property, people, or animals. Without intervention, children who display externalizing behaviors are at an increased risk for a host of other, more serious problems throughout life such as teenage pregnancy, drug or alcohol abuse, criminal activity, and antisocial

http://dx.doi.org/10.1037/14776-010
Play Therapy in Middle Childhood, A. A. Drewes and C. E. Schaefer (Editors)

behaviors (Mental Health America, 2009). Adlerian play therapy may be particularly helpful with children with externalizing or disruptive behaviors.

BASIC RATIONALE AND THEORY

Adlerian theory, also known as *individual psychology*, holds that people are social beings who are searching for a sense of belonging and connectedness in the world, behavior is purposeful and goal directed, and people are creative and unique (Adler, 1927/1998). Adlerian theory is among the play therapy theories most widely used by mental health professionals in their work with children (Lambert et al., 2007). It is a popular choice because of its comprehensive system of conceptualizing human personality and the inclusion in the therapeutic process of important adults in children's lives, such as parents and teachers (Kottman, 2003, 2011; Meany-Walen & Kottman, 2015). For a more thorough description of each concept and how each relates to Adlerian play therapy, readers can consult *Partners in Play: An Adlerian Approach to Play Therapy* (Kottman, 2003).

People are social beings. From birth, they strive for connection and belonging (Adler, 1927/1998). First with family, and later with people outside of the family, children and adults search for ways to connect with and feel valued by others. Physical and emotional connections are important for optimal growth and well-being (Adler, 1956, 1927/1998). Consider an infant who cries to be held, fed, or cleaned or an infant who coos and giggles delightfully at the sight of his or her mother. Crying and cooing are ways an infant can express desires and needs and get them met by others in his or her life. The behaviors are intentional, even if not within the infant's awareness, and create opportunities for adults to physically and emotionally connect with the child. As the child matures, he or she continues to need to find ways to belong and gain significance with others. In Adlerian play therapy, the therapist seeks to understand the patterns of how the particular child client connects with others and achieves a sense of belonging.

One of the cornerstones of Adlerian theory is what translates to English as *social interest* or *community spirit*. Adler wrote that social interest contributes to a person's character development and how he or she behaves in the world. It is a way of being that concerns the welfare of the world, including people and the environment (Adler, 1927/1998). The level of a person's social interest is influenced by the person's lifestyle and beliefs about how he or she belongs in the world. Readers can think of social interest on a continuum. An example of someone with a great deal of social interest is Mother Teresa. On the opposite end, someone with little or no social interest is Charles Manson. A person with social interest cares about others and the future of the universe. Demonstrations of social interest include being empathic, volunteering, sharing resources or wealth, recycling, driving safely, and feeding animals.

According to Adler (1927/1998), people are born with the capacity to develop social interest, but they have to be taught to value and connect with others. This responsibility belongs to parents, teachers, and other influential people in children's lives. One of the primary functions of the Adlerian play therapist is to work with children to enhance their concern for others and increase their ability to connect with others.

Adlerians believe that all people's behaviors are goal driven (Adler, 1927/1998). People behave in ways that can be described as socially useful (e.g., helping others with homework, sharing resources with people in need, being funny) or socially unuseful (e.g., gang activity, prejudice or bigotry, isolation). Both options evoke a response from the social world. People interpret the responses they receive and choose to maintain or change their patterns of behavior. Their interpretation is based on their *lifestyle*, which is how they make meaning of self, others, and the world. Part of the Adlerian play therapy process is understanding the goals of children's behavior and helping them shift from socially unuseful goals to more socially useful goals.

Each person's lifestyle is unique and creative and different from every other person's lifestyle, hence the term *individual psychology*. Lifestyles are fairly stable and develop over the course of a person's early childhood on the basis of how that person perceived the way in which he or she fit in the family or original social group (Adler, 1927/1998). Lifestyles are the combination of emotion, thought, and behavior patterns and are based on the person's perceptions that develop into the person's personality (Adler, 1956). These perceptions need not be rational or logical. For example, a child may interpret the death of a puppy as being a result of not sharing a toy with a sibling. This child may develop a belief that he or she can control the life and death of others through good or bad behaviors. Another example is a child who grows up in a family that frequently moves. This child might develop a belief that the world is unpredictable, that others are in control, and that he or she is a misfit who doesn't belong. The child could become good at quickly building superficial relationships while not creating relationships with depth. If the child avoids building meaningful relationships, he or she reduces the risk of feeling sad when he or she inevitably moves. Perhaps this child might become the school bully, which could create predictability and control. Being the bully could ensure that others will not like the child and provide a sense of power in choosing to not be friends rather than others choosing to not befriend him or her.

In this way, people set things up so that they re-prove what they already believe about themselves, creating a kind of confirmation bias feedback loop.

They act as if the things they believe about themselves, others, and the world are true; then when they get feedback from the social world, it confirms what they already believe. In Adlerian play therapy, understanding clients' (children and their parents, teachers, and other important people in their lives) lifestyles is the primary objective in the conceptualizing and treatment planning process.

DEVELOPMENTAL ISSUES

Adler wrote frequently about the importance of play in children's lives. He described play as being necessary for their development and the primary way children communicate to others: "In observing children at play we can see their whole attitude towards life; play is of the utmost importance to every child" (Adler, 1927/1998, p. 83). Adlerian play therapy is appropriate for use with children of various ages, including children as young as 3 years through adolescence (Kottman, 2003).

Because people make their own meaning about life and how they fit into the world, therapy is tailored to the individuality of each client (Adler, 1927/1998). On the basis of this idea, Adlerian play therapists work to understand their clients as unique and creative individuals. Adlerian play therapy differs from client to client depending on individual characteristics, developmental considerations, and cultural influences (Kottman, 2003, 2009). Play techniques, activities, and the level of abstraction in interpretation vary depending on the developmental level of the client. Sessions for a typical 6-year-old may be quite different from those for a 12-year-old. For example, Adlerian play therapy with a 6-year-old might consist of play activities that rely on concrete expression such as puppets, dollhouse and dolls, and role-play. The focus of the session might be on the activity rather than discussion. These activities are also helpful to the Adlerian play therapy process with 12-year-olds, but the Adlerian play therapist may also engage the client in abstract reasoning skills using discussion and future planning. Similarly, cultural considerations must be taken into account. An Adlerian play therapist is intentional about including doll families, books, and other toys and materials that represent a variety of skin colors and family dynamics (e.g., multiracial families, same-sex parents).

PLAY INTERVENTION PROCEDURES AND SETTINGS

Adlerian play therapy is described as having four phases: (a) building the therapeutic relationship, (b) investigating the client's lifestyle, (c) helping the client gain insight, and (d) reorienting and reeducating the client

(Kottman, 2003). The term *phases* is used intentionally because counseling is a cyclical process rather than a linear path. Thus, the counselor does not finish one stage and move to the next. Rather, the counselor seamlessly moves through the phases and sometimes revisits earlier phases or approaches several phases within a single session. This pattern of phases holds true in the play therapy with the child and in the consultation with parents and teachers. Adlerian play therapy is equally appropriate for school settings and for mental health settings such as agencies and private practice.

Phase 1: Building the Therapeutic Relationship

Phase 1 typically begins with the parents, teachers, or other adult caregivers of the child client. Most often, an adult brings the child to counseling and has a vested interest in the outcome of therapy. Additionally, because the family of origin is the most influential group to which the child belongs, the Adlerian play therapist works to build a relationship with these adults (Kottman, 2003, 2009). Giving a tour of the playroom, describing the play therapy process, sharing information about the counselor's credentials and experience, and gathering information about the goals for the child's counseling are useful strategies to start building the relationship with caregivers.

During this initial phase, the client and counselor work to build a collaborative relationship in which the child and the counselor share decision making (Kottman, 2003). Within the session, sometimes the counselor decides the activities and sometimes the client picks the activities. During the first meeting, the Adlerian play therapist might introduce the playroom to the child in this way: "Here is our playroom. Sometimes you will get to decide what we do, and sometimes I will decide what we do." This is a time when the counselor is getting to know the client and the client is getting to know and trust the counselor. The relationship begins to develop during this phase. The counselor continues to maintain and strengthen the therapeutic relationship over the course of the counseling process. Some of the skills used to build the relationship in Adlerian play therapy are tracking, restating content, reflecting feeling, playing actively with the child, metacommunicating, role-playing, creating therapeutic metaphors, answering or asking questions, cleaning the room together, and using art, games, or a sand tray in the session.

Limit setting is also used in all phases of Adlerian play therapy. There are four steps to limit setting. First, the Adlerian play therapist informs the child of the playroom rules: "It's against the playroom rules to cut the doll's hair." Next, the play therapist reflects a feeling or makes a guess about the purpose of the behavior that needs limiting: "I'm guessing you want to cut the doll's hair to show me how mad you are." The third step is when the counselor engages the client in generating alternative appropriate behavior to promote client responsibility and self-control: "I bet you can think of something else to cut. What can you find in here that would be OK to cut?" In many cases, this procedure is enough to involve the child in redirecting his or her own behavior. There are times, however, when the child may choose to continue the inappropriate behavior, in which case the play therapist initiates the final step of limit setting, generating consequences: "Let's think of something that could be a consequence if you decide to continue to cut the doll's hair."

Phase 2: Investigating the Client's Lifestyle

The Adlerian play therapist is like a detective. The second phase is a search for clues that help the therapist to better understand the lifestyle and goals of the client. During this phase, the counselor is active and directive (Kottman, 2003, 2009). The play therapist gathers developmental, environmental, familial, and situational information about the child. Gaps or leaps in development are noteworthy; behavior in the home, school, and other social settings is important; and adults' perceptions of the child are telling. The Adlerian play therapist is also interested in the lifestyle of the parents and other adults. The ways in which the lifestyles sync or clash will be important as the counselor plans interventions for the adults and child.

In exploring the family dynamics, family constellation, and family atmosphere, the counselor might ask the client to create a picture or sand tray of his or her family. This activity yields information about how the child connects with others and gains a sense of belonging in the family. Another activity is building a block tower together. This activity gives the therapist information about how the child interacts with others, how he or she solves problems, and how birth order has affected the child's perceptions of self, others, and the world. For example, a child who is overbearing or bossy in the process of building the tower is likely that way with peers. Perhaps the child is an oldest child and has created a lifestyle based on the belief that is it his or her responsibility to be in charge. Another child might be invited to play a game of tic-tac-toe with the counselor as a vehicle for discovering the child's capacity for rule-governed behavior, pattern of reaction in stressful situations, and sportsmanship. For instance, during the game, the child might cheat or create situations in which he or she is guaranteed to win in reaction to the belief that he or she must always be the best to be loved and valued. Interpretations vary depending on the client and what the counselor knows about the client's life experiences.

Several concepts should be considered when developing a hypothesis about a client's lifestyle and designing a treatment plan for the child and the significant adults in his or her life. These concepts include culture, family atmosphere, birth order, life tasks, personality priorities, goals of misbehavior, Crucial Cs, and assets.

Culture

Cultural influences are not necessarily positive or negative. Rather, they might be considered an overarching concept that influences individuals and families (Gil, 2005). The counselor must consider how culture impacts the family and the family constellation. Differences in discipline practices; education and academic or professional achievement expectations; dating and partnering timing and styles; multigenerational living arrangements and influences; and spiritual or religious beliefs, holidays, and practices, among other cultural variables, must be considered as the counselor develops a hypothesis of the child and child's caregivers' lifestyles.

Family Atmosphere

Adler stated, "Before we can judge human beings we must know the situation in which they grew up" (Adler, 1927/1998, p. 126). Exploring family atmosphere is essential to understanding children and how they create their lifestyles. *Family atmosphere* is the synthesis of several family factors, including but not limited to the following: number, gender, and order of children; mental or physical illness within the family; relationship between parents or caregivers; discipline styles; and parents' lifestyles. Family atmosphere might be thought of as the personality of the family (Kottman, 2003).

Birth Order

Birth order is the position of the child within his or her sibling group (Adler, 1956). Even when children share similar experiences related to being in the same family, their psychological experience is influenced by the order of their succession. Like all tenets of Adlerian theory, birth order is subjective. Differences in gender, gaps in birth, death of a sibling, and other unforeseen events can alter the interpretation of birth order for children.

Oldest children were once only children. The change in birth position and attention received from caregivers can impact oldest children's worldview and lifestyle. Oldest children may strive to protect and help younger siblings, may be organized and prepared, and may prefer their fathers because of the change in attention they receive from their mothers once the new baby arrives (Adler, 1956). Oldest children might go to extremes and become overly protective and rigid. They may become independent in ways that reject other people (Kottman, 2003).

Like oldest children, middle children have changed positions. They were once the youngest and were pushed into middlehood. They might become competitive with the oldest or youngest, or they might be the mediator between the oldest and youngest. They are typically quite democratic and easygoing. Some middle children become so adept at making peace that they have difficulties making decisions or speaking up for themselves (Kottman, 2003).

Youngest children might be revered because they are always the baby of the family and do not have to earn attention (Adler, 1956; Kottman, 2003). Because they are provided instant playmates, they have stimuli and people to chase after them. Youngest children are often competitive and strive to outshine their older siblings or become unique. For example, a younger child might choose to be an athlete if an older sibling excels in music.

Only children receive a lot of attention due to not having to share the limelight with other siblings. The only child is typically adept at interacting with adults and may be hesitant to leave the side of his or her caregiver (Adler, 1956). The only child does not have constant playmates as do children with siblings. Only children might become overly dependent on others or may become self-reliant. They usually have creative imaginations and a strong ability to verbally communicate (Kottman, 2003).

Life Tasks

Life tasks are challenges individuals must master in their development of personal wellness and positive mental health (Adler, 1956). The five life tasks for adults include work, love, friendship, spirituality, and self (Mosak & Maniacci, 1999). Adlerians assess how people are functioning at each of these five tasks to gauge their overall functioning. For children, Kottman (2003) described the five life tasks as school, family, friendship, purpose, and self.

The school life task includes functioning at the academic work and the social processes of school. Interactions with teachers and willingness to follow school and classroom rules are assessed. The family life task includes the child's relationship with other family members and the feeling of being connected with siblings, parents, and extended family. The attitudes about and relationships with other people of the same general age are evaluated as part of the friendship life task. Because children do not have the same abstract reasoning capacity as adults, they typically do not ponder the ideas of spirituality or religion. Instead, Kottman evaluated children's beliefs about their role in life and their beliefs about the possibility of some kind of greater being. The self life task is similar for children as it is for adults. It includes the child's ability to find humor, fun, and enjoyment in life; the child's self-worth and optimism; and the child's emotional response to self, others, and the world.

Personality Priorities

Personality priorities are patterns of feelings, thoughts, and behaviors that people create in response to their early experiences. They are based on a person's belief about how he or she fits into and find significance in the world (Kefir, 1981; Kottman & Ashby, 2015). The four personality priorities are pleasing, comfort, control, and superiority.

Children with the personality priority of pleasing are often agreeable and believe their role in life is to make others happy. Children with the comfort priority avoid stress and discomfort. They may not offer alternative suggestions or find solutions to their own problems as the process of creatively thinking might feel too taxing. Children with the control priority might test limits or demonstrate their desire to avoid being controlled; they can also rigidly follow rules or make sure rules are followed by others. Children with the superiority priority work to achieve a status of supreme understanding and capabilities. They believe they must be the best and might argue their position, thoughts, or behaviors with others to be validated or demonstrate their superiority (Kottman, 2003).

Goals of Misbehavior

Adlerian theory holds that all behavior is purposeful. Dreikurs and Soltz (1964) described all children's misbehavior as able to be funneled into four goals: attention, power, retaliation, and inadequacy. The goal of children's behavior is to meet a perceived need. Adlerian play therapists identify their clients' goals and channel children's misbehavior into more productive and socially useful behaviors (Kottman, 2003). To identify the goal of misbehavior, the play therapist considers children's behavior, the thinking and feelings underneath their behavior, the reaction of adults when confronted with the misbehavior, and the children's reactions when they are corrected.

Children who misbehave with the goal of attention might believe they are significant only when they are the center of attention. Adults might feel annoyed or exasperated when they interact with these children. Children with the goal of power believe they must show others they cannot be controlled. They meet their need for security by being powerful and in control. Children with the retaliation and revenge goal show verbal or physical cruelty to possessions, animals, children, or adults. Children with this goal may overtly or passively demonstrate their desire for revenge. Passive retaliation might be withdrawal of affection toward others. Many times, these children have been hurt or abused and believe they must hurt others before others can hurt them. Children with a goal of inadequacy protect themselves from failure and disapproval by demonstrating their inability to be successful. They are typically more discouraged than the other three types of children because they no longer have the motivation to try (Kottman, 2003).

Crucial Cs

Lew and Bettner (1996) noted that children need to have mastered four necessities, the Crucial Cs, to meet the challenges of life. The four Crucial Cs are connect, capable, count, and courage. Children who have mastered connection believe that they belong; they cooperate with others. Those who are capable hold the belief that they are competent in a way that is not competitive but demonstrates self-reliance. Children who believe they count know that they matter, are significant, and are valuable. They believe that they contribute to others and the greater good of society. Children who have mastered courage take risks and try things even when there is no guarantee of success. They believe they can handle challenges and are hopeful.

Assets

It is important to learn about the assets and strengths of the child (Kottman, 2003). Building on assets and encouraging strengths is helpful when creating treatment plans and encouraging children. For example, a child who is a good reader but is lousy at making friends might join a book club at school. A child who is lazy but loves butterflies might benefit from the counselor's use of the metaphor of a butterfly emerging from a cocoon to understand how struggle is necessary for the butterfly to be able to fly.

Adlerian play therapists conceptualize children with these elements in mind. How a counselor assesses a child on each of these domains helps the counselor set counseling goals, create interventions for the child and caregivers in Phase 3, and assess the child's progress.

Phase 3: Helping the Child Gain Insight

During Phase 3, the Adlerian play therapist uses what he or she knows about the child through the conceptualization to create interventions to help the child and adults in the child's life to gain insight into current patterns of feelings, thoughts, and behaviors. Along with all the skills used in the initial phases of Adlerian play therapy, interventions or strategies used during Phase 3 might include unstructured play, movement activities, games, role-plays, sand trays, bibliotherapy, problem solving, "spitting in the client's soup" (i.e., confronting the client's dysfunctional behavior), and techniques such as challenging the client's thoughts and behaviors, giving homework, and giving feedback to the client.

One of the primary skills used in the third phase of Adlerian play therapy is metacommunication, a skill in which the play therapist comments about what is going on with the child and (in many cases) what it means. *Metacommunication* "is kind of an umbrella skill that . . . can involve reflection of feelings, questions, speculation about underlying messages, interpretation of the meaning of reactions or behaviors, and so forth" (Kottman, 2003, p. 111). Depending on how directly the child usually communicates about specific situations, the play therapist may also develop stories or metaphors designed to help the child gain insight into his or her patterns.

All interventions should be tailored specifically to the needs of the particular client. For example, with a client who prefers to do sand trays, the play therapist uses sand trays to communicate with the client, and with a client who is a kinesthetic learner, the therapist develops interventions that incorporate movement and action.

Phase 4: Reorienting and Reeducating the Client

During Phases 1 through 3, the counselor is working with the client and the important adults in the client's life to gain information, help the client understand himself or herself more completely, and help teachers and parents to gain a more positive picture of the child and his or her behavior and motivation. Phase 4 is a more directive and didactic phase in which the therapist engages in teaching the child new ways of looking at self, others, and the world; provides opportunities for the child to practice applying more constructive patterns of thinking, feeling, and behaving; and helps the child acquire more constructive ways of building relationships and solving problems. Depending on the child, this reorienting and reeducating can happen directly or through stories and metaphors.

Sometimes helping the child make changes happens during play therapy sessions, sometimes through homework assignments, and sometimes through parent or teacher consultation. For example, with a child who believes that he does not connect with others and is unable to share power, the Adlerian play therapist might invite another child into the playroom with the purpose of helping the client learn to connect and share power with a new peer. With a child who believes that she is not capable and is proving her inadequacy by giving up easily, the therapist might instruct the parent or teacher to set up small tasks that the child can complete successfully. The therapist instructs the parent or teacher on what to say to encourage the child to reinforce success and counterbalance the mistaken goal of misbehavior.

Just as the counseling process is unique to individual clients, the termination process meets the individual needs of the client and adults. When the counseling goals have been met, as evidenced by self-report, parent or teacher report, or in-session demonstration, the counselor can start the termination process. One or two family or individual sessions might be conducted and future check-ins might be scheduled, depending on the child's and adult's lifestyles. It can also be helpful for children and adults to know that there will be continued challenges that can be expected. Normalizing the process can reduce anxiety for all participants.

EMPIRICAL SUPPORT

Although Adlerian play therapy is the third most frequently used play therapy theory by mental health professionals who work with children (Lambert et al., 2007), only recently have accounts been published of empirical support for this approach. Meany-Walen (2010) conducted her dissertation on the effectiveness of Adlerian play therapy with children who demonstrated externalizing behaviors in the classroom. This was the first known study investigating the effectiveness of Adlerian play therapy, and her findings were later published in an article in the *Journal of Counseling & Development* (Meany-Walen, Bratton, & Kottman, 2014). Since then, researchers have begun building a foundation of research supporting the effectiveness of Adlerian play therapy with children who present with problematic behaviors (Akay, 2013; Dillman Taylor & Meany-Walen, 2015; Meany-Walen, Bullis, Kottman, & Dillman Taylor, in press; Meany-Walen, Kottman, Bullis, & Dillman Taylor, in press). According to evidence provided by these studies, Adlerian play therapy has shown success at reducing problem behaviors and improving on-task behaviors. Although the groundwork of evidence is relatively new, Adlerian play therapy is a promising intervention for children.

CASE ILLUSTRATION INCLUDING PARENTAL INVOLVEMENT

Simon was a 7-year-old White boy who was brought to counseling by his father at the advice of Simon's teacher because of her concerns with his behaviors in school. His father, Thomas, had been a single father since Simon was 2 years old, when his wife unexpectedly left him and moved to another state. Simon had an older sister, Stacy, who lived with Simon and Thomas and was a junior in high school. Stacy was fairly involved with Simon and helped with cooking, babysitting, completing homework, disciplining, and playing with Simon.

Upon entering the waiting room, Thomas and Stacy sat and watched television quietly. Although they sat in adjoining chairs, they did not talk or interact with one another. Simon appeared engrossed in the game he played on a tablet he brought to the waiting room. The play therapist, Marie, knelt by Simon and introduced herself. She informed Simon that she was going to meet briefly with his father and then would come to get him. He nodded and said nothing.

Marie and Thomas met for 20 minutes. During this time, Marie asked questions about Simon's developmental and family history, which was normal. Academically he did well, but he was disruptive in class and did not have many friends. He frequently blurted out during work time and played aggressively with peers during free play or recess. Thomas shared that the family was financially stable; he worked full time, was home every night, and wanted the best for Simon. Throughout the consultations with Thomas, he was pleasant and eager to answer Marie's questions. She asked for permission to talk with Simon's teacher, and Thomas signed the consent forms.

Next, Marie asked Simon to come to the playroom. With his tablet in tow, he readily followed Marie. She asked him to leave the tablet with his father, which he did reluctantly. Upon entering the playroom, Marie said, "This is our playroom, and we'll play in here when you come to see me. Sometimes, I will decide what we will do, and sometimes you'll get to decide what to do. Today, first you get to decide." Excitedly, Simon explored the playroom. He touched several of the toys and committed to playing with the gun and darts. He quickly and clumsily loaded and shot the dart gun at the row of animals that sat on the shelf. He exclaimed that his goal was to knock them over. To test his willingness to follow directions, Marie invited Simon to work with her to build a tower with the blocks and then aim the dart gun at the blocks. He was intrigued by this idea but was quick to correct Marie when she was not building the tower the way he thought it should be built, saying, "Let me do it by myself. You don't do it right." Because this was their first meeting, Marie decided to not challenge Simon and let him build the tower on his own. Her goal was to start to build a collaborative and trusting relationship with Simon.

Following the initial session, Marie contacted Simon's teacher. His teacher informed Marie that Simon was academically competent, but his acting out behaviors were concerning and were interfering with the other students' ability to learn. She described Simon's many good qualities but stressed that he needed to change his externalizing behavior to stay in the classroom. Marie and the teacher agreed to stay in contact to discuss progress and consider suggestions Marie might have for ways the teacher could help support changes in Simon's behavior over the course of the next several weeks.

The next week, Simon, Thomas, and Stacy came to the counseling center. Again, Thomas and Stacy sat quietly watching the television in the waiting room, and Simon was on his tablet playing violent games. Marie started the session with Thomas so she could learn more about the family constellation and Thomas's lifestyle. Thomas appeared to openly answer any question that Marie asked. He was pleasant and funny. He seemed warm and yet a bit cautious about genuinely connecting with Marie. When he was asked about his own upbringing, Thomas described himself as being "dirt poor," harshly disciplined, and the son of an alcoholic mother and father. He was the oldest of three brothers and was responsible for all aspects of taking care of them and keeping them safe. Because he was amenable to her questions and suggestions, Marie asked Thomas to think about what he wanted for his son, write down his answers, and bring them back the following week.

Marie then had a session with Simon. Simon went straight to the dart gun, shooting the animals and shouting with joy when they fell over. He aimed the dart gun at Marie and she set a limit:

> I am guessing you want to see what I would do if you shot me with a dart, but it's against the playroom rules to shoot people. I bet you can think of something else to shoot that would be OK in the playroom.

Without missing a beat, Simon shot at the beanbag chair. He said, "I'm pretending this is you." Marie wanted to encourage his ability to follow the rules and metacommunicated with him, as follows: "You decided to shoot the beanbag and pretend it was me. You want me to know that you like to do things your way." Simon exclaimed, "Right! I'm in charge, and I will shoot you if I want to!" She replied, "You like to let people know that you don't like to do what they tell you to do." Simon smiled and nodded.

Marie was getting a sense of his lifestyle, but she wanted to know a bit more about his perceptions of his family dynamics. She knew that being in control was important to him and guessed that many of the externalizing behaviors he demonstrated and the difficulties he seemed to have with authority figures were the result of him believing that he needed to be in charge, which resulted in power struggles. To engage him in sharing power, she needed to provide him with choices. She said, "I would like for you to draw a picture. You can choose to draw one now, or you can choose to draw one in 5 minutes. Which do you choose?" Because she had given him a choice, he did not seem to feel a need for a power struggle and decided that he would draw the picture then.

In the spirit of sharing power, she offered him crayons, markers, or paint with which to make his picture. She instructed him to make a picture of his family. Simon chose the colors and drew a picture of his father, sister, and mother. They were not touching, and there was no background or other drawing in the picture. He did not include himself. When discussing his picture, his demeanor softened a bit, and he said he missed his mother and loved her very much. Marie asked where he was. He said, "I forgot about myself. I'm probably in my room playing video games."

Following this activity, he began playing with the animal figures: a big dolphin he identified as Dad, a medium elephant he identified as Mom, a medium zebra he identified as Stacy, and a large, aggressive-looking lion for himself. The dolphin, zebra, and lion interacted, while the elephant was placed to the side. It appeared that he wanted his mother included and didn't know how she was a part of his family. During his interactions with the three animals, Marie used several nondirective skills, such as restating content, reflecting feelings, and tracking his play. The lion consistently played rough and did things that could be described as externalizing behaviors. The lion appeared to want attention and received none from the dolphin and only minimal attention from the zebra. Marie metacommunicated to Simon, "That lion wants some attention. He needs to know that his family loves him."

The next session started in the same way. Marie met with Thomas and confirmed that she had spoken with Simon's teacher. Because she had given Thomas an assignment during the previous session, she followed up with the question about what he wanted for his son. Thomas responded, "I wasn't sure what you were specifically asking, so I wrote down a lot of answers." Essentially, he wanted Simon to have a fun and carefree childhood, and he felt guilty that Simon did not have an involved mother. He allowed Stacy to help as much as possible to make up for Simon not having a mother figure, and he admitted that he did not know how to parent a teenage daughter. Marie learned that Thomas had no rules for Simon and feared punishing him too harshly as he had been punished when he was a child, and thus he resorted to no consequences and no emotional involvement. Marie intentionally did not include Stacy in the sessions because she believed that Stacy was too parentified (i.e., took on too much of a parenting role). Marie encouraged Thomas to relieve Stacy of parenting responsibilities for Simon. Thomas and Marie discussed parenting roles and effective discipline strategies such as logical and natural consequences.

When she met with Simon, he started the session playing with the dart gun and then transitioned to playing with the animals. He seemed to pick up where he left off in the previous session. Marie had started to conceptualize Simon from her first observation of the family in the waiting room. Consultations with Thomas and the teacher, as well as sessions with Simon, helped Marie to create many hypotheses about his lifestyle. She continued to observe his play and interact with him in a playful and inquisitive way. At the end of the sixth session, Marie had formulated a conceptualization of Simon and his father (see Table 9.1).

Having the conceptualization helped Marie create goals for Simon and Thomas. Marie introduced Thomas to the concepts of personality priorities, goals of misbehavior, and Crucial Cs. She knew that because of Thomas's pleasing personality priority, he would follow through at home with suggestions made during consultations. Marie requested that Simon and Thomas have a playdate once each week. This could be going to the park, building a house of blocks, reading a book, washing the car, or playing catch. The only rules were that they do it at least once a week with no tablet or video games, they had to both agree on the activity, and they had to tell Marie about it

TABLE 9.1
Case Conceptualization of Thomas and Simon

Lifestyle concept	Thomas	Simon
Family atmosphere	Thomas's upbringing and fear of repeating the patterns of his childhood with Simon have created an environment of no rules and no expectations, which has resulted in Simon having too much power in the family. Thomas is unsure of how to show affection and does not build close relationships for fear of rejection and abandonment as occurred with his estranged wife.	Because of Thomas's parenting style, Simon feels alone, rejected by his mother and father, and spends much of his time playing violent video games by himself.
Birth order	Thomas is an oldest child. His family role was to protect and care for his brothers. He sacrificed play and spontaneity to ensure the safety of his brothers.	Chronologically, Simon is the youngest child. Psychologically, he is an only child. His sister is 10 years older, and he is being raised by her and his father. Simon is independent and accustomed to getting his way. He has a great deal of power in the family.
Life tasks	*Work*—Thomas is financially successful and independent and feels competent and valuable in his work.	*School*—Simon is academically successful but struggles to behave appropriately in the classroom.
	Family—Thomas feels isolated from his family of origin and disconnected from his current family. He is unsure of how to show affection and desires a more intimate relationship with his children.	*Family*—Simon does not feel connected to his father or mother. He feels mostly connected to his sister. His family members do not communicate affection and warmth with one another.
	Love—Thomas is single and fears finding love or starting romantic relationships because of his failed previous relationships. He does not trust others and believes it is easier to be alone than risk being rejected.	*Friendship*—Reports indicate that Simon is capable of building relationships and is generally liked by peers. His over-the-top and aggressive behaviors interfere with his ability to maintain friendships.
	Spirituality—Thomas was raised Baptist and spent many of his teenage and early adult years rejecting faith and religion. He believes there is a higher power and has recently become more interested in understanding his own beliefs about religion and spirituality.	*Purpose*—Little is known about Simon's spirituality. Simon knows that he impacts the world but believes that he can only do so in a negative fashion.

TABLE 9.1
Case Conceptualization of Thomas and Simon (*Continued)*

Lifestyle concept	Thomas	Simon
	Self—Thomas feels competent in most areas of his life. He believes he is a good person and wants the best for others.	*Self*—Simon can be funny and adventurous. He takes risks and believes he will physically and academically succeed at new tasks. He does not believe he is valued by others and typically shows feelings of hurt or fear through aggression and other externalizing behaviors.
Personality priorities	*Pleasing* personality priority (maladaptive). Thomas tries to make others happy and fears being rejected by others. Thus, he caters to Simon's demands. In this way, both of their personality priority needs are being met but not in a productive manner.	*Control* personality priority (maladaptive). Simon believes he must be in control of himself to feel safe. He also believes he needs to overpower others to make sure he can be in control of himself and situations.
Goals of misbehavior	Not applicable.	Simon's goals of misbehavior are to gain attention and power. He strives to be noticed and receive affection. By acting out in class, he receives attention from his peers and teacher. He has learned that any attention is better than no attention. He also seems to want power—he believes that he must show others they cannot control him and that he needs to be in control of himself and others, resulting in externalizing behaviors and resultant power struggles.
Crucial *C*s	Not applicable.	Simon knows that he is capable and has courage. He knows that he can connect with others and typically does so in a socially unuseful fashion. He could benefit from learning new ways to connect in socially useful and cooperative ways. Simon also needs help at increasing the Crucial *C* of *count*. He does not believe that he matters in the world.
Assets	Thomas is friendly, has social interest, desires well-being for his family, has financial resources, and is intelligent and resilient.	Simon is friendly, competent, able to follow directions, and loving and desires a relationship with his family.

the following week. She considered setting limits on Simon's video game and tablet times. However, the combination of Simon's control and Thomas's pleasing personality priorities might doom this effort to failure and result in ongoing power struggles that would counterbalance positive gains in their relationship. She was concerned that Simon would feel vulnerable not being in control and that Thomas would give in because of his fear of being rejected and Simon being angry with him.

For the next several months, Marie moved through the third and fourth phases of play therapy, continuing to see Simon in play therapy. She tailored their play activities and her metacommunication with the goals of helping Simon gain insight into some of his behaviors and giving him practice in new patterns of thinking and feeling and in behaving in a more cooperative manner. When Simon chose the activities, Marie and Simon usually played with the animals and infused nurturing themes such as feeding and brushing the animals. As they played, Marie metacommunicated about the experience: "The lion likes when the zebra and dolphin all eat together." "The dolphin wasn't sure how to take care of the lion, but he is trying hard." "I noticed the lion isn't getting into trouble as much anymore. Maybe the lion only acted like that to get the dolphin's attention." Marie also introduced more directive activities as a way of giving Simon a chance to practice sharing control.

Marie also consulted with Simon's teacher about creating ways for him to positively receive attention and power. For example, the teacher let Simon be the line leader, erase the whiteboard, and take lunch count. The opportunities allowed for Simon to experience getting attention for doing socially useful tasks. Marie also coached Simon's teacher in offering him limited choices—for example, did he want to do the first 15 math problems or the last 15 first? Did he want to sit on the floor or in a chair during group time? Simon felt encouraged and more in control without needing to overpower others. It did not take long before his school behaviors improved tremendously.

As the counseling relationship approached termination, because Simon reached the goals of decreased externalizing classroom behavior and feeling more connected to his father, Marie decided to conduct the last few sessions at Simon's school and meet only every other week. In this way, she could get permission to have another child join Simon and her in session. As the final part of the reorientation and reeducation phase of play therapy, conducting sessions with another child allowed Simon to practice and demonstrate his peer relationship skills. During the group sessions, Simon demonstrated an improvement in being able to share belongings and ideas with peers. He was initially uncertain about sharing "his" play therapist with another child, as this threatened his sense of belonging and amped up his fear of abandonment. Yet, in session this proved not to be a problem. The reduced frequency of sessions helped Simon to transition to termination.

Over the course of the next 2 months, Marie and Thomas had infrequent phone conversations to check in about the progress that the family was continuing to make. Thomas reported that for the first time, he enjoyed parenting! He described the weekly playdates as helping to improve his relationship with Simon, and he was able to set up logical consequences without being afraid of repeating the patterns of his own parents or being rejected by Simon. He also reported that he felt more confident as a parent of a teenage girl and noticed a positive change in Stacy's attitude as well. Before the end of their last conversation, he wanted Marie to know that for Simon's 8th birthday, he asked for a toy dolphin, zebra, and lion.

CONCLUSION AND FUTURE DIRECTIONS

The future looks bright for Adlerian play therapy and therapists. Terry Kottman developed the groundwork, including a treatment manual for play therapists to use as they conduct their own research (Kottman, 2009). The evidence supporting Adlerian play therapy is rapidly expanding and suggests that Adlerian play therapy is an effective intervention for use with children with externalizing behaviors and other troubling situations and behavior problems. Play therapists who identify with this theoretical approach to helping recognize and honor the unique qualities of every human being and creatively respond to those qualities. Whereas the primary goal is to help individual clients, the greater goal of an Adlerian play therapist is to create a world of respect, belonging, and togetherness.

REFERENCES

Abidin, R. R., & Robinson, L. L. (2002). Stress, biases, or professionalism: What drives teachers' referral judgments of students with challenging behaviors? *Journal of Emotional and Behavioral Disorders, 10*, 204–212. http://dx.doi.org/10.1177/10634266020100040201

Achenbach, T. M., & Rescorla, L. A. (2001). *Manual for the ASEBA school-age forms and profiles*. Burlington: University of Vermont, Research Center for Children, Youth, & Families.

Adler, A. (1956). *The individual psychology of Alfred Adler: A systemic presentation in selections from his writings* (H. L. Ansbacher & R. R. Ansbacher, Eds.). New York, NY: Harper & Row.

Adler, A. (1998). *Understanding human nature*. Oxford, England: Oneworld. (Original work published 1927)

Akay, S. (2013). *The effects of Adlerian play therapy on maladaptive perfectionism and anxiety in children* (Unpublished doctoral dissertation). University of North Texas, Denton.

Dillman Taylor, D., & Meany-Walen, K. K. (2015). *A single case design: Adlerian play therapy with elementary aged children and teachers*. Manuscript submitted for publication.

Dreikurs, R., & Soltz, V. (1964). *Children: The challenge*. New York, NY: Hawthorn/Dutton.

Gil, E. (2005). From sensitivity to competence in working across cultures. In E. Gil & A. Drewes (Eds.), *Cultural issues in play therapy* (pp. 3–25). New York, NY: Guilford Press.

Kefir, N. (1981). Impasse/priority therapy. In R. Corsini (Ed.), *Handbook of innovative psychotherapies* (pp. 400–415). New York, NY: Wiley.

Kottman, T. (2003). *Partners in play: An Adlerian approach to play therapy* (2nd ed.). Alexandria, VA: American Counseling Association.

Kottman, T. (2009). *Treatment manual for Adlerian play therapy*. Unpublished manuscript.

Kottman, T. (2011). *Play therapy: Basics and beyond* (2nd ed.). Alexandria, VA: American Counseling Association.

Kottman, T., & Ashby, J. (2015). Adlerian play therapy. In D. Crenshaw & A. Stewart (Eds.), *Play therapy: A comprehensive guide to theory and practice* (pp. 32–47). New York, NY: Guilford Press.

Lambert, S. F., LeBlanc, M., Mullen, J. A., Ray, D., Baggerly, J., White, J., & Kaplan, D. (2007). Learning more about those who play in session: The National Play Therapy in Counseling Practices Project (Phase 1). *Journal of Counseling & Development, 85*, 42–46. http://dx.doi.org/10.1002/j.1556-6678.2007.tb00442.x

Lew, A., & Bettner, B. L. (1996). *A parent's guide to understanding and motivating children*. Newton Centre, MA: Connexions Press.

Meany-Walen, K. K. (2010). *Adlerian play therapy: Effectiveness on disruptive behaviors of early elementary-aged children* (Unpublished doctoral dissertation). University of North Texas, Denton.

Meany-Walen, K. K., Bratton, S., & Kottman, T. (2014). Effects of Adlerian play therapy on reducing students' disruptive behaviors. *Journal of Counseling & Development, 92*, 47–56. http://dx.doi.org/10.1002/j.1556-6676.2014.00129.x

Meany-Walen, K. K., Bullis, Q., Kottman, T., & Dillman Taylor, D. (in press). Group Adlerian play therapy with children with externalizing behaviors: Single case design. *Journal for Specialists in Group Work*.

Meany-Walen, K. K., & Kottman, T. (2015). Adlerian play therapy with children affected by externalizing behavioral disorders. In E. Green & A. Myrick (Eds.), *No child forgotten: Integrating play therapy and evidence-informed interventions with unique pediatric populations* (pp. 177–194). Lanham, MD: Rowman & Littlefield.

Meany-Walen, K. K., Kottman, T., Bullis, Q., & Dillman Taylor, D. (in press). Adlerian play therapy with children with externalizing behaviors: Single case design. *Journal of Counseling & Development*.

Mental Health America. (2009). *Recognizing mental health problems in children*. Retrieved from http://www.mentalhealthamerica.net/recognizing-mental-health-problems-children

Mosak, H., & Maniacci, M. (1999). *A primer of Adlerian psychology: The analytic–behavioral–cognitive psychology of Alfred Adler*. New York, NY: Taylor & Francis.

Price, J. M., Chiapa, A., & Walsh, N. E. (2013). Predictors of externalizing behavior problems in early elementary-aged children: The role of family and home environments. *Journal of Genetic Psychology, 174*, 464–471. http://dx.doi.org/10.1080/00221325.2012.690785

III

PLAY INTERVENTIONS TO STRENGTHEN RELATIONSHIP SKILLS

10

CHILD–PARENT RELATIONSHIP THERAPY WITH PREADOLESCENTS

KARA CARNES-HOLT, KRISTIN K. MEANY-WALEN,
AND PEGGY CEBALLOS

Although preadolescents spend increasingly more time with peer groups and less time with family units, their healthy development relies strongly on the security of their relationship with their parents (Jacobs, Bleeker, & Constantino, 2003; Papalia, Olds, & Feldman, 2007). Past research shows that a strong relationship between preadolescents and their parents mitigates externalizing and internalizing problems (Crocker & Hakim-Larson, 1997; Jaffe & Baker, 1999; Lederman & Mian, 2003) during this developmental stage when considerable socioemotional and cognitive changes occur (Steinberg & Monahan, 2007). Despite the importance of this relationship, parents commonly report being most concerned about their parenting abilities when their child embarks on preadolescence (Baril, Crouter, & McHale, 2007).

Parts of this chapter are reprinted from "Child–Parent Relationship Therapy: A Model for Pre-adolescents," by K. Meany-Walen, K. Carnes-Holt, P. Ceballos, and E. Michero, 2014, *British Journal of Play Therapy*, *10*, pp. 6–19. Reprinted with permission.

http://dx.doi.org/10.1037/14776-011
Play Therapy in Middle Childhood, A. A. Drewes and C. E. Schaefer (Editors)

RATIONALE AND THEORY

Bernard and Louise Guerney developed filial therapy in the 1960s as a therapeutic intervention to teach parents how to become therapeutic agents for their own children (Guerney, 1964). Garry Landreth later refined filial therapy into a structured 10-session group-training model, child–parent relationship therapy (CPRT; Bratton, Landreth, Kellam, & Blackard, 2006; Landreth & Bratton, 2006). In CPRT, parents are taught child-centered play therapy skills and philosophy to enable them to enhance the parent–child relationship. The CPRT model seeks for parents to develop appropriate expectations of themselves and an accurate understanding of their child's development. CPRT leaders use teaching, group process, and supervision of parent–child interactions to enhance parenting skills.

The current model of CPRT and its treatment manual (Bratton et al., 2006; Landreth & Bratton, 2006) are tailored toward parents of children between the ages of 3and 10 years, leaving a gap in services specifically designed for older children (Packman & Solt, 2004). CPRT training components include listening with full attention, demonstrating nonjudgmental acceptance, being aware of the child's emotions, showing compassion, and parent self-regulating. Research indicates that these skills improve protective factors and reduce risks during adolescence (Coatsworth, Duncan, Greenberg, & Nix, 2010). Therefore, adaptations of CPRT for preadolescents are essential.

Despite the importance of the parental relationship to the healthy socioemotional development of preadolescents, parents may struggle to adapt their interaction style as preadolescents' developmental needs require a change in relationship dynamics (Baril et al., 2007; Packman & Solt, 2004; Vernon, 2009). Teaching parents how to effectively communicate with their growing child is essential, as research indicates that emotional distancing in the parent–child dyad does not enhance healthy individuation for preadolescents (Freeman & Newland, 2002). Thus, providing parenting programs that seek to enhance the parent–preadolescent relationship is optimal (Harter, 1999). In response, Packman and Solt (2004) provided a rationale and some general ideas for applying CPRT with preadolescents.

CPRT for preadolescents assists parents in facilitating and maintaining the basic conditions needed for healthy attachment. Secure attachments develop when caregivers are attuned to the child's emotional needs and offer a relationship in which the child has recurring experiences of feeling understood, connected, and protected (Bowlby, 1980; Schore, 1994; Siegel & Hartzell, 2004). Thus, parents' ability to offer a relationship based on safety and predictability provides the needed socioemotional support for preadolescents' healthy individuation and independence (Schore, 1994). CPRT for preadolescents provides a model to facilitate such a relationship between parents and preadolescents by teaching parents how to communicate acceptance, empathy, and understanding (Landreth & Bratton, 2006). With the implementation of CPRT for preadolescence, the primary caregiver is emotionally responsive and consistent in parent–child interactions. Weekly CPRT activity times can promote a secure attachment relationship, which contributes to the fundamental healing dynamic of CPRT.

DEVELOPMENTAL CHARACTERISTICS OF PREADOLESCENTS

Preadolescence, ages 8 to 12 years, is a turning point in children's lives, a time of significant physical, emotional, social, and cognitive development characterized by new challenges and transitions that have the potential to change people's feelings, thoughts, and behaviors (Graber & Brooks-Gunn, 1996). An important and influential difference between children and preadolescents is the social context in which preadolescents spend their time (Graber & Brooks-Gunn, 1996; Jacobs et al., 2003; Steinberg & Monahan, 2007). During childhood, children spend the majority of their time with the family of origin. As children develop, much of their family time is replaced by time spent with peers and other social groups. Because of the increasingly limited time together and the developmental characteristics of preadolescents, the parent–child relationship needs to be redefined by parents and preadolescents as they embark on this phase of life.

Emotional Development

A combination of age, gender, timing of puberty, and hormonal development increase the heightened emotional reactions and moodiness characterizing preadolescence (Papalia et al., 2007). Because of the dramatic hormonal changes combined with a lack of emotional maturity and coping skills, preadolescents tend to react with anger when they feel stressed or vulnerable (Papalia et al., 2007). Emotionally, preadolescents begin to become autonomous before they are prepared to handle such extreme emotional polarities, causing them to feel confused about their inability to control their emotions (Steinberg & Monahan, 2007) and overwhelmed as they attempt to mask their vulnerability (Vernon, 2009). They often think parents do not understand, and they prefer to spend time with peers, whom they believe understand their feelings (Packman & Solt, 2004). This reaction causes tension in the parent–child relationship as preadolescents start to pull away from parents at a time when parents can serve as a guide to help them navigate their emotions (Bulanda & Majumdar, 2009).

Preadolescents' perceptions of themselves and the variables through which they define themselves change; they are increasingly concerned about external judgments and comparisons. They begin to feel as if nobody understands, increasing their dissatisfaction with current relationships, mainly with parents, and aligning themselves with others who have similar experiences, mainly with peers. Elkind (1980) described a phenomenon that occurs during adolescence as the *imaginary audience*; adolescents believe that others are constantly watching and evaluating them. Regardless of the accuracy of their evaluation, their perceptions of what others are thinking contribute to their self-identity.

Cognitive Development

Preadolescence is characterized by a substantial increase in maturity and reasoning abilities compared with childhood (Schachter, Kleinman, & Harvey, 2005; Tillett, 2005). Preadolescents are shifting from concrete to formal operational thinking (Elkind, 1980; Vernon, 2009). Thus, preadolescents are beginning to think abstractly. Because this new way of thinking is a gradual and nonlinear process, the preadolescent may fluctuate between child and adolescent reasoning capabilities. Even though preadolescents may be capable of operational thinking, they may not be comfortable with expressing themselves strictly through verbal expression. At times, they still engage in play behaviors to communicate their experiences (Packman & Solt, 2004).

Beginning in preadolescence, a dramatic change in brain activity, primarily in the frontal lobe, begins to occur (Papalia et al., 2007; Schachter et al., 2005; Tillett, 2005). Reasoning, emotional regulation, planning, and impulse control are among the tasks handled by the frontal lobe. This part of the brain assists in the cognitive maturation process and is not fully developed until young adulthood. In part because of the immaturity of the developing brain, preadolescents are susceptible to making rash choices and not rationally analyzing the immediate or long-term consequences of their decisions (Casey, Jones, & Somerville, 2011; Schwartz, 2008; Tillett, 2005). Youth in this age group value immediate gratification and typically disregard long-term consequences (Schachter et al., 2005). Tillett (2005) described preadolescents as capable of making responsible decisions but at times lacking realistic expectations of the consequences of their actions. They often believe they are invincible, and although they understand risk, they may not fully understand how it applies to their own life, acting as if risks belong to other people and they have an invisible cloak that protects them from all harm (Elkind, 1980; Tillett, 2005).

Parents' lack of understanding of these cognitive changes may cause unrealistic expectations for preadolescents that result in conflict between parent and preadolescent. In addition, preadolescents typically lack an understanding of how they are instrumental in their own life dissatisfaction. They are quick to blame others such as parents, siblings, and teachers for their unhappiness. These cognitive and emotional changes happen along a flux of physical changes that may cause preadolescents to experience anxiety, stress, worry, and dissatisfaction (American Academy of Child and Adolescent Psychiatry [AACAP], 2011).

Physical Development

Puberty, the process of maturing sexually and attaining the ability to reproduce, was once associated primarily with adolescents. Although several hypotheses exist with no definitive explanation, many children enter puberty at an earlier age (i.e., preadolescence) than past generations (Papalia et al., 2007). Girls experience increased breast size, menarche followed by menstruation, and widening of the hips (AACAP, 2011; Papalia et al., 2007). Boys typically experience physical changes at an older age than girls, usually between late preadolescence and adolescence (AACAP, 2011; Papalia et al., 2007). Some associated physical changes for boys are growth of the testes and penis, ejaculation of semen and nocturnal emission, deepening of the voice, and broadening of the shoulders. Both genders experience the emergence of underarm and pubic hair, changes in skin, increased muscle capacity, and a growth spurt (Papalia et al., 2007).

The physical changes within and between the sexes may create additional stress, worry, and dissatisfaction in preadolescents who feel bigger or smaller than the rest of their peers (AACAP, 2011). These changes affect preadolescents' self-esteem and the development of their self-concept (Nyarko, 2012). The physical changes that accompany puberty can also create confusion for the parent. Because the child looks mature, the parent may have expectations that the child can act mature. When a child's behavior and a parent's expectations do not match, frustration in both parties can negatively impact the relationship.

Healthy parent–child relationships can act as a buffer to the development of low self-esteem and negative self-concept. Children with higher self-esteem are more likely to make safe and positive decisions throughout preadolescence. Thus, an improved parent–child relationship can be a protective factor (Chowdhury & Pancha, 2011; Crocker & Hakim-Larson, 1997; Jaffe & Baker, 1999; Lederman & Mian, 2003).

Internalizing and Externalizing Behaviors

The terms *internalizing behaviors* and *externalizing behaviors* are commonly used to describe modes of expression clustered together and labeled as a disorder according to the *Diagnostic and Statistical Manual of Mental Disorders*

(5th ed.; American Psychiatric Association, 2013). Internalizing behaviors include problems within the individual such as symptoms of anxiety, depression, withdrawal, and somatic complaints (Achenbach & Rescorla, 2001). When people have internalizing behavior patterns, they may avoid other people, activities, and events. They may complain of discomfort such as stomach cramps or fatigue (American Psychiatric Association, 2013). Because parents and teachers often make referrals for youth counseling based on observed behavioral concerns (Abidin & Robinson, 2002), young adolescents with internalizing behaviors may unintentionally be ignored and not receive intervention. Essentially, preadolescents with internalizing behaviors do not create a problem for others; thus, their feelings of sadness, anxiety, or low self-esteem may go unnoticed.

On the contrary, externalizing behaviors are expressions that can be observed by others. These behaviors interfere with the rights and dignity of other people, create interpersonal problems, and are usually the result of more significant underlying problems (Abidin & Robinson, 2002; Achenbach & Rescorla, 2001; American Psychiatric Association, 2013). Fighting, yelling, stealing, breaking rules, being impulsive or hyperactive, and using drugs or alcohol are examples of externalizing behaviors. Because preadolescents experience a roller-coaster of emotions, are practicing with higher level cognitive functioning, have more resources for independence, and are more physically capable, it may not be uncommon for preadolescents to exhibit externalizing behaviors.

CHILD–PARENT RELATIONSHIP THERAPY FOR PREADOLESCENTS: PROCEDURE AND SETTING

Mental health professionals who conduct CPRT with preadolescents follow the same procedures described in the CPRT treatment manual (Bratton et al., 2006) with developmentally responsive adjustments. It is strongly recommended that mental health professionals have an understanding of traditional CPRT protocol and terminology that are explained in the CPRT treatment manual before applying the suggested modifications for preadolescents. Parents attend 2-hour group meetings for 10 sessions. The first three sessions focus on teaching parents CCPT basic skills to prepare them for the special time with their child. Sessions 4 through 10 are used to supervise parents' special time with their child, teach advanced CCPT skills, and help parents generalize the skills outside of the special times. Table 10.1 highlights the modifications that need to be done when conducting CPRT with preadolescents.

TABLE 10.1
Modifications for Preadolescents of the Child–Parent Relationship Therapy (CPRT) Model

CPRT with younger children	CPRT with preadolescents
Toys are used for weekly play sessions.	Developmentally appropriate materials and activities are used for weekly special times. Materials may change each week.
30-minute "play sessions" are used.	45- to 60-minute "activities" are used.
Emphasis is placed on use of tracking.	Emphasis is placed on reflection of content and esteem-building responses because tracking can seem childish to a preadolescent.
The parent selects "special playtimes."	The parent and child determine "special times," which may vary from week to week depending on schedule. Preadolescents participate in determining the content and timing of the activity to respond to their developmental need to participate in decision making.
The CPRT leader provides education about child development.	The CPRT leader provides education about preadolescent development.
Parents are expected to share their experiences as children.	Parents are expected to process and share their experiences during their own adolescence.
Child care is made available.	Supervision of preadolescents and adolescents may be requested. Movies, games, and activities are made available that are developmentally appropriate for this age group.
The parent focuses on frequent verbal statements to let the child know he or she is present.	The parent places more emphasis on being genuine and casual, avoiding use of the current popular slang of preadolescents as a means to connect.
ACT limit setting is used: • Acknowledge the feeling • Communicate the limit • Target an alternative	ACE limit setting is used to respond to preadolescents' developmental need for participation in decision making: • Acknowledge the feeling • Communicate the limit • Explore possible alternatives
Choice giving is used.	Choice giving is used, providing examples that are developmentally appropriate. The preadolescent takes an active role in developing some of the choices.

CHILD–PARENT RELATIONSHIP THERAPY: EMPIRICAL SUPPORT

Bratton, Ray, Rhine, and Jones (2005) conducted a meta-analysis of 93 outcome-controlled research studies examining the efficacy of play therapy and found a large treatment effect size (1.25) for filial therapy. CPRT, in particular, has more than 35 research studies with a variety of presenting issues; 27 of these studies are controlled-outcome studies involving more than 1,000 participants (Baggerly, Ray, & Bratton, 2010). CPRT has also been shown to be effective with ethnically diverse groups (e.g., Glover & Landreth, 2000; Sheely-Moore & Bratton, 2010), immigrant parents living in the United States (Ceballos & Bratton, 2010; Lee & Landreth, 2003; Yuen, Landreth, & Baggerly, 2002), and adoptive parents (Carnes-Holt, 2010).

Considering the positive outcomes of CPRT with young children, it seems reasonable to believe that CPRT with parents of preadolescents can also be effective. The explanations and examples given in the CPRT parent notebook are based on the developmental needs of children under age 10 (Bratton et al., 2006). CPRT leaders of parents with preadolescents need to link concepts and skills taught in each session to the developmental needs of preadolescents. Having a thorough understanding of preadolescents' development can help CPRT leaders answer parents' concerns and spontaneous questions that may arise. It is also important to show video clips that exemplify special times with preadolescents to help parents have realistic expectations of their at-home sessions.

CASE ILLUSTRATION OF A PREADOLESCENT WITH INTERNALIZING BEHAVIORS, INCLUDING PARENT INVOLVEMENT

Marco and Kate were the parents of Julia, an 11-year-old girl who was in fifth grade. Julia's parents contacted the therapist and expressed interest in joining the CPRT group. Marco and Kate expressed concerns that Julia's behaviors "shifted overnight." Kate stated that their loving, affectionate, and outgoing child suddenly appeared quiet, withdrawn, and anxious.

Julia was the oldest of three children, and her parents reported that she had always been a high-achieving student and active in sports. Julia had a previous history of individual play therapy when she was 5 years old to support her with the adjustment of having a younger sibling. Julia's parents stated that she had recently started at the middle school in their local community; however, she was still with her peer group from elementary school. Marco and Kate expressed interest in wanting to "get to the bottom of this" before it was "too late."

Intake Session

Bonnie, one of the coleaders for the CPRT group, met with Marco and Kate to initiate a therapeutic relationship, gather Julia's developmental history, and provide an overview of the philosophy and structure of CPRT. Bonnie informed Marco and Kate that some modifications would be made to the traditional CPRT model to respond to Julia's preadolescent developmental needs.

CPRT leaders can follow the therapist study guide found in the CPRT treatment manual (Bratton et al., 2006) when conducting CPRT with parents of preadolescents. However, specific adjustments should also be made to each session. In the following sections, we suggest changes to the sessions and handouts found in the parent handbook located in the hard copy of the CPRT treatment manual (Bratton et al., 2006). CPRT leaders can change the handouts by accessing the Microsoft Word version of the parent notebook found in the CD that comes with the CPRT treatment manual (Bratton et al., 2006).

Sessions 1 to 3

In the same way that CPRT leaders teach parents of young children to reflect the child's feelings and behaviors (Landreth & Bratton, 2006), parents of preadolescents are taught to use reflective skills to convey empathy and enhance the relationship. The skill of reflecting feelings remains the same, but because preadolescents are self-conscious and believe others are watching them (Elkind, 1980), tracking (i.e., verbally stating what the parent sees and observes) may be distracting and create uncomfortable feelings, reconfirming to preadolescents that in fact, people are always watching and evaluating them. Instead of tracking, caregivers use reflection of content by paraphrasing. When the preadolescent is not talking, the parent may use tracking, but with caution. In general, CPRT leaders remind parents of the importance of being genuine and casual when using the skills while avoiding using current popular slang as a means to connect.

In the original CPRT model, one-on-one parent–child interactions were called *special playtimes*. The purpose of special playtimes is to enhance the parent–child relationship through parents' ability to convey empathy and unconditional acceptance (Landreth & Bratton, 2006). This same principle applies to CPRT with preadolescents; however, play sessions are structured in ways that respond to the preadolescent's development. Play sessions are called "special times," and instead of using toys as the medium for interaction, parents engage in different activities that promote parent–child interactions. Although parents are taught to use traditional play therapy skills, preadolescents may perceive the term *playtimes* as juvenile, which might reconfirm to growing children that their parents do not understand them. Additionally, toys may not be age appropriate for preadolescents, who still need nonverbal means of communication but through developmentally appropriate mediums (Bratton, Ceballos, & Meany-Walen, 2014).

Preadolescents can engage in higher levels of abstract thinking than younger children, and they are socially developing their sense of independence (Sprenger, 2008). Therefore, they can be included in deciding the activity for the special time, which is a variation on the original model, which included the same play materials and objectives for each session. In general, when deciding on the activity for the special time, it is critical to follow the same three guidelines specified in the CPRT model for younger children (Landreth & Bratton, 2006): (a) the activity allows for parent–child interaction to occur and avoids external stimuli that do not promote parent–child contact (e.g., playing video games, watching movies), (b) the special time is conducted once a week for durations that allow for completion of the activity (e.g., 45 minutes to bake, 90 minutes for fishing), and (c) distractions (e.g., interaction with other children, phone calls) are avoided during this time.

In contrast to the guidelines for the play sessions (Landreth & Bratton, 2006), the parent and preadolescent can choose different weekly activities. Once an activity is chosen, it is important for parents to understand that the activity should not be evaluated but rather should be experienced. Parents should not be concerned about the child doing the activity "right" or improving a skill; instead, parents need to focus on the improved relationship and the experience of being with their child and using play therapy responses.

Marco and Kate eagerly attended the first CPRT session and met other parents attending the group. After a brief introduction, the coleaders introduced concepts such as strength focusing and reflective responding. The CPRT coleaders invited Marco and Kate to share with the group daily scenarios of Julia that created opportunities for reflective responding. Kate shared that when Julia arrived home from school, she was often quiet and irritable and made comments about difficult social relationships at school. Kate shared that she tried to question and problem solve these situations with Julia. Through this activity, Kate realized that using reflective responding, such as "You feel frustrated when your friends do not eat lunch with you," could convey more understanding and empathy in her relationship with Julia.

During the second CPRT session, Marco and Kate reported that they had noticed that the reflective responding had been successful, with Julia sharing more about what she was thinking and feeling with decreased irritability. During this session, the CPRT coleaders introduced the concept of having a weekly special time with Julia. Marco and Kate explored activities that Julia might enjoy and weekly times they had available to spend with her. The CPRT leaders encouraged Marco and Kate to involve Julia in the process of selecting the time and activity for each week. Marco and Kate participated in a role-play to practice skills of reflective responding and following Julia's lead in the activity chosen for the special time. The CPRT coleaders emphasized that "be with" attitudes were to be the guiding philosophy for these special times with Julia.

The focus of the third CPRT session was to help parents practice introducing the special time to the child and reminding them of the core principles during this time. Marco and Kate expressed anxiety about how receptive Julia would be to special times. The CPRT coleaders normalized this fear and acknowledged the relationship struggle that is often present for parents of preadolescents. The parents were reminded that affirming Julia's strengths, being genuine and empathic, and communicating acceptance were the emphasis when being with Julia. Marco and Kate shared that they would both talk to Julia about starting a special time with each parent beginning the following week.

Sessions 4 to 6

In CPRT, parents learn to set limits following the ACT model: **a**cknowledge the feeling, **c**ommunicate the limit, and **t**arget an alternative (Landreth, 2012). These steps enhance children's ability to engage in problem solving and responsible decision making. Because preadolescents are socially and emotionally learning to be independent and are developing their abilities to engage in abstract thinking (Sprenger, 2008), the third stage of limit setting is slightly modified to an ACE model: **a**cknowledge the feeling, **c**ommunicate the limit, and **e**xplore possible alternatives. This adjustment allows the preadolescent to feel more in control of the situation while practicing decision-making skills.

Landreth (2012) stated that providing children with age-appropriate choices empowers children, develops their problem-solving and decision-making skills, and reduces power struggles between the adult and the child. Thus, CPRT leaders are intentional about helping parents brainstorm choices that are age appropriate (Landreth & Bratton, 2006). Problem solving an acceptable choice is within preadolescents' ability to think abstractly (Papalia et al., 2007) and reinforces their sense of independence. Parents who engage in discussions and reasoning when establishing limits and giving choices contribute to their preadolescents' development of a healthy self-concept (Nyarko, 2012).

Homework assignments within the CPRT model are structured to create memorable family moments that strengthen the parent–child relationship. This goal remains the same when providing CPRT to preadolescents. The key to success is to find activities that are developmentally appropriate (e.g., sending text messages). Because the developmental stage of preadolescents can vary greatly from one year to another, and because each child enjoys different things, it is important for therapists to brainstorm these activities with parents to ensure they adapt to the culture and developmental needs of the preadolescent.

During Sessions 4 through 6, Marco and Kate learned advanced skills (e.g., limit setting) and shared with group members their experience in special times with Julia. Julia chose to do different activities with each of them. Marco shared that he rode bikes and went out to lunch at a special restaurant with Julia. He disclosed that Julia was shy and did not say much regarding her experiences at school. The CPRT leader helped Marco focus on the importance of having the special times and how much they both enjoyed them regardless of Julia's level of self-disclosure.

Marco expressed his concern about how to talk to Julia when she was quiet; he described these moments as "awkward and uncomfortable." The CPRT leader engaged in role-playing with Marco to help him practice how to use reflective skills during these moments.

Kate shared that she did craft activities with Julia at home and went out for ice cream during their special time. Videotaping the special times is not required because the type of activities that preadolescents agree to do vary greatly and often take place outdoors; however, parents in the group were encouraged to videotape their special times if the logistics could be worked out. Thus, Kate videotaped some of the special times spent at home doing craft activities. It is important to note that Julia was aware of the videotaping and gave consent for Kate to show the videotapes during group time, knowing that Marco and additional group members would be present. Kate's supervision focused on her ability to listen empathetically instead of giving advice. As Kate and Marco shared different moments, the CPRT leader helped them brainstorm how to respond using reflections of feelings and content and guided them to think about the importance of strengthening their individual relationship with Julia as a means to open communication with her. Both Marco and Kate noted that Julia appeared more comfortable with the special times as time went by and they did more sessions.

During Session 4, the CPRT leader introduced limit setting. Julia's parents identified times when they could use limit setting with her, such as cleaning her room and occasional struggles with sibling relationships. Similarly, during Session 6, the CPRT leader introduced choice giving and helped Kate and Marco come up with real-life situations when they could use choices. They both reported that when they engaged Julia in deciding the consequence for not cleaning her room, they felt less responsible for applying the rules.

In summary, throughout Sessions 4 through 6, Marco and Kate were able to practice learned skills while exploring their unique challenges in applying them. The CPRT leader was able to help them find ways to work on their challenges and focus on strengthening their relationship with Julia.

Sessions 7 to 10

Parents who participate in CPRT learn to substitute praise for encouragement as a way to encourage children's sense of self-motivation and self-control (Landreth & Bratton, 2006). This skill applies to parents of preadolescents in the same way as in the CPRT model for parents of younger children. Thus, this skill does not require any modification other than providing age-appropriate examples.

Parents may choose to continue to meet for support from one another; this continued gathering may or may not include the leader. Because every group creates its own personality, each group has a different idea of what they need following termination of CPRT. Furthermore, should a particular family, parent, or child need ongoing professional support, the group leader makes recommendations or follow-up arrangements for continued services based on the individual needs of that person or family.

Sessions 7 through 10 continue in much the same way as the previous sessions. Supervision of recorded special times or discussion about special times is conducted. Kate and Marco both reported noticing changes in Julia's interactions at home. They shared that the use of limit setting and choice giving allowed Julia the opportunity to make responsible decisions, and they were pleased with the outcomes. Parents also learn the importance and benefit of encouraging their child. Bonnie described the differences between encouragement and praise. Kate and Marco, with the guidance of Bonnie and other group members, brainstormed many opportunities to encourage Julia.

Session 7 includes homework for the parents to write a letter to their child. Bonnie stated that Marco and Kate could send this letter as a text message to Julia. The letter was to follow the format outlined by Bratton et al. (2006): "Dear ___________, I was just thinking about you, and what I was thinking is you are so _________ (thoughtful, responsible, considerate, loving, etc.). I love you, ______ (Mom, Dad)." (p. 61). Kate and Marco wrote individual messages to Julia and sent them to her on different days. In Session 8, they reported that Julia did not verbally acknowledge the messages but did write a text-message response to both of them. As Kate shared this experience, her eyes began to water. She stated, "I feel like I have my daughter back. We're getting the old Julia." Several group members nodded in agreement and offered encouraging words to Kate and Marco.

During Sessions 8 and 9, group leaders work with parents to transition the skills used during special times to use outside of the special time. Kate and Marco reported that they found themselves reflecting Julia's feelings outside of the scheduled activity times. Kate shared that she caught Marco reflecting her feelings, and she believed that their relationship had strengthened from learning these skills.

In addition to supervision, Session 10 allows the group members to process their feelings and experiences in the group. Parents can share what they have learned and the changes they have seen in themselves and their children. Bonnie and Marco stated that their daughter shared more about her peer relationships with them and that she was more loving and engaged with them compared with before the CPRT group. They commented on their improved communication skills with Julia and with each other. They also described feeling a sense of relief to know that other parents struggled with similar things as they did. Although Kate and Marco described being very thankful for the group and were sad to see it end, they were thankful for the opportunity and all they had learned. After the group dismissed, Kate and Marco pulled aside Bonnie and said,

> This group changed our family. We were worried about Julia's future as she became more independent and started middle school. Because of what we've learned and how we've improved our relationship with Julia, we are much less worried and know that we can handle many things that will come our way. Thank you for strengthening our family.

REMINDERS AND STRATEGIES FOR SUCCESS

CPRT with preadolescents is considered successful when the parent and child improve their relationship. Although the expectation is for both the parent and the child to build a relationship together, pressure is put on the parent to make the initial effort and apply the learned CPRT skills with his or her preadolescent child. The following reminders to parents will help increase opportunities for success with CPRT and the parenting of preadolescents:

- In CPRT, activities are a means to an end. The goal is to improve the parent–child relationship. Even if the activity does not work out as planned, the time spent with the preadolescent was not wasted.
- There are no gender rules in CPRT. Boys like to bake, and girls like to fish. Do not limit activities to those that may seem traditionally male or female.
- Be patient. Avoid looking for perfection, and start looking for opportunities to connect.
- Find a time that works for you and your child. Scheduling the special time when both parent and preadolescent can be physically and emotionally available communicates respect for each other.

- Throughout the week, notice the television programs your preadolescent watches, the books he or she reads, and the music he or she likes. Try to use these as relationship builders.
- You cannot control your preadolescent; however, you can guide. Build a relationship in which your child feels safe sharing with you difficult moments and decisions.
- Preadolescence is challenging for most caregivers. Parents and children alike have a hard time during this stage of development.
- Parents can understand without agreeing. For example, a parent can communicate caring about a daughter's feelings of devastation after a fight with her best friend without agreeing that her life is ruined. At this moment, she needs to know you understand.
- Most of the time, preadolescents do not learn about life through their parents' mistakes. When safe and appropriate, allow your child to experience making mistakes and overcoming the consequences.
- Allow preadolescents to engage in problem solving. Help your child become part of the process of deciding rules and consequences for misbehavior. When preadolescents are part of the decision-making process, they are more likely to follow the expectations. Practice in making decisions and planning responsibly provides a valuable life skill.

CONCLUSION

Preadolescence is a time of significant physical, emotional, social, and cognitive development characterized by new challenges and transitions (Graber & Brooks-Gunn, 1996; Steinberg & Monahan, 2007; Vernon, 2009). Because these developmental changes affect the parent–child relationship (Packman & Solt, 2004), both parents and preadolescents may feel apprehensive about this transitional time, which frequently includes excitement, frustration, and confusion. Providing interventions that help parents develop a relationship that includes emotional closeness and open communication can serve as a significant protective factor for families (Coatsworth et al., 2010; Hemphill & Littlefield, 2006). Additionally, strengthening the parent–child relationship during preadolescence can help minimize externalizing and internalizing behavioral problems for preadolescents (Jaffe & Baker, 1999; Lederman & Mian, 2003). Past research supports the effectiveness of CPRT with parents of young children (Baggerly, Ray, & Bratton, 2010; Bratton et al., 2005), so CPRT is a promising intervention that can be adapted for use with this age group.

REFERENCES

Abidin, R. R., & Robinson, L. L. (2002). Stress, biases, or professionalism: What drives teachers' referral judgments of students with challenging behaviors? *Journal of Emotional and Behavioral Disorders, 10*, 204–212.

Achenbach, T. M., & Rescorla, L. A. (2001). *Manual for the ASEBA school-age forms and profiles*. Burlington: University of Vermont, Research Center for Children, Youth, and Families.

American Academy of Child and Adolescent Psychiatry. (2011, December). *Facts for families: Normal adolescent development Part I*. Retrieved from https://www.aacap.org/App_Themes/AACAP/docs/facts_for_families/57_normal_adolescent_development.pdf

American Psychiatric Association. (2013). *Diagnostic and statistical manual of mental disorders* (5th ed.). Washington, DC: Author.

Baggerly, J. N., Ray, D., & Bratton, S. (2010). *Child-centered play therapy research: The evidence base for effective practice*. Hoboken, NJ: Wiley. http://dx.doi.org/10.1002/9781118269626

Baril, M. E., Crouter, A. C., & McHale, S. M. (2007). Processes linking adolescent well-being, marital love, and coparenting. *Journal of Family Psychology, 21*, 645–654. http://dx.doi.org/10.1037/0893-3200.21.4.645

Bowlby, J. (1980). *Attachment and loss* (Vol. 3). New York, NY: Basic Books.

Bratton, S. C., Ceballos, P. L., & Meany-Walen, K. K. (2014). Play therapy. In R. J. R. Levesque (Ed.), *Encyclopedia of adolescence* (pp. 2091–2100). New York, NY: Springer Science + Business Media.

Bratton, S. C., Landreth, G. L., Kellam, T., & Blackard, S. R. (2006). *Child parent relationship therapy (CPRT) treatment manual: A 10-session filial therapy model for training parents*. New York, NY: Routledge.

Bratton, S. C., Ray, D., Rhine, T., & Jones, L. (2005). The efficacy of play therapy with children: A meta-analytic review of treatment outcomes. *Professional Psychology: Research and Practice, 36*, 376–390. http://dx.doi.org/10.1037/0735-7028.36.4.376

Bulanda, R. E., & Majumdar, D. (2009). Perceived parent–child relations and adolescent self-esteem. *Journal of Child and Family Studies, 18*, 203–212. http://dx.doi.org/10.1007/s10826-008-9220-3

Carnes-Holt, K. (2010). *Child–parent relationship therapy (CPRT) with adoptive families: Effects on child behavior, parent–child relationship stress, and parental empathy* (Doctoral dissertation). Available from ProQuest Dissertations and Theses database. (Order No. 3417739)

Casey, B., Jones, R. M., & Somerville, L. H. (2011). Braking and accelerating of the adolescent brain. *Journal of Research on Adolescence, 21*, 21–33. http://dx.doi.org/10.1111/j.1532-7795.2010.00712.x

Ceballos, P., & Bratton, S. (2010). Empowering Latino families: Effects of a culturally responsive intervention for low-income immigrant Latino parents on children's behaviors and parental stress. *Psychology in the Schools, 47*, 761–775. http://dx.doi.org/10.1002/pits.20502

Chowdhury, U., & Pancha, A. (2011). Posttraumatic stress disorder in children and adolescents. *Community Practitioner, 84*(12), 33–35.

Coatsworth, J. D., Duncan, L. G., Greenberg, M. T., & Nix, R. L. (2010). Changing parent's mindfulness, child management skills and relationship quality with their youth: Results from a randomized pilot intervention trial. *Journal of Child and Family Studies, 19*, 203–217. http://dx.doi.org/10.1007/s10826-009-9304-8

Crocker, A. D., & Hakim-Larson, J. (1997). Predictors of preadolescent depression and suicidal ideation. *Canadian Journal of Behavioural Science, 29*, 76–82. http://dx.doi.org/10.1037/0008-400X.29.2.76

Elkind, D. (1980). Child development and counseling. *Personnel and Guidance Journal, 58*, 353–355. http://dx.doi.org/10.1002/j.2164-4918.1980.tb00413.x

Freeman, H. S., & Newland, L. A. (2002). Family transitions during the adolescent transition: Implications for parenting. *Adolescence, 37*, 457–475.

Glover, G. J., & Landreth, G. L. (2000). Filial therapy with Native Americans on the Flathead Reservation. *International Journal of Play Therapy*, 9(2), 57–80. http://dx.doi.org/10.1037/h0089436

Graber, J. A., & Brooks-Gunn, J. (1996). Transitions and turning points: Navigating the passage from childhood through adolescence. *Developmental Psychology, 32*, 768–776. http://dx.doi.org/10.1037/0012-1649.32.4.768

Guerney, B., Jr. (1964). Filial therapy: Description and rationale. *Journal of Consulting Psychology, 28*, 304–310. http://dx.doi.org/10.1037/h0041340

Harter, S. (1999). Symbolic interactionism revisited: Potential liabilities for the self constructed in the crucible of interpersonal relationships. *Merrill–Palmer Quarterly, 45*, 677–703.

Hemphill, S. A., & Littlefield, L. (2006). Child and family predictors of therapy outcome for children with behavioral and emotional problems. *Child Psychiatry and Human Development, 36*, 329–349. http://dx.doi.org/10.1007/s10578-005-0006-1

Jacobs, J. E., Bleeker, M. M., & Constantino, M. J. (2003). The self-system during childhood and adolescence: Development, influences, and implications. *Journal of Psychotherapy Integration, 13*, 33–65. http://dx.doi.org/10.1037/1053-0479.13.1.33

Jaffe, P. G., & Baker, L. L. (1999). Why changing the YOA does not impact youth crime: Developing effective prevention programs for children and adolescents. *Canadian Psychology, 40*, 22–29. http://dx.doi.org/10.1037/h0086824

Landreth, G. (2012). *Play therapy: The art of the relationship* (3rd ed.). New York, NY: Brunner-Routledge.

Landreth, G., & Bratton, S. (2006). *Child–parent relationship therapy (CPRT): A 10-session filial therapy model.* New York, NY: Brunner-Routledge.

Lederman, R. P., & Mian, T. S. (2003). The Parent–Adolescent Relationship Education (PARE) program: A curriculum for prevention of STDs and pregnancy in middle school youth. *Behavioral Medicine, 29*, 33–41. http://dx.doi.org/10.1080/08964280309596173

Lee, M., & Landreth, G. L. (2003). Filial therapy with immigrant Korean parents in the United States. *International Journal of Play Therapy, 12*(2), 67–85. http://dx.doi.org/10.1037/h0088879

Nyarko, K. (2012). The influence of peer and parent relationships on adolescents' self-esteem. *IFE Psychologia: An International Journal, 20*, 161–167.

Packman, J., & Solt, M. D. (2004). Filial therapy modifications for preadolescents. *International Journal of Play Therapy, 13*(1), 57–77. http://dx.doi.org/10.1037/h0088885

Papalia, D. E., Olds, S. W., & Feldman, R. D. (2007). *Human development* (10th ed.). New York, NY: McGraw-Hill.

Schachter, D., Kleinman, I., & Harvey, W. (2005). Informed consent and adolescents. *Canadian Journal of Psychiatry, 50*, 534–540.

Schore, A. N. (1994). *Affect regulation and the origin of self*. Mahwah, NJ: Erlbaum.

Schwartz, K. D. (2008). Adolescent brain development: An oxymoron no longer. *Journal of Youth Ministry, 6*(2), 85–93.

Sheely-Moore, A., & Bratton, S. (2010). A strengths-based parenting intervention with low-income African American families. *Professional School Counseling, 13*, 175–183. http://dx.doi.org/10.5330/PSC.n.2010-13.175

Siegel, D., & Hartzell, M. (2004). *Parenting from the inside-out: How a deeper self-understanding can help you raise children who thrive*. New York, NY: Jeremy P. Tarcher/Putnam.

Sprenger, M. (2008). *The developing brain: Birth to age eight*. Thousand Oaks, CA: Corwin Press. http://dx.doi.org/10.4135/9781483329758

Steinberg, L., & Monahan, K. C. (2007). Age differences in resistance to peer influence. *Developmental Psychology, 43*, 1531–1543. http://dx.doi.org/10.1037/0012-1649.43.6.1531

Tillett, J. (2005). Adolescents and informed consent: Ethical and legal issues. *Journal of Perinatal & Neonatal Nursing, 19*, 112–121. http://dx.doi.org/10.1097/00005237-200504000-00007

Vernon, A. (2009). *Counseling children and adolescents* (4th ed.). Denver, CO: Love.

Yuen, T., Landreth, G., & Baggerly, J. (2002). Filial therapy with immigrant Chinese families. *International Journal of Play Therapy, 11*(2), 63–90. http://dx.doi.org/10.1037/h0088865

11

PAIR COUNSELING TO PROMOTE SOCIAL COMPETENCIES AMONG SCHOOL-AGE CHILDREN

MICHAEL J. KARCHER, KRISTI McCLATCHY, AND COURTNEY BORSUK

Peer problems and peer interventions have typically been the focus of research and interventions in the early teen years, when peer dynamics are found to relate most strongly to a host of behavioral, emotional, social and academic problems; but the seeds of interpersonal ineffectiveness are sewn several years prior and therefore interventions to address this problem should be provided to preteens. Yet, traditionally most interventions for children have had the adult clinician as the child's main partner in therapeutic efforts. We, the authors and members of the Group for the Study of Interpersonal Development at Harvard and the University of Texas at San Antonio, feel that other children can be much more influential in facilitating the growth of interpersonal competence. Of course, sometimes in the treatment of socially struggling children, they are involved in group counseling or play therapy. However, we feel such interventions provide only limited opportunities for children to put new self-awareness and social skills they may learn in these therapeutic modalities into action in authentic relationships with peers.

http://dx.doi.org/10.1037/14776-012
Play Therapy in Middle Childhood, A. A. Drewes and C. E. Schaefer (Editors)

This chapter rests on the premise that, without involving peers—that is, interventions only involving an adult clinician or providing formal, structured group interactions, many struggling children are not provided the full range of opportunities for emotional expression or skill development needed to facilitate effective transfer of newly learned competencies to real relationships outside the therapy hour.

This chapter presents a model of a dyadic peer-driven child play therapy called *pair counseling*. It is a more structured, short-term approach to the pair therapy intervention detailed first by Selman and Schultz (1990). In pair counseling, two children meet with a counselor for an hour each week to learn, practice, and develop key social-cognitive skills (Karcher, 2002). The goal is to help emancipate children from maladaptive ways of relating by encouraging them to take one another's perspective and to act in ways that allow both children to get their needs met.

Pair counseling is a play therapy treatment modality that aims to teach problem-solving skills and interpersonal negotiation strategies in a therapeutic relationship through authentic interactions with a same-age, same-sex but interpersonally different peer. The approach helps teach skills by modeling and doing, and provides a unique context in which children can receive the support they need from the adult (and sometimes the peer) to implement or test out, practice and evaluate, and subsequently reflect on the use of more developmentally mature behaviors.

When employed to treat (or "develop") older children, pair counseling can help them learn to understand how others may see them, to observe and interpret the consequences of their behaviors on their peer relationships, and to see themselves and others more complexly and, from a developmental standpoint, more maturely. These older children also can come to view themselves more positively by learning what their peers view as interesting about them. We assume, and research suggests, that many of the lessons resulting from this experiential learning better equip participants with new, more effective interpersonal skills to extend to relationships outside "the pair."

Pair therapy began in the Judge Baker Children's Center in Boston in the 1980s. Building on his theoretical work describing the growth of interpersonal understanding (Selman, 1980) and the corresponding negotiation strategies used by both successful and struggling children and youth (Selman & Schultz, 1990), Selman and Schultz applied this developmental theory to provide clinical-developmental guideposts to form a long-term, minimally directive, dyadic approach to working with interpersonally struggling children. Similar to Rogers's and Kohut's efforts to mobilize normative humanistic and psychodynamic growth (viz. developmental) processes, pair therapy provides a therapeutic way to cultivate more sophisticated interpersonal perspectives and negotiation strategies using the vehicle of a real peer relationship in which these competencies can be learned, practiced, and reflected on. It was first applied to working with children in this residential treatment setting, and has since been extended to the treatment of children of varying ages, in a range of different contexts, and in service of a variety of developmental and clinical problems (Selman, Watts, & Schultz, 1997).

Pair counseling (or *pairs*) is described in this chapter in terms of its role in treating common childhood psychological, behavioral, and emotional problems. The contexts in which it can be used, its appropriateness for and the therapeutic opportunities it presents when working with children of different sexes and cultural backgrounds, and the techniques from the Pair Counseling Manual (Karcher, 2012) for structuring sessions are also described.

Why is a manual needed for conducting pair counseling? Shifts in the child intervention landscape, with both the increasing role played by managed care organizations and the emergence of evidence-based practice as an essential foundation for intervention, have led to the need for shorter, more focused treatment methods and, consequently, to their manualization. The emergence of the evidence-based approach is built on the use of manuals and the specific techniques described within them to assess implementation fidelity and intervention efficacy (Westen, 2002). Though there is debate about the utility of breaking therapy into its component processes to estimate its effectiveness relative to other approaches (Wampold, 2001), this trend shows no signs of abating.

Additionally, empirical evidence suggests that the use of therapy manuals can enhance intervention impact (Drake, 2001). This is particularly so when used in a way that accommodates clinical wisdom, flexibility, and situational needs (Kendall & Beidas, 2007; Messer & Wampold, 2002).

BASIC RATIONALE, CLINICAL POPULATIONS, AND DEVELOPMENTAL THEORY

There are several clinical problems that may first interfere with children's social and academic success in the early elementary years for which pair counseling may be helpful. These can be conceptualized into two separate categories: internalizing and externalizing problems. We link these to self-transforming and other-transforming negotiation strategies later in this chapter.

Externalizing and Internalizing Problems and Behaviors

As a diagnostic characterization of types of disorders among children and youth, externalizing disorders are characterized by the chronic use of maladaptive behaviors that direct outward the expression of problematic experiences and feelings. Such children act aggressive, oppositional, and disruptive. Conversely, internalizing disorders reflect a chronic and maladaptive containment or withdrawal of social and personal problems inside oneself, manifesting in depression and anxiety, as two examples.

Externalizing and internalizing problems in childhood have long-term social and developmental implications, including increased risk-taking behaviors (e.g., substance use, delinquency, unprotected sex, running away, violent behavior), in adolescence (Thompson et al., 2010; Leadbeater, Hellner, Allen, & Aber, 1989; Loeber & Burke, 2011). For example, maladaptive externalizing behaviors in childhood also are correlated with the higher rates of disruptive behavioral disorders, such as oppositional defiant disorder, conduct disorder, and antisocial personality disorder (Loeber & Burke, 2011; Snoek, Van Goozen, Matthys, Buitelaar, & van Engeland, 2004).

Before these later problems emerge, children who present with internalizing and externalizing behaviors frequently experience interpersonal challenges with their peers. Many have similar social-cognitive developmental competencies as their peers but lack equally mature interpersonal negotiation strategies necessary for developing and maintaining friendships (Selman, Beardslee, Schultz, Krupa, & Podorefsky, 1986; Selman et al., 1992; Yeates, Schultz, & Selman, 1991). As one example, the capacity to solicit peer support through empathic and cooperative interactions with peers contributes to problematic internalizing and externalizing behaviors but is even more strongly predictive of academic, social, and behavioral difficulties (Kwon, Kim, & Sheridan, 2012).

To respond to the relational, dyadic nature of these behavioral problems, pair counseling can be used to facilitate the development of more mature peer relationships by teaching perspective-taking and negotiation skills that contribute to these social competencies. A primary goal of pair counseling is to help children close the "thought-action gap," which is a discrepancy between the complexity of children's social-cognitive development and their interpersonal negotiation strategies (Karcher, 2002; Yeates et al., 1991). More specifically, the goal is to help children move away from reliance on less mature negotiation resolution approaches like fight-or-flight by learning to articulate their needs in a more direct and acceptable tone and learn to coordinate their needs with those of others. Narrowing the thought-action gap by acquiring more mature social skills can then provide an alternative to externalizing and internalizing behaviors.

Developmental Parallels With Externalizing and Internalizing Behaviors

Several theoretical concepts and techniques that pair counselors draw upon, which are not considered necessary or "specific ingredients" in most other child intervention approaches (Wampold, 2001), inform a developmental view of the origins of these internalizing and externalizing behaviors and provide a road map for therapeutic intervention.

The most important, unique, or specific therapeutic ingredients in pair counseling, which are likely unfamiliar to most readers, are the developmental theory of perspective-taking skills and associated interpersonal negotiation strategies introduced above. Selman and Schultz (1990) also introduced two developmentally informed interpersonal styles that parallel, and in some ways, provide less pathology-based explanation of the nature and origin of externalizing and internalizing behaviors. Specifically, as we suggest below, children with externalizing behaviors rely upon *other-transforming strategies* (i.e., forceful and demanding), while children with internalizing behaviors overuse *self-transforming strategies* (i.e., self-transforming; Karcher, 2002; Karcher & Lewis, 2002; Moody, 1997a; Selman & Schultz, 1990). In this section, we elaborate this developmental theory to reveal how it affords a therapeutic road map or guideposts for pair counselors but also other clinicians as well.

Negotiation Strategies

Although it is perspective-taking skills that drive children's negotiation strategies, it is the interpersonal negotiation strategies that are most similar to the internalizing and externalizing clinical behaviors that are the target of most child therapies. Therefore a pair counselor must understand and appreciate that the children participating in pair counseling bring different methods of interacting in relationships, that these are symptomatic of many presenting problems, and that this often reflects delays in developmental maturity (cognitive or behavioral). This view can inform a different way of viewing and treating internalizing and externalizing disorders. We think most clinicians can benefit from seeing the links between these clinical disorder profiles and Selman and Schultz's (1990) interpersonal orientations.

To resolve conflict, children often use negotiation strategies that fall into one of two categories. Children who struggle interpersonally often use extreme and immature (for their age) strategies that either transform their own actions or needs (internalizing conflict) or transform the other's actions or needs (externalizing conflict; see Figure 11.1). Whether a child is acting in an other-transforming or a self-transforming way depends on whose needs the child tries to transform or change in a given interaction. Some children are other-transforming. They insist that other children adapt (or "transform") in moments of conflict. They are seen by their peers as bullies and by adults as externalizing. They rely on the "fight" stress response. Other children are more self-transforming and overuse the "flight" response. In conflict, they transform themselves to reduce tensions or resolve disagreements, not unlike the autoplastic and alloplastic styles O'Connor (1991) described.

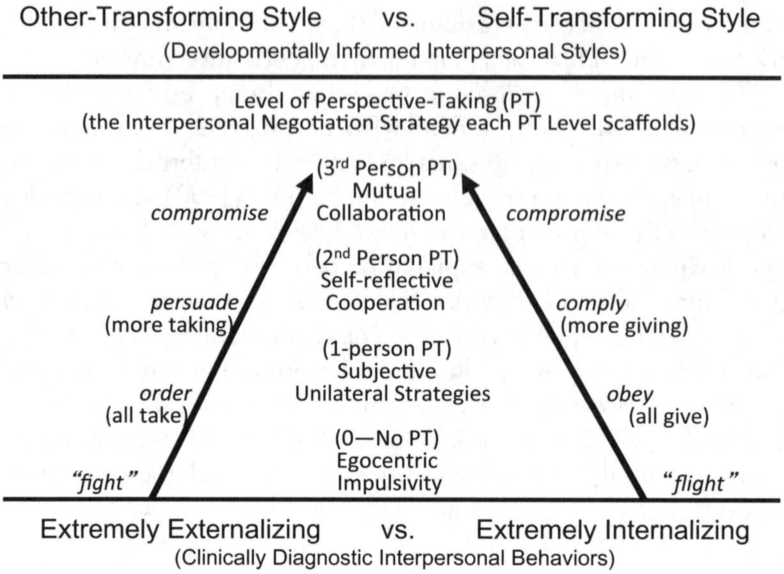

Figure 11.1. Developmental levels, interpersonal orientations, and their relationship to externalizing and internalizing behaviors.

As applied to the practice of pair counseling, it is through supervised activities and discussions that the pair counselor provides a safe context where children can become aware of their own interpersonal orientations. Second, the pair counselor helps the child develop friendship-making and -maintaining skills by structuring the children's interactions so that they can develop more balanced repertoires of interpersonal negotiation skills. For example, a child in pairs may develop social skills that allow her to escape a long-standing role as victim through the use of more competent, direct, and assertive strategies in pairs. Often, as we illustrate in our case study, in the beginning of pair counseling the child may rely solely on self-transforming strategies; afterwards they may use both self- and other-transforming strategies more effectively.

Perspective-Taking Skills

The negotiation-strategies children reflect their perspective-taking abilities as well as their emotional lives (e.g., fears, feelings, goals), attachment experiences and history of interpersonal conditioning. Whether the gap in maturity between their thoughts and actions is solely developmental or relational (i.e., attachment-based) is immaterial to the extent that the pair counselor works from the view that all youth can benefit from learning to better articulate their needs, better understand the needs of others, and coordinate multiple perspectives in their relationship with others.

A detailed description of Selman's perspective-taking skills and the negotiation strategies they support is provided by Selman and Schultz (1990), but for our present purposes, a brief summary is necessary. Between childhood and adolescence, youth advance in their ability to articulate and coordinate their own and others' wants, feelings, and beliefs (i.e., perspectives). Children who cannot articulate any perspective use *egocentric* thought, resulting in *impulsive* behaviors. When they can articulate either their own or another's (but not both) *subjective perspectives*, they can act *unilaterally* from that one view. When *self-reflective capacities* allow two perspectives—those of two people or an individual's own conflicting—to be coordinated, *cooperation* is possible. When a "birds-eye," or third-person, view on two perspectives occurs, collaboration (i.e., shared goals) is possible and one can see how relationships grow over time.

Pair counselors help children become aware of two common discrepancies. The first is the difference between what one child wants and what his or her pair partner wants—to do, to have, or to be. The second is that, often when relationships flounder, there is a thought-action gap between the developmental level of a child's perspective-taking and negotiation style. That is, one's level of perspective taking does not match the maturity of their social behaviors.

PAIR COUNSELING INTERVENTION PROCEDURE

The main goals of pair counseling are to help both children in the pair learn how to become better friends, to establish and maintain enduring relationships, and to negotiate effectively within relationships by better coordinating social perspectives. Through guided interaction with peers, opportunities to try out new skills and social perspectives emerge. In this section we overview the specific ingredients of pair counseling approach (Karcher, 2002, 2012), and later illustrate this approach in a case study of two school-age children.

An Overview

Typically in pair counseling, two previously unconnected children, who are of the same sex and who demonstrate similar levels of social-cognitive or perspective-taking skills, meet once a week. In the treatment of more severe problems, children often meet twice a week. The counselor helps the pair work through their interpersonal conflicts as they occur. This is why each pair includes youth whose different interpersonal orientations are most likely to create conflict in order to show both children different approaches to negotiating conflict.

Critically important for pair counselors is to remember that in pair counseling, children *learn* to make friends even if the two children do not actually *become* friends outside of the pair itself. It is a testing ground. The relationship is considered real, and the friendship skills they learn and practice are real, but becoming friends is not the goal. Rather, the goal is helping children learn to use perspective-taking and negotiation strategies effectively as a way to establish a healthy balance of autonomy and intimacy within relationships. The expectation is that they will then transfer this new repertoire of social skills to their relationships outside the pair. The pair counselor's job is to teach and guide the practice of using friendship-making and friendship-maintaining skills in the lived experience of the pair counseling dyad, not to make them friends.

Pair Counselors

All sessions begin with the pair counselor facilitating a discussion of the participants' relational successes in prior sessions and helping the children recall areas in which they each felt improvement was needed, as revealed in their struggles in prior sessions. Following this reflection time, the pair counselor shifts into a less directive role. The pair counselor abstains from engaging in play, yet actively uses praise and process comments to increase the children's awareness of the relationship dynamics that unfold as the session progresses.

Consistent with current views on motivation and self-understanding, pair counselors praise the children's use—not just the success—of specific strategies and also the children themselves as being caring, thoughtful, and compassionate people (see Grant, 2014). Pair counselors intentionally comment on the use of statements and behaviors that reflect cooperation, assertiveness, and demonstrate compassion in the pair's interactions, both to praise their effort ("Great idea to suggest taking turns") and to reinforce their view of themselves as caring people ("When you offered to go second, it really showed me how much you care about her feelings").

Counselors prompt children to articulate their own or the other's perspective and to try to use more developmentally mature negotiation strategies. Pair counselors interrupt and intervene with suggestions mostly when the children need immediate assistance in resolving conflicts that otherwise could undermine or damage the relationship. During such conflicts, pair counselors navigate the pair toward using discussion, cooperation, or compromise, whichever reflects a one level step-up from the negotiation and perspective-taking capabilities typically used in the pair.

Therapeutic Strategies

Selman and Schultz (1990) describe three scaffolding techniques pair counselors use during sessions to help the children step up to using more mature strategies: empowering, linking, and enabling. Counselors *empower* children to verbalize their personal perspectives (level one) rather than rely upon physicalistic and egocentric self-transforming or other-transforming strategies (level 0). Counselors *link* children's different perspectives (level one) so that children learn to manage two perspectives simultaneously (level two). Counselors *enable* older children to recognize the longevity of their relationships and how their behaviors may foster or hinder the development of a "we" or third-person perspective (level three).

Three Guidelines

Pair counselors are responsible for implementing the following three main guidelines or "ground rules":

1. The pair must reach a decision together about what play activities they will engage in before touching the toys and materials.
2. Once this decision is reached, the pair must engage in the activity together (i.e., no isolated or parallel play) and stop play to renegotiate if either decides to discontinue playing the activity they jointly selected.
3. The children are not to hurt one another, the pair counselor, the play items, or other property in the play space (Karcher & Lewis, 2002; Selman & Schultz, 1990).

For older pairs, it may be important to explain that talking about what happens in the pair with peers outside of the pair is not appropriate because it can lead to hurt feelings. Early on in the pair counseling relationship, these guidelines should be verbally reviewed at the start of each session.

Three Session Phases

Pair counseling sessions consist of three distinct components (Karcher, 2012). Each session begins with a review of the ground rules and a time for reflection. During this reflection, the counselor assists the children in remembering or identifying their relational successes and failures in the previous session. The second and longest component of the session involves the children selecting a play activity and doing this activity and, subsequently, doing jointly-chosen activities together. Throughout this playtime, counselors use the scaffolding techniques (i.e., empowering, linking, and enabling) to help the pair step up the developmental ladder (see Figure 11.1) toward compromise, cooperation, or collaboration. The pair also uses expressions of praise and makes process comments on the developing relationship. The last component involves reflecting, praising, and planning. Pair counselors help the children discuss their successes and failures to identify areas of growth to address in future sessions. Using the *3-2-1 Activity*, the counselor asks the pair to identify *three* things that went well during the session, *two* things that did not go well, and *one* goal for their next session together. It can be used to both begin and end sessions. To end on a positive note, the pair chooses an activity they might play in the next session. It also helps reduce children's resistance to reflecting on their relationship by making it clear how long this reflection process takes and what it entails.

Developmental Activities

Games and activities that pair counselors provide for children to choose from are most useful when they invite physical interaction, rule-dependent play, and friendship-fostering conversations. Such games parallel the interpersonal negotiation strategy (INS) levels described above, allow both the sharing of personal experiences and direct (e.g., Ungame) and indirect (e.g., puppets) discussions of friendships. Physical and rule-based games (e.g., Twister, Uno, Nerf basketball) invite physical negotiation, conflict, and subsequent discussions of the consequences of the egocentric, impulsive, and inconsiderate actions by one partner on the other. Parallel-play activities (only requiring turn-taking; e.g., playing a video game) or disconnected art (e.g., drawing or journaling separately) do not afford practicing the higher-level negotiation strategies that pair counselors coach.

EMPIRICAL SUPPORT

Other dyadic peer interventions for participants with clinical disorders have been described in the literature. Using the same peer dyadic (triadic when you add in the counselor), Curtis (2010) created structured dyadic behavior therapy (SDBT). It uses operant and classical conditioning techniques to help children ages 7 to 12 to facilitate social learning and self-regulation skills through peer interaction, modeling behavior, and incorporating feedback in a structured peer relationship. Although Curtis (2014) suggested SDBT offers a way of providing treatment that does not require parental involvement, the only research on SDBT was performed as an adjunct to parent management training, thus clouding any interpretations of a main effect of SDBT (Curtis, 2010).

Pair counseling appears to be most useful in lessening the use of externalizing behaviors among children. Research on externalizing disorders and behavioral problems associated with immature negotiation strategies in childhood (Leadbeater et al., 1989; Moffitt, 1990) suggests that to prevent long-term antisocial behavior, this link must be broken prior to adolescence.

This may explain why pair counseling appears more useful for children than teens and for boys more than girls.

In a pilot study designed to assess the effects of pair counseling on externalizing and internalizing behavior problems in residential treatment, Karcher and Lewis (2002) provided 15 to 18 fifty-minute sessions of pair counseling to nine boys and 11 girls in an inpatient mental health institute in the Midwest. The children had to demonstrate problem severity sufficient to warrant a stay of at least three months to maximize treatment completion. The comparison was of the effects of pair counseling for 10 participants diagnosed with mood internalizing behaviors and 10 with behavioral problems or externalizing behaviors. The findings revealed children diagnosed with externalizing behavior disorders increased their interpersonal understanding and decreased in delinquent behaviors. Pair counseling participation was associated with an increase in interpersonal understanding equivalent to one year of normal developmental growth. The positive effects of pair counseling on misconduct were explained, or mediated, by increases in interpersonal understanding, and the externalizing group that benefitted the most were both younger and had more males than the internalizing group, who were older and included more females.

Two studies of a version of pair counseling that did not enlist the manualized approach described by Karcher (2012) with older youth suggested no impact on delinquent or regular education students. Using a similarly small sample, but focusing on delinquent adolescents, Moody (1997a) found no effect of 20 sessions of pair counseling on moral reasoning or criminal recidivism for the 14 delinquent boys receiving treatment (compared with 14 controls in an alternative "training" school for youth offenders). However, the treatment and control group differed considerably on starting variables (e.g., moral reasoning), and these pre–post differences were not factored into outcome analyses, which lessen the faith one can have in these findings. Nevertheless, the case studies revealed why Moody felt that pair counseling fostered better relationships with peers and helped youth learn social skills that helped them be more effective with others. Horton (2008) conducted 10 sessions of pair counseling with 16 high school students and found that, compared with the 16 youth not receiving pair counseling, there were no posttest differences. However, using case studies, Horton still argued for pair counseling's promise in schools.

In conclusion, the limited research on pair-counseling effectiveness is not strong. All three studies had small samples, two of three used nonmanualized approaches, and the only one suggesting effectiveness did not include a no-treatment comparison group. The only statistically significant finding in that study, which suggested younger boys and those with externalizing disorders benefited most, was not adequately powered from a statistical standpoint. Regardless of these inadequacies, all authors felt the approach was promising and in need of additional studies with stronger research designs.

IN WHAT SETTINGS AND WHO MAY BENEFIT THE MOST

There are a variety of settings in which pair therapy and pair counseling have been used. Both have been delivered to pairs across a wide age range and to treat a wide array of disorders. Because pair counselors need to have consistent access to both children, outpatient treatment poses problems because caregivers often bring children inconsistently to counseling in this setting, leaving one child to meet alone with the counselor. Conducting pair counseling in schools and residential treatment settings can increase rates of attendance by both participants. *Fostering Friendship* (Karcher, 2002; Moody, 1997b; Selman, Watts, & Schultz, 1997) provides multiple case studies and descriptions of pair therapy and counseling in schools, inpatient and residential settings.

Children ages 7 to 12 are the most common participants in pair counseling, partly because play and peer relationships are key developmental competencies and interests at these ages. However, the developmental issues of autonomy and relatedness which pair counseling addresses are present before the period of formal schooling and do not end with the conclusion of compulsory education. In *Fostering Friendship*, Kane, Raya, and Ayoub (1997) described using pair therapy with toddlers. McClain and Sampson (2013) suggested pair counseling is a cost-effective approach to career counseling, to facilitating adjustment to college, and to helping students learn from one another (e.g., time management) and to interact with diverse peers.

Although some research has reported that boys benefit more than girls from pair counseling, contrary research suggests that it may be particularly well-suited to support girls' social and developmental needs. Gender differences in the timing and focus of gender role socialization may help explain why girls seem to place greater value of interdependence and the use of verbal and relational (as opposed to nonverbal) interpersonal negotiation strategies than boys. Males, whose gender socialization starts in early childhood, engage in more level-one type externalizing behaviors, with externalizing disorders especially common among boys in childhood. Given the link between behavioral problems, academic success, later delinquency, elementary-age boys demonstrate higher rates of academic challenges than girls (Kwon, Kim, & Sheridan, 2012) and adolescent boys—particularly those who in childhood relied most heavily on other-transforming strategies—engage in more delinquency, drug use, and unprotected sex (Leadbeater et al., 1989).

Females, whose gender socialization pressures to make interpersonal sacrifice to maintain relationships peaks in early adolescence, report higher rates of self-reflective (level two) type internalizing disorders, like depression, anxiety, and eating disorders than boys and far more in adolescence than during childhood. Females continue to present higher rates of internalizing problems in adulthood than males do (Bachrach, Bekker, & Croon, 2012).

One consequence of the gender socialization of girls to prioritize connection in relationships may lead them to be less likely to overuse physicalistic and unilateral (other-transforming) strategies to meet their needs but a greater use of self-transforming approaches or more verbal strategies to negotiate them in ways that don't cause interpersonal conflict. Cross-cultural studies reveal girls—in both collectivistic and individualistic societies—are more likely to compromise with peers during conflict than are boys (Martinez-Lozano, Sanchez-Medina, & Goudena, 2011), suggesting pair counseling goals are more aligned with girls' socialization.

Cultural differences also may influence children's comfort with working toward the more relational negotiation strategies targeted in pair counseling. This research suggests children in Western societies may even have a greater need for the developmental assistance provided in pair counseling because people living in individualistic cultures tend to engage in negotiations less frequently, and when they do, they are less likely to find compromise compared with people from more collectivistic societies (Gelfand et al., 2002). Martinez-Lozano et al. (2011) found children in individualistic societies were more likely to end peer conflict by using low-level physical strategies (i.e., fight-or-flight); children in collectivistic societies more often utilize negotiation and then continue peer interactions after the conflict. It has been argued that, when children in multicultural societies are matched with children from backgrounds (e.g., race, religion, class status) different from their own, pair counseling can deepen their intergroup understanding (Karcher, 1996). These children may learn about the other's background, and question their own beliefs and prejudices (Karcher & Nakkula, 1997; Schneider, Karcher, & Schlapkohl, 1999).

CASE ILLUSTRATION INCLUDING PARENT/CAREGIVER INVOLVEMENT

The following case study[1] reveals the value of pairing children who not only have opposing interpersonal styles for resolving conflict but whose cultural backgrounds differ, even though both are what society would otherwise label black. Kenny and Carl are two sixth-grade boys who attended an urban underresourced school and who were selected by the school counselor to participate in pair counseling. Kenny, whose mother and he emigrated a year prior from the Caribbean, described himself as "lonely." He had few friends,

[1]The dialogue and some case study details are from *Fostering Friendship: Pair Therapy for Treatment and Prevention* (pp. 121–144), by R. L. Selman, C. L. Watts, and L. H. Schultz (Eds.), 1997, New York, NY: Aldine de Gruyter. Reprinted with permission.

either at school or home. Things were also difficult for him at home, given the long hours his mother worked each day. But it was at school that he faced his most serious problems. He had been referred to the school counselor by his teacher, who had seen him withdraw into an apparent depression—hiding his head in his hoodie, not playing during recess, and most recently not completing assignments. The teacher saw Kenny being bullied on several occasions and Kenny also identified the teasing and bullying he received from some of his peers as his most pressing problem. Some students avoided him because his skin was considerably darker than most other African-American students in the school. Then, when other students found out that Kenny was both bright and committed to his academics, he was ridiculed for being a nerd. Kenny relied on internalizing-coping strategies that manifested in an egocentric, self-transforming style when interacting with peers—egocentric in that he did not express his needs verbally and negotiated conflict (i.e., bullying) by withdrawing.

His nemesis was a boy named Carl. Kenny described Carl as the biggest bully in class, (i.e., overreliant on externalizing, other-transforming behaviors). Carl was unlike Kenny in many ways. Carl was larger than Kenny. He was tall with big broad shoulders, which he used to advantage by playing sports and learning karate. Carl idealized fighting and liked to play rough. At home, with several men and older boys around, Carl had a lot of opportunities to roughhouse. Yet, Carl was not really aware that his peers at school saw him as aggressive and intimidating—he viewed most of his classmates as friends. This suggested Carl was not very skillful at understanding social or emotional perspectives other than his own; therefore, he regularly relied on impulsive other-transforming strategies to navigate his peer interactions.

Kenny and Carl had one thing in common: both boys desired friendships. Kenny referred to a few classmates as friends, but he did not turn to them for support. Carl, on the other hand, believed he had more friends than likely was the case, and might be hard-pressed to evoke a sympathetic response from most classmates when he was in need. For both, their increasing inability to engage effectively in peer relationships was accompanied by declines in the quality and quantity of their academic work. Kenny and Carl both needed to develop better friendship-making skills if they were to get back on track in school. For these two boys, developing specific friendship-making skills was not a luxury but a very real necessity. The teachers saw this, and for this reason, they allowed the boys to participate in weekly pair counseling for several months.

At the beginning of their participation in pair counseling, Carl and Kenny attempted, most unsuccessfully, to use their own negotiation strategies to influence what activities they, "the pair," would engage in during the sessions. Carl demanded his interests guide their time together, while, at least initially, Kenny meekly agreed to Carl's demands in order to avoid confrontations. On the few occasions early in their relationship that Kenny was courageous enough to suggest a game to play, Carl would typically demand obedience, ordering they do something such as, "No, let's play Jenga. I'm up first." Kenny would comply with "OK." The pair counselor saw this power imbalance, but did not intervene immediately because he realized this allowed their classroom dynamics to be replicated and later discussed in the sessions.

It became clear to both boys by the third weekly meeting, in their second month of pair counseling, that these strategies were not working well. During the fourth session, Kenny played his power card, so to speak. Knowing he had to agree in order for Carl to get to play his game of choice, Kenny refused to speak. For the next two meetings, Carl resisted attempting to guess why Kenny was being defiant, uncooperative, and disconnected. Carl was also unwilling to imagine how he would feel if someone else regularly demanded their way during their session. By the seventh session, the counselor encouraged the pair to consider using the sock puppets as a way of creating a safer context in which to express their feelings and needs. After the boys used markers to make the white tube socks they were given into characters for their play, they realized the purpose of their puppets and decided together to perform a puppet show. Kenny suggested it, and Carl agreed—Carl likely thought it was the obvious thing to do with their puppets.

It was in this session that the children began to truly articulate their own perspectives and illustrate their typical negotiation styles using the puppets. But they did two other things as well that are considered (vis-à-vis our developmental theory) to represent developmental advances and therapeutic progress. First, they used their puppets to attempt more advanced negotiation strategies, actions not typical of their maladaptive, egocentric, and impulsive self- and other-transforming strategies. Second, they conveyed to one another, through the medium of the puppet actors, their feelings about each other, their respective curiosity but ambivalence about the other's interpersonal style, and their shared conflicted interest in being more successful academically and socially. This was, for example, the first time Carl used words to describe his subjective experience of feeling resentment toward Kenny and other more academically successful students. Kenny also shifted away from his typically egocentric, withdrawing, self-transforming approach toward verbalizing his real interests, feelings, and needs. Both shared for the first time their beliefs about friendship (i.e., what it entailed and what it can cost individuals), and their views on working hard at school versus joining a gang.

In the first of three sequential weeks of puppet shows, Carl shared his experience of being actively recruited by a neighborhood gang. He used level two reflective, perspective-taking skills to convey that he knew the gang was trying to make him think they alone had his best interests in mind. We saw he had done to Kenny and other classmates what was done to him on the streets. He also shared for the first time that he desired to connect with and befriend Kenny.

However, the interpersonal maturity of their puppets changed like the wind. This is common and characteristic of the bumpy, uncomfortable developmental growth processes of *differentiating* and subsequently *hierarchically reintegrating* what is currently known for a more developmentally mature and relationally enhancing social understanding. As the children attempted to cognitively maintain multiple perspectives simultaneously, they both encountered the utter confusion that can occur with the differentiation of one's own from another's feelings and beliefs—which was a monumental shift for these equally egocentric, impulsively behaving boys—and seeing their interrelatedness. Whether coordinating their two perspectives or trying to integrate competing, seemingly contradictory views of themselves, the process of interpersonal development, through the hierarchical integration of perspectives, is a precarious bargain.

Coordinating Internal Dialogues and Articulating One's Own Perspective

Below, Carl uses two puppets ("CC" and "Bob") to act out conflicting feelings about befriending Kenny.

CC *(Carl)*: Bob, you know that kid over there? His name is Kenny.

Bob (Carl): Yeah, what about him?

CC: Why don't you just go over there and tell him to take this (drug)?

Bob: Them are drugs. Kenny never took drugs before. I knew Kenny before I knew you.

In this interchange, the part of Carl that does not care about Kenny (CC) battles with the part of Carl that wants Kenny as a friend (Bob), someone to defend, assist, and care about. It occurs in the context of the drug pushing Carl experiences from gang members on the streets. Then, it incorporates his racial biases, which Bob uses to reject and demean Kenny during the session.

CC: Bob, he ate the "candy." What's gonna happen to him?

Bob: Ah, nothing. He's just gonna be acting funny for a few days.

CC: A few days. But he's like my best friend.

Bob: But I hate him.

CC: Why do you hate him?

Bob: Cause he's different . . . You're whiter than he is.

These characters convey Carl's love–hate relationship with Kenny (i.e., his feelings), and Carl also articulates his confusion about seemingly contradictory, societally based beliefs about race, skin color, and worth, which it appears inform his conflicting feelings toward Kenny. Drawing on long-standing cultural biases about skin color, Carl *thinks* that because Kenny has darker skin, Carl should be less interested in having a friendship with Kenny, but he *feels* a desire to befriend Kenny. Perhaps he only feels this because he knows he is supposed to learn to be friends in pair counseling, but he seems to truly find Kenny interesting. Carl *thinks* Kenny should be less intelligent than himself because of Kenny's darker skin, but Carl *experiences* in class daily that Kenny is more intelligent. Then Kenny stands up for himself and asserts his perspective.

Kenny: Man, I want to go to school.

Carl: School? You never can go to school. You want to be cool, stay outta school.

Kenny: I like going to school and am gonna stay outta here. It's cold out here.

Carl: Cold? In school it's warm, but out here man this is life. Right here man. In school is all you do is be smart. You should be dumb like me.

Kenny: All I know is that I'm going to school so bye.

This process of externalizing one's feelings in concrete interactions is the first step in "taking a perspective" on one's own feelings to coordinate them with another's. Of course, this can be done in individual play therapy in which the adult, using figures and puppets, tries to convey this view, but a child voicing his or her own view like this directly to a peer (especially one who happens to be the source of one's anger and self-doubt), may better prepare children to do this more effectively and sooner with other peers outside of therapy.

Trying on the Other's Point of View

How scary it must be for a bully to consider the perspective of his victim and for a victim to consider the motivations of his assailant. As the puppet show progressed, each child began to try out the other's negotiation strategies and social perspective. Carl's puppet became the victim of bullying and advocated prosocial behaviors, as he feels Kenny does. Kenny's puppet becomes the aggressor who used other-transforming strategies to dismiss the importance of schools and the value of nurturing and protecting friends.

Carl: Momma he hit me in my head. Why? (Carl instructs) Say "I want to be in a gang?"

Kenny: Because I want to be in the gang.

Carl: Gangs? Gangs is bad for you.

Kenny: No they ain't.

Carl: But you shoot people and everything like that.

Kenny: Oh, shut up.

The movement in and out of one another's perspective in puppet play was a first small step up the developmental ladder, from using impulsive responses to self-directed verbalizations. Until that point, Kenny relied on self-transforming, nonverbal responses (i.e., either passively agreeing or, more recently, digging in his heals in response to Carl's demands). In the excerpt above, Kenny first demonstrates an assertiveness he had never shown. He may have learned how to from Carl. Then, after differentiating (i.e., trying on) Carl's assertiveness using Carl's words, Kenny courageously expresses his own feelings as assertively as Carl, hierarchically integrating his feelings with this new strategy—verbal assertion. In the puppet show, he first attempts what he would do in class only a month later in the heat of a disagreement with Carl. In front of the whole class, Kenny restates almost verbatim what his puppet had said to Carl in the final performance: "I got something to say to your face right now you big bully! Those are my friends and you're not, you're a bully. So I don't want to be your friend no more."

CONCLUSION AND FUTURE DIRECTIONS

To fill a critical void in the therapeutic armamentarium for supporting child development, dyadic interventions can be used to provide real-world therapeutic interactions with peers that help children build the interpersonal skills they need to be more effective behaviorally, emotionally, and socially, and by extension academically. Pair counseling provides one such therapeutic modality for contexts wherein shorter approaches necessitate accelerated efforts to help youth learn to take one another's perspective, see its effect on their immediate relationship, and use both to more effectively cultivate deeper, effective, and satisfying peer relationships. In pair counseling, children can articulate new interpersonal understandings and practice new negotiation strategies in the context of a developing friendship. Because the children who are referred for pair counseling typically lag their peers in the development of friendship-making skills—either perspective-taking or negotiation skills, or both—they often have missed opportunities to practice age-appropriate skills with peers. Peers who already possess these skills expect their peers to use them as well, so many shun or withdraw from these less competent children.

As illustrated in our case study, as late as in middle school, many children still need help escaping the rigid use of fight-or-flight responses to peer negotiation. Using pair counseling to help such children move from physicalistic responses toward articulating and defining their own and others' needs can help them immensely. Concomitantly, using less verbally aggressive or regressive methods of interacting with peers also decreases the internalizing and externalizing behaviors characteristic of the presenting problems of many school-age children. The utility of this or any peer approach is in the degree of transfer of these skills to the larger world, and pair counseling may provide children a way to bridge therapeutic growth and real-world competence.

REFERENCES

Bachrach, N., Bekker, M. H. J., & Croon, M. A. (2012). Autonomy-connectedness and internalizing-externalizing personality psychopathology, among outpatients. *Journal of Clinical Psychology*, 69, 718–726. http://dx.doi.org/10.1002/jclp.21940

Curtis, D. F. (2010). ADHD symptom severity following participation in a pilot, 10-week, manualized family-based behavioral intervention. *Child & Family Behavior Therapy*, *32*, 231–241. http://dx.doi.org/10.1080/07317107.2010.500526

Curtis, D. F. (2014). Structured dyadic behavior therapy processes for ADHD intervention. *Psychotherapy*, *51*, 110–116. http://dx.doi.org/10.1037/a0033984

Drake, L. (2001). The culture-negotiation link: Integrative and distributive bargaining through an intercultural communication lens. *Human Communication Research*, *27*, 317–349.

Gelfand, M. J., Higgins, M., Nishii, L. H., Raver, J. L., Dominguez, A., Murakami, F., . . . Toyama, M. (2002). Culture and egocentric perceptions of fairness in conflict and negotiation. *Journal of Applied Psychology*, *87*, 833–845. http://dx.doi.org/10.1037/0021-9010.87.5.833

Grant, A. (2014, April 11). Raising a moral child. *The New York Times*. Retrieved from http://nyti.ms/1hp5Uon

Horton, J. K. (2008). *Pair counseling for high school students: Improving friendship skills, interpersonal relationships, and behavior among aggressive and withdrawn adolescents* (Unpublished doctoral dissertation). The College of William and Mary, Williamsburg, Virginia.

Kane, S. R., Raya, P. A., & Ayoub, C. C. (1997). Pair play therapy with toddlers and preschoolers. In R. L. Selman, C. L. Watts, & L. H. Schultz (Eds.), *Fostering friendship: Pair therapy for treatment and prevention* (pp. 185–206). New York, NY: Aldine.

Karcher, M. J. (1996). Pairing for the prevention of prejudice: Pair counseling to promote intergroup understanding. *Journal of Child and Youth Care Work*, *11* (Fall), 119–143.

Karcher, M. J. (2002). The principles and practice of pair counseling: A dyadic developmental play therapy for aggressive, withdrawn, and socially immature youth. *International Journal of Play Therapy, 11*, 121–147. http://dx.doi.org/10.1037/h0088868

Karcher, M. J. (2012). *The pair counseling manual: A developmental intervention for counseling children in dyads*. San Antonio, TX: Developmental Press.

Karcher, M. J., & Lewis, S. S. (2002). Pair counseling: The effects of a dyadic developmental play therapy on interpersonal understanding and externalizing behaviors. *International Journal of Play Therapy, 11*, 19–41. http://dx.doi.org/10.1037/h0088855

Karcher, M. J., & Nakkula, M. J. (1997). Multicultural pair counseling and the development of expanded worldviews. In R. L. Selman, C. L. Watts, & L. H. Schultz (Eds.), *Fostering friendship: Pair therapy for treatment and prevention* (pp. 207–227). Hawthorn, NY: Aldine.

Kendall, P. C., & Beidas, R. S. (2007). Smoothing the trail for dissemination of evidence-based practices for youth: Flexibility within fidelity. *Professional Psychology: Research and Practice, 38*(1), 13–20. http://dx.doi.org/10.1037/0735-7028.38.1.13

Kwon, K., Kim, E., & Sheridan, S. (2012). Behavioral competence and academic functioning among early elementary children with externalizing problems. *School Psychology Review, 41*, 123–140.

Leadbeater, B., Hellner, I., Allen, J., & Aber, L. (1989). Assessment of interpersonal negotiation strategies in youth engaged in problem behaviors. *Developmental Psychology, 25*, 465–472. http://dx.doi.org/10.1037/0012-1649.25.3.465

Loeber, R., & Burke, J. D. (2011). Developmental pathways in juvenile externalizing and internalizing problems. *Journal of Research on Adolescence, 21*, 34–46. http://dx.doi.org/10.1111/j.1532-7795.2010.00713.x

Martinez-Lozano, V., Sanchez-Medina, J. A., & Goudena, P. P. (2011). A cross-cultural study of observed conflicts between young children. *Journal of Cross-Cultural Psychology, 42*, 895–907. http://dx.doi.org/10.1177/0022022110381361

McClain, M. C., & Sampson, J. P. (2013). Using pair counseling to improve the cost-effectiveness of college career counseling. *The Professional Counselor, 3*, 82–92. http://dx.doi.org/10.15241/mcm.3.2.82

Messer, S. B., & Wampold, B. E. (2002). Let's face facts: Common factors are more potent than specific therapy ingredients. *Clinical Psychology: Science and Practice, 9*, 21–25. http://dx.doi.org/10.1093/clipsy.9.1.21

Moffitt, T. E. (1990). Juvenile delinquency and attention deficit disorder: Boys' developmental trajectories from age 3 to age 15. *Child Development, 61*, 893–910. http://dx.doi.org/10.2307/1130972

Moody, E. E., Jr. (1997a). Lessons from pair counseling with incarcerated juvenile delinquents. *Journal of Addictions & Offender Counseling, 18*, 10–25. http://dx.doi.org/10.1002/j.2161-1874.1997.tb00122.x

Moody, E. E., Jr. (1997b). Pair counseling: An intervention for disturbed children when nothing else works. *Elementary School Guidance & Counseling, 31*, 171–179.

O'Connor, K. J. (1991). *The play therapy primer: An integration of theories and techniques*. New York: Wiley InterScience.

Schneider, B. H., Karcher, M. J., & Schlapkohl, W. (1999). Relationship counseling across cultures: Cultural sensitivity and beyond. In P. Pedersen (Ed.), *Multiculturalism as a fourth force* (pp. 167–190). Washington, DC: Taylor & Francis.

Selman, R. L. (1980). *The growth of interpersonal understanding: Developmental and clinical analysis*. New York, NY: Academic Press.

Selman, R. L., Beardslee, W., Schultz, L. H., Krupa, M., & Podorefsky, D. (1986). Assessing adolescent interpersonal negotiation strategies: Toward the integration of structural and functional models. *Developmental Psychology, 22*, 450–459. http://dx.doi.org/10.1037/0012-1649.22.4.450

Selman, R. L., & Schultz, L. H. (1990). *Making a friend in youth: Developmental theory and pair therapy*. Chicago, IL: University of Chicago Press.

Selman, R. L., Schultz, L. H., Nakkula, M., Barr, D., Watts, C., & Richmond, J. B. (1992). Friendship and fighting: A developmental approach to the study of risk and prevention of violence. *Development and Psychopathology, 4*, 529–558. http://dx.doi.org/10.1017/S0954579400004867

Selman, R. L., Watts, C. L., & Schultz, L. H. (1997). *Fostering friendship: Pair therapy for treatment and prevention*. New York, NY: Aldine de Gruyter.

Snoek, H., Van Goozen, S. H., Matthys, W., Buitelaar, J. K., & van Engeland, H. (2004). Stress responsivity in children with externalizing behavior disorders. *Development and Psychopathology, 16*, 389–406. http://dx.doi.org/10.1017/S0954579404044578

Thompson, R., Tabone, J. K., Litrownik, A. J., Briggs, E. C., Hussey, J. M., English, D. J., & Dubowitz, H. (2010). Early adolescent risk behavior outcomes of childhood externalizing behavioral trajectories. *The Journal of Early Adolescence, 31*, 234–257. http://dx.doi.org/10.1177/0272431609361203

Wampold, B. E. (2001). *The great psychotherapy debate: Models, methods, and findings*. Mahwah, NJ: Erlbaum.

Westen, D. (2002). Manualizing manual development. *Clinical Psychology: Science and Practice, 9*, 416–418. http://dx.doi.org/10.1093/clipsy.9.4.416

Yeates, K. O., Schultz, L. H., & Selman, R. L. (1991). The development of interpersonal negotiation strategies in thought and action: A social–cognitive link to behavioral adjustment and social status. *Merrill-Palmer Quarterly, 37*, 369–405.

IV

PLAY INTERVENTIONS FOR AUTISM SPECTRUM DISORDER

12

PLAY THERAPY FOR SCHOOL-AGE CHILDREN WITH HIGH-FUNCTIONING AUTISM

KAREN STAGNITTI

Children with high-functioning autism may no longer be diagnosed under the *Diagnostic and Statistical Manual of Mental Disorders* (5th edition [*DSM–5*], American Psychiatric Association, 2013; Turygin, Matson, Beighley, & Adams, 2013) as being on the spectrum for autism. This is because under the *DSM–5*, children with autism spectrum disorder (ASD) are diagnosed on the basis of significant and persistent impairments in the area of social/communication and significant and persistent impairments in the area of restricted and/or repetitive behaviour (Turygin, Matson, Beighley, et al., 2013; Turygin, Matson, Adams, & Belva, 2013). Turygin and colleagues argued that children diagnosed with ASD using the *DSM–5* will have more severe symptoms than children diagnosed on the *DSM–IV–TR* or *DSM–IV*. However, they conceded that children with high-functioning autism still required intervention as they will continue to present with social difficulties.

Diagnosis for ASD under the *International Classification of Diseases* (10th ed; *ICD–10*; World Health Organization [WHO], 2015) includes

http://dx.doi.org/10.1037/14776-013
Play Therapy in Middle Childhood, A. A. Drewes and C. E. Schaefer (Editors)

children diagnosed with childhood autism showing impaired development before three years of age with abnormal functioning in social interaction, communication, and behaviour that is repetitive and stereotyped. Asperger's syndrome is included as a separate section under the *ICD–10* (WHO, 2015) with children showing similar characteristics to those with childhood autism but having no general delay in language or cognitive development.

This chapter outlines the basic rationale and theory underlying the Learn to Play program, the play ability of children with high-functioning autism (or Asperger's syndrome as described in the *ICD–10* [Version: 2015]), the Learn to Play intervention, the empirical support, and a case study.

BASIC RATIONALE AND THEORY

The main aim of the Learn to Play program is to develop in children who cannot play the ability to spontaneously initiate their own play. This therapy program grew out of clinical work with children who were referred for treatment to specialist early intervention childhood teams because of concerns related to their development. Research on the development of the Child-Initiated Pretend Play Assessment (Stagnitti, 2007) had led to the realization that the majority of children who were referred to early intervention childhood services had low developmental levels in pretend play. It is not uncommon for these children to be 2 to 4 years delayed in their development in pretend play. The rationale behind the Learn to Play program is that a child's ability to self-initiate their own play is vital for their well-being as play gives a foundation for the child's self-regulation, language, and social–emotional development (see Gray, 2011).

The theory behind the Learn to Play program (Stagnitti, 1998, 2009, 2014) draws from Axline (based on Rogerian psychology, 1974), cognitive developmental play theories, and developmental theory. Virginia Axline worked in the 1940s and developed nondirective play therapy after being influenced by Carl Rogers and his person-centered therapy. With Axline's technique, the child enters a room with toys displayed and is instructed to play with whatever he or she would like. Destruction of the toys and harm to the therapist are not acceptable and children are told the session will be ending five minutes before the session ends. The principles of Axline's approach underpin the Learn to Play program. These are: a warm relationship is developed by the therapist with the child; the therapist accepts the child unconditionally; the therapist creates an atmosphere of permissiveness so the child is free to self-initiate; the therapist respects the child's capacity to develop; the child leads the way; the therapist responds to the child; and the only limits established are those that allow the play to flow. Unlike Axline's approach, the therapist predetermines which toys are placed out for the child to play with and the child is praised during the play. The reason for these two departures from Axline's approach are that children with low developmental levels of play are overwhelmed by large numbers of toys, so limiting the toys is one way to help them focus, and children who cannot play do not find play interesting, and so praising their engagement in play is one method to enhance their motivation to continue in the play scene.

Vygotsky's approach to the developmental cognitive theories of play has been more influential in the Learn to Play program than Piaget's approach. Vygotsky (2004) maintained that play "was a creative reworking of the impressions he has acquired" (p. 11). In play, then, children experiment with what they have experienced, seen, or physically engaged in. Vygotsky (1976) maintained that through play children developed cognitive skills. Most important, he took a constructivist approach and asserted that children's development could be extended by capable peers or adults (Vygotsky, 1976).

One of the assumptions of the Learn to Play program is that pretend play is an ability. It is influenced by a child's natural ability and physical and social environments. However, not all children develop ability in pretend play, which is understood to be the most complex, or mature, form of play between the ages of 12 months and 10 to 12 years (Vygotsky, 1976). Children who are developing typically tend to engage spontaneously in pretend play because it is the most intellectually and emotionally challenging play type within this age group. Pretend play includes the skills of (a) play scripts (i.e., the stories in the play), (b) logical sequencing of play actions, (c) object substitution (i.e., symbols used in play), (d) social interaction, (e) role play, and (f) play with an object outside of the self (e.g., a doll or teddy, also called *decentration*; Stagnitti, 1998). Pretend play, as it is understood in the Learn to Play program, encompasses both solitary play and social play, simple single actions of pretend to complex sequences with scripts carried out over 3 weeks. Symbolic play, role play, sociodramatic play, projection play, construction play and narrative play are embedded within pretend play. When children begin to engage in pretend play, they use single actions with single objects and symbols represent physically similar objects (Stagnitti, 1998). By 5 years of age, children can engage in any story script—over 2 to 3 weeks—with a group of peers, using roles and ambiguous symbols, and can incorporate an object outside the self, such as puppets, dolls, or teddy bears. For children with delays in pretend play, skills within pretend play can be varied and uneven.

DEVELOPMENTAL ISSUES

The focus of this chapter is on children with high-functioning autism. High-functioning autism is also used interchangeably with Asperger's syndrome (Lawson, 2008). Using the *ICD–10* (Version: 2015; WHO, 2015), children who are diagnosed with Asperger's syndrome would present similarly to children with high-functioning autism as there is no delay in language or cognitive function while still showing abnormalities in social interaction and repetitive or restricted interests. While controversy persists over the finer details of the diagnoses of autism, Asperger's syndrome, and even pervasive developmental disorders (PDD; Volkmar, Klin, & McPartland, 2014), these children have significant functional issues (Turygin, Matson, Beighley, et al., 2013; Volkmar et al., 2014).

Children with autism, regardless of whether they have a diagnosis of high-functioning autism or Asperger's syndrome, have difficulty with pretend play development, and this is one reason these children are literal in their thinking. A boy who was traveling on a train serves as an example of literal thinking. He had bought a ticket and put it in his pocket. When the conductor came through the train to check on tickets, the conductor asked, "Can I see your ticket?" The boy said, "No." He had interpreted the conductor's words literally because his ticket was in his pocket and the conductor couldn't see it. Such literal thinking can result in social difficulties. In the example of the train ticket, the conductor was about to throw the boy off the train when his friend, who was traveling with him, asked him to take his ticket out of his pocket and show the conductor. Children with high-functioning autism or Asperger's syndrome have impairments in complex social skills (Lawson, 2008; Volkmar et al., 2014). Pierce-Jordon and Lifter (2005) found that children with PDD, compared with typically developing children, had less complex play within a social interaction than outside a social interaction.

Functioning within society is not an easy task for children who have high-functioning autism. Apart from difficulties in complex social interactions and in reading emotional cues and others' nonverbal behaviors and intentions (i.e., *theory of mind*; see Hughes & Leekam, 2004), these children have restricted repetitive and stereotyped patterns of behaviors, interests, and activities, inflexibility, stereotyped mannerisms, and preoccupation with parts of objects (Lawson, 2008).

Children with high-functioning autism may have some ability in pretend play, but this is limited. Pretend play involves reading socioemotional cues and nonverbal behavior and understanding the imposed meanings within play scenarios. When children engage in pretend play, they undertake roles and use objects outside of themselves (e.g., a doll or teddy). Children who play well self-initiate their play and can play on their own or negotiate and cooperate with peers in play. Children with autism play with fewer objects, can become intensely preoccupied with parts of an object or toy, spend less time playing, and tend to be more functional than symbolic in their play (Charman & Baron-Cohen, 1997; Naber et al., 2008). An example of functional play is when a child plays with objects by relating them together (e.g., putting animals in a truck or pushing the truck) but the play has no narrative or no complexity as there are no logical sequences, object substitutions, character development, or overall script. For children with autism, play actions can be repetitive, and they experience difficulties with spontaneous, self-initiated pretend play (Charman & Baron-Cohen, 1997; Naber et al., 2008). Earlier play scripts that reflect body scripts (e.g., pretending to drink, eat or sleep) are commonly missed in the play development of children with high-functioning autism; instead, they may appear to have a higher level of play script ability because their play script is an imitation of a screen scene (e.g., television, iPad) that has captured their intense interest. Poor ability to play is linked with difficulties in social interaction and play with peers (Naber et al., 2008). As a consequence, these children can often be observed on the sidelines of the play, disconnected socially.

Repetition of play actions, fewer play actions, and difficulty with self-initiated pretend play are associated with poor narrative understanding (Stagnitti, in press). Narrative is storytelling, and this in turn is associated with understanding context of the play scene. If a child understands narrative, then she or he can "think forward" (Stagnitti, in press), meaning she or he can think about what might happen next. For children with autism, thinking forward (or predictive thinking within a narrative) is not the way they think, and this also contributes to their literality. Another example of this is David (pseudonym), who used to watch over a holiday house (i.e., a vacation home/accommodation) when his mother was away. David had a diagnosis of Asperger's syndrome. When a neighbor came over to check if David was coping with the new guests, she reminded him to "take the dirty sheets off the bed after the guests had left." When David's mother came home, the dirty sheets were in a pile on the floor. David had carried out the instruction literally, and in so doing, had missed the unsaid narrative of the context. The unsaid narrative of "taking dirty sheets off the bed" meant that you took the sheets off the bed, washed them, dried them, folded them, put them in the cupboard, and in the meantime, put a clean set of sheets on the bed. For children with high-functioning autism, it cannot be assumed that they know the narrative. Another example is of a friend of mine, who, when she was a girl, would scream and cry each time her mother said, "Put your shoes on, we are going out." As my friend has a diagnosis of high-functioning autism, the comment "Put your shoes on, we are going out" was her complete understanding of the situation. If this is all you know, then you don't know what is going to happen. Will you ever come back? Where are you going? So my friend would scream each time. If her mother had given her the full narrative, it would have sounded something like this: "Put your shoes on. We are going out. We are going to the shop to buy bread and milk, then we are going to pick up your brother, then we are coming back home. You can take your shoes off when we come back home." This would not have been scary, and my friend would have understood what was going to happen and most probably would not have screamed. When working with children with high-functioning autism, they will need the full narrative each time.

Children with high-functioning autism have difficulty with pretend play. This results in (a) decreased use of symbols in play, (b) decreased play actions in a logical sequence, (c) decreased use of role play or characters in play, and (d) decreased understanding of the play context and narrative. The next section explains the Learn to Play program, which aims to build in children the capacity to self-initiate their own pretend play.

PLAY INTERVENTION PROCEDURES

The Learn to Play program was first published in 1998 (Stagnitti, 1998). It was developed as a one-on-one therapist–child program. The aim the program is to give children the ability to self-initiate their own play to the highest level of complexity that is possible for the particular child.

Self-initiation of play is vital to a child's ability to play because it comes from within. Neurologically effective play is self-controlled and self-directed by the child (Gray, 2011; Sunderland, 2007). Ayres (1972) noted that when children engaged in self-initiated play within therapy, "the child must organize his own brain" (p. 256). Play is meaningful to a child if the play ideas have been developed from within the child because then he or she takes control of the play.

The following are the principles and then an explanation of the techniques involved in the Learn to Play program. This is then followed by an explanation of the Learn to Play School-Based program and the evidence supporting this approach to building a child's self-initiated play ability.

Accept Children for Who They Are

When working with children with high-functioning autism, the therapist accepts that they need routine and structure, and they are less anxious if they are given an explanation of what is going to happen. During the therapy session, if the child becomes distracted, the therapist will need to bring the child back to the play scene, but in so doing, it may be necessary for the child to finish their train of thought. For example, Rodney (pseudonym) was playing with a train and animals. The animals were going for a ride and coming home. After several repetitions of this play scenario, the therapist asked, "What will the animals do now?" This question requires predictive thinking and is linked to narrative understanding. Rodney could not answer the question in relation to the play scene. Being a bright boy, he answered by explaining a computer game that included animals. However, in his explanation, he began to talk about his prowess in playing computer games and was no longer engaged with the play scene. When bringing Rodney back to the play, the therapist was aware that he needed to finish his explanation of his computer prowess before he could reengage once more with the play.

Introduce Play Skills That Match the Child's Developmental Level

Before you begin to work with children, it is necessary to understand their developmental play level. For children with high-functioning autism, it is not uncommon for their developmental play age to be on the 18-month-old level of pretend play development, even though their chronological age may be 6 years. That is, their play reflects body scripts (e.g., drinking, eating, sleeping), no logical sequences of pretend play actions, repetition of play actions, no object substitutions, and minimal use of a character in play such as a doll or teddy bear. Even though children with high-functioning autism may have a play level that is 2 to 4 years below their chronological age, they may show obsessions in their play. For example, they may have a focused interest in trains or a movie they have seen. In such cases, trains or characters from the movies will appear repeatedly in their play. This is also called *scripting* or *template play*, where the child reproduces exactly what they have seen on a screen. This is not self-initiated original play. It is imitating verbatim what has been seen. While these play scenes may be used to initially engage a child in play, these play scenes are a false level of developmental ability in self-initiated play.

Use Both Variation and Repetition

When working with a child with high-functioning autism to build his or her ability to self-initiate play, the therapist begins by introducing play scenes at the child's developmental play level and repeats these scenes with variation until the child's interest wanes. This is one of the key principles of the Learn to Play program. As long as children are engaged in the play scene, keep playing out the scene but vary the scene each time the scenario is played out. For example, when playing tea parties, the therapist continues to engage in "drinking" their tea for as long as the child is interested. As the therapist repeats the drinking imitation, the scene can be varied by (a) blowing on the "hot" tea, (b) stirring a spoon in the cup, (c) putting the cup up to the mouth, (d) making sipping noises, (e) offering the cup to a teddy bear, (f) offering a drink to the child, (g) having more sips of tea, or (h) spilling the tea.

Gain the Child's Focused Attention

Focused attention is necessary for neurological change (Doidge, 2010). If the child is not focusing on the toys or play materials, the therapist cannot begin to model the play actions for the play scene. Gaining the focused attention of a child with high-functioning autism is one of the challenging principles in the Learn to Play program. This is because children with high-functioning autism who cannot play, do not recognize the play, and are not interested in what the therapist is doing. Hence the therapist exaggerates their pleasure in playing by using their voice, face, body, and actions. Initially, the child may focus on the task only because the therapist is so animated about the play. Focused attention is getting the child's engagement in the play. Therapy cannot proceed until the therapist establishes the child's attention. With children with high-functioning autism, focused attention can also be aligned with interest. A child's strong interest can be used to gain her or his focus on the play. For example, the therapist may start by pushing a train along the floor or using a figure from the child's movie passion. However, as the child engages in and begins to understand the play, her or his obsession is used less and less as the child begins to develop their original play ideas.

Talk About the Play as the Play Progresses

For children with high-functioning autism, talking about the play as it progresses is a principle because (a) it gives the child the language for the play scene and (b) you cannot assume the child knows how to use the toys. Talking about the play as you play describes for the child how to use the toys. You cannot assume that because a child has a truck or a teddy bear at home, they know how to play with it. An early Learn to Play session may be the therapist showing the child how to use a truck with the accompanying talk reflecting exactly the play actions: "We are pushing the truck. The truck is driving. The truck is stopping. Go. Stop. Go. Stop." In the earlier sessions for Learn to Play, the therapist will be describing what they are doing (Stagnitti, 2009). As the child begins to understand play and recognize what the therapist is doing, the therapist's language changes to the narrative of the play. For example, "The teddy is going for a ride. Let's take teddy to the park. Teddy is going to the park. Drive. Drive. Teddy is happy he is going to the park." By talking about the play as you play, the play action and the language that accompanies it will connect more strongly neurologically (Doidge, 2010; Stagnitti, 2014, p. 158).

Engage Emotionally in the Play With the Child

For children with high-functioning autism, emotional engagement in the play is connected with increased understanding of the play (Sherratt, 2002; Stagnitti & Casey, 2011). Play brings joy, which is one of its benefits for the mental health of a child (Gray, 2011). Joy is an emotion that brings with it a sense of happiness and well-being. The child's emotional engagement in play brings a deeper, more meaningful experience for the child and embeds the learning in a deeper way. The therapist and child emotionally engage together in the play.

Allow the Child to Self-Initiate Play Ideas

The therapist sets up the sessions so that there is a permissive atmosphere in which the child is given the opportunity to initiate his or her own ideas within the play. The aim of the Learn to Play program is for children to take over the play by adding their own ideas that are logical and sequential to the play scene. Ayres (1972) noted that when setting up a session with permissiveness that allowed the child to initiate their own play, that "often the child takes over the direction of the treatment" (p. 257) and that the "child's response is often characterized by intense emotional involvement and excitement" (p. 257). This emotional engagement together with the child's own initiation of play ideas is a powerful combination for change in the child's play ability to attain a higher level of complexity.

TECHNIQUES AND SETTINGS

The techniques of Learn to Play are detailed in Table 12.1. This table sets out more specific information in how to build a child's play ability.

The Learn to Play program has also been developed into a program for use in schools. For the Learn to Play School Program, teachers and therapists working in the schools are trained in the Learn to Play program by understanding 10 play skills. These play skills are: (a) sequences of play actions, (b) describing the play, (c) object substitution, (d) decentration (i.e., the use of an object outside of the self, such as a puppet, doll, or teddy bear, as if it is alive), (e) play scripts, (f) role play, (g) property attributions, (h) reference to absent objects, (i) adding problems to the play narrative, and (j) predicting what will happen next. The Learn to Play School program was developed from

TABLE 12.1
Techniques of Learn to Play When Working With Children With High-Functioning Autism

Technique	Reason
Early sessions, therapist chooses the toys.	When beginning the program, the therapist chooses play scenes that match the child's developmental play level and that will raise some interest for the child. The therapist has spoken with the parent or guardian about any particular interests the child may have.
Early sessions, minimal toys are used.	Children with limited play ability are overwhelmed by large numbers of toys. They cannot focus. They are distracted and will want to move from toy to toy instead of focusing and playing with the toys.
No other toys are visible to the child.	The toys and play materials for the sessions are put aside in the playroom but out of reach of the child. As each toy set for each play scene is played with, the therapist puts them out of sight.
Use the floor.	Using the floor space allows greater freedom of movement and physically allows the play to move around the room.
Begin with play scenes that reflect the child's life experiences.	Children with autism are literal thinkers with limited play skills. For meaningful engagement in play, the play scene needs to reflect the child's life experience (do not include traumatic events). For example, eating, drinking, shopping, school.
The therapist models the play action/s.	The therapist shows the child how to use the toys in play by modeling play actions with the toys. As the child imitates the therapist, the child learns how to use the toys and in turn, how to play using the toys. The therapist needs to be playful and be able to play in order to engage a child to do the same.
Move from directed to cofacilitated to non-directed therapist play.	The Play Therapy Dimensions Model by Yasenik and Gardner (2012) has four quadrants. Of these quadrants, Learn to Play techniques fit in their Quadrant III and Quadrant IV. This is respectively, nonintrusive responding and co-facilitation. In Learn to Play, the therapist begins in Quadrant IV, co-facilitation, by modeling the play action for the child and then cofacilitating the play. As the child begins to add logical sequential actions to their play showing an increasing understanding of narrative and character utilization and role play, the therapist moves to Quadrant III, where the child takes over the play completely and the therapist responds to the child. In Learn to Play the therapist will need to move back and forth from co-facilitation to nonintrusive responding as the therapist challenges the child to increase the complexity of their play ability, support the child in the challenge, and consolidate the child's play ability. Put another way, the therapist models the play actions and as the child initiates their own play ideas, the therapist consolidates the child's play before challenging the child to the next developmental level of play.

TABLE 12.1
Techniques of Learn to Play When Working With Children With High-Functioning Autism *(Continued)*

Technique	Reason
Variety of play scenes on the same developmental level.	Playing is not rote learning. Playing reflects the ability of the child to process their world, to understand it, and to act upon it. Using a variety of play scenes from the same developmental level will expand the child's attention and assist the child in generalizing the play skills across different play scenarios. For example, the therapist is not showing the child how to place a block to their face and talk; they are demonstrating that a block can be a cell phone. As the child develops in ability, the therapist will also use the block in various other representations such as a pillow, a train, a tree trunk, and so on.
Therapist reinforces the child's play ability.	When the child varies the play action or adds their own self-initiated ideas to the play, the therapist imitates the action, or talks about what the child is doing, or adds to the child's action. In this way the therapist is reinforcing to the child that the child is a capable being, and is giving power to the child.
Watch the child for fatigue.	When children with high-functioning autism begin Learn to Play sessions, they will become tired as they are working very hard during the sessions. They are interacting in ways that are new to them. Some children may only be able to cope with 20 minutes for the first session. As their play skills increase, they will be able to easily play for one hour. However, stop the session when the child shows signs of fatigue as children don't want to play when they are too tired.
Challenge the child when ready.	For children with high-functioning autism, pretending in play is a new way to interact with the world. When they reach new levels of play ability, often they will be content to stay at this level. More than any other group of children, children with high-functioning autism will need to be challenged to move their play to more complex levels. The therapist challenges the child in several ways such as adding: (a) more actions to the play sequence, (b) a character such as a doll, (c) a problem to the play scenario, or (d) symbols in play (i.e., object substitution).
The therapist is always cognizant of the child's play ability across six domains.	Play is a complex ability and when working with children to increase their ability to self-initiate their play, the therapist is aware of the child's play development across the domains of: (a) play scripts, (b) sequences of play actions, (c) object substitution, (d) social interaction, (e) role play, and (f) doll or teddy play (see Stagnitti, 1998). Working with children on an individual level, the therapist is always aware of the child's ability in: (a) play scripts, (b) number of actions in a sequence, (c) object substitution, (d) use of the doll or teddy in play, and (e) child's role play ability.

(*continues*)

TABLE 12.1
Techniques of Learn to Play When Working With Children With High-Functioning Autism *(Continued)*

Technique	Reason
Therapist can focus on one or several play skills.	During the Learn to Play sessions, the therapist may be focusing on one particular play skill. For example, the therapist may spend several sessions focusing on object substitution ability. However, when doing this, the therapist is also aware to plan for the child's developmental ability in play scripts and sequences of play actions and doll or teddy play that may be part of the play scenarios where object substitution is used. For example, the therapist may introduce using a block as a cell phone (20 months) within the play script of ringing a friend (play script inside of the home [20–24 months]), short logical sequence of play actions (24 months), friend is a teddy bear—the teddy bear is real (24 months).

the Parent Learn to Play program (see Stagnitti, 2014). In 2015 in Australia, the program was launched in specialist schools, which are schools that specifically cater to children with multiple developmental issues, including autism, who have an IQ between 55 and 70.

In the specialist schools, the Learn to Play School program has been incorporated as part of the school curriculum, and therapists and teachers work together in the classroom. One school that had been running the program for 2 years when this chapter was written had a dedicated space for the program. Each week, in preparation, teachers and therapists create four short videos demonstrating the play scenarios that were set up in the room. These videos are recorded on iPads. When a class comes to the dedicated space for the program, the class is shown the videos. The children enjoy these as they recognize the staff from the school who are playing in the videos. The teacher then discusses each of the play scenarios with the group. The children then choose which play area they wish to go to. One child is designated as the reporter for the group. Each play area is set up with props for one of the play scenarios they have just seen on the video. For example, four scenarios could be "going to the hairdresser," "shopping," "playing with a train set," and "cooking a meal in the kitchen." The play areas that reflect these scenarios would be: (a) a hairdresser with props being a chair, combs, brushes, towels, and rollers; (b) a table with food items on it, a basket, and money; (c) a train with people; and (d) a play kitchen with table, chairs, sink, stove, saucepans, utensils, and plates. The children spend time in their chosen play area and there is at least one staff member for each area. After 45 minutes, the children are given a 5-minute warning that play time is nearly over, then they gather together and the reporter tells the teacher what the children played. The teacher encourages the other class members to ask the reporter questions and vice versa. The play scenarios for the week are also embedded within the daily classroom activities, and children engage in the Learn to Play School program each week of the year.

EMPIRICAL SUPPORT

The Learn to Play program evidence to date has been reported as case studies. A longitudinal case study of a child with autism found that after 18 months in the program, the child had improved 2 standard deviations in the ability to self-initiate play as assessed on the Child-Initiated Pretend Play Assessment (ChIPPA; Stagnitti, 2004, 2007). Symbolic play was within normal limits for his age when the child was 6 years old. This child completed schooling when he was 18 years old, showing some difficulties in higher level problem solving in his final year at school.

A multiple case study of four children with autism found that after seven sessions, three of the four children reached levels of play ability that included (a) initiation of spontaneous actions within pretend play, (b) imposing on the doll independent thoughts from the child (i.e., decentration and evidence of understanding other's minds), (c) increased object substitution, (d) increased number of logical sequential play actions, (e) recognition of how to use the toys, (f) property attributions, and (g) the child's own emotional engagement in the play. After seven sessions of Learn to Play, the early childhood intervention staff reported, to their surprise, changes such as increases in the children's social turn-taking, play engagement in early childhood settings, and increased language utterances (Stagnitti & Casey, 2011). At the time of this writing, data were being analyzed from a study that included data on oxytocin and cortisol from saliva samples of parents and children pre- and post-four sessions over a 10-month period. Other data collected for this study were the Parent-Child Relationship Inventory, video footage of sessions, and the child's play ability. Clinical research over the past 16 years has determined that Learn to Play is effective with children who have at least a developmental age of 12 to 18 months, one meaningful gesture or word, or focused attention on a play action performed by an adult. If a child has no meaningful verbal or nonverbal communication, then Learn to Play is not appropriate for that child.

For the Learn to Play School program a pre–post group comparison research design was carried out in one specialist school over 22 weeks. It was found that children in the Learn to Play group significantly improved in their social interaction compared to the non–Learn to Play group. The Learn to Play group also decreased significantly in play deficits and increased in language scores (O'Connor & Stagnitti, 2011; Stagnitti, O'Connor, & Sheppard, 2012).

To gauge the levels of evidence on the Learn to Play program, refer to the Australian National Health and Medical Research Council's Levels of Evidence (NHMRC, 1998, 2007) for quantitative studies. For the NHMRC (2007) there are six levels of evidence, with Level I being the highest (e.g., systematic reviews of randomized controlled trials) and Level IV being the lowest (e.g., case series with either posttest or pretest and posttest outcomes; NHMRC, 2007). The evidence level for the Learn to Play School research is level III–2. For the qualitative studies the NHMRC level of evidence is level VI. However, the Rosalind Franklin—Qualitative Research Appraisal Instrument (Henderson & Rheault, 2004) is specifically designed to measure the rigor in qualitative studies. Five levels of evidence are used to ascertain a study's credibility, transferability, dependability, and conformability (e.g., objectivity by reducing bias; Henderson & Rheault, 2004). Level I is assigned when the study meets all four criteria; Level II is assigned when the study meets three aspects, and so on to Level V. The multiple-case study is rated at Level I and the longitudinal-case study is rated at Level III. More research is needed on the Learn to Play program.

CASE ILLUSTRATION INCLUDING CAREGIVER OR PARENT INVOLVEMENT

Robert was 7 years old when he began the Learn to Play program. Robert had a diagnosis of high-functioning autism based on an assessment by his child psychiatrist. He had also been assessed by a speech therapist and an occupational therapist. On his first visit to the Learn to Play playroom, Robert was screaming. He did not want to come. His mother calmed him down, which took most of the session. On his second visit, he was still upset but calmed down in half the time. A play assessment (Stagnitti, 2007) was completed in this session to ascertain Robert's play ability. He was 3 standard deviations below his peers in his play ability, which translated to a 5-year delay in his pretend play ability. By the fourth session, Robert was beginning to realize that the Learn to Play playroom was a nonthreatening, safe place to come.

The program began on the 20- to 24-month developmental play skill level. This translated into repetitive single action play scenarios with some evidence of two to three logical-sequential actions, object substitution use with physically similar objects, interaction with a teddy bear on a repeated one-to-two play action basis, and play scripts on the body level such as drinking, eating, sleeping, as well as within the home. To meet Robert's play needs, the program began with play activities that he would succeed at, such as throwing a ball to a large doll that had arms long enough to catch it. Robert would throw the ball in the air, and the doll—which was moved by the therapist—would make running movements to get it. When the therapist judged Robert was feeling safe and was laughing as the doll ran to the ball, the doll began to tackle Robert for the ball. The doll could do this as it was nonjudgmental and separate from the therapist. Robert enjoyed this and laughed even more. He engaged directly with the doll (i.e., decentration) and looked directly at her. He spoke to her and tried to hide the ball from her. This turn-taking between Robert and the doll continued until he began to disengage from this play scenario (repetition with variation and response to the child). A tea set was brought out. This play scenario involved short logical sequences of play actions (e.g., stir a spoon in the cup and drink from the cup), early play scripts (e.g., body and within the home), object substitution (e.g., ice-cream stick for a spoon), and allowed for decentration (i.e., the teddy joined us for a cup of tea which Robert offered to the teddy). The next few sessions remained on this level of play with increases in variations to the play actions. For example, food was introduced to the tea party. The therapist was careful not to include too many play objects as Robert would be overwhelmed. By the seventh session, Robert was beginning to recognize what was happening in the play and was beginning to initiate his own actions within the play scenes. For example, he could put plastic food items in a cooking pot, stir it, and offer a meal on a plate to his mother. His mother reported that at school, staff had reported that during recess he could spontaneously engage in play such as pretending to cook a toy pizza in a toy oven. Robert placed the pizza pieces on a plate, put on an oven mitt, turned the dials on the toy oven, opened the door, placed the pizza in the toy oven, closed the door, waited for a minute, and then took out the pizza and pretended to eat a slice. He was generalizing his skills across settings.

After 6 months in the program, the play scenarios had progressed to road scenes with cars, block buildings, and service stations. Robert could now include less physically similar object substitutions in his play. For example, he could use a thick crayon as a cell phone, he could use a box lid as a ramp from the gas station to the road, and he could use sticks as people. At this point, the Learn to Play sessions were now operating in Quadrant III of Yasenik and Gardner's (2012) play therapy dimensions model. The model is an integrative one that provides play therapists with a framework that conceptualizes decisions about therapy using two intersecting dimensions: directiveness and consciousness. Quadrant III of the model represents nonintrusive responding while relating to the child within the symbols of play. Within the Learn to Play program, children who move into Quadrant III are initiating their own play and showing more complex levels of symbols in their play. The therapist could now leave the toy cupboard door open on one side and Robert could now come in, look in the cupboard, and choose the toy he wanted to play with. He would set up a play scene, play out a narrative, and use more complex object substitutions in the play (e.g., use a shoe as a cell phone). The therapist would respond to him and join in his play at his request. At his afterschool center, the staff were reporting that Robert could organize several pieces of equipment and create scenes. Staff commented to his mother that they needed to provide Robert with more complex play scenarios. As Robert's play ability increased, he also became a happy child. Gray (2011) included joy as a benefit of play, and this could be observed in Robert's behavior. He enjoyed himself. He saw pleasure in playing and being challenged, and he could include others in his play—albeit at a younger level than his chronological age.

Over the time period in the Learn to Play program, the therapist modeled to Robert's mother how to join her son in play and how to challenge him to achieve higher levels of complexity in his play. His mother could identify when to come into his play and extend his play ideas without disrupting his play. When she joined him in play—often on his invitation—he would smile and show greater enthusiasm in his social interactions. Robert was now a little boy who knew how to play and how to engage in his social world.

CONCLUSION AND FUTURE DIRECTIONS

The Learn to Play program provides therapists and parents with knowledge on the value of pretend play for children up to 8 years old. Pretend play during this time is the predominant form of play for children. Over the past 16 years, knowledge has been gained as to why the program is effective, how to engage children in play, and the importance of self-initiated pretend play. For children with high-functioning autism, the Learn to Play program provides a therapy that targets areas of their development in which they have difficulties. Children with high-functioning autism can be shown and can learn how to engage in pretend play. Many of the children who have gone through the program have generalized their skills to other settings, and school staff have commented on increases in social turn-taking, language, and ability to engage in play with peers.

Research in the future will be designed with Learn to Play as a complex intervention (Campbell et al., 2000). This is because the program has many elements, and randomized controlled trials are not always possible with young children with complex developmental needs. A study with a new intervention based on the Learn to Play program was given a trial with adolescents who had a diagnosis of high-functioning autism (Goldingay et al., 2015). This study was based on the assumption that adolescents who experience social interaction difficulties may be lacking in abilities that are based on pretend play abilities. This research found that parents rated significant improvements in empathy and cooperation and decreases in hyperactivity.

Engaging with children to develop their ability to self-initiate their own play ideas is a powerful therapeutic intervention. For children with high-functioning autism, changes have included increases in happiness, in social turn-taking, in play ability, and in language utterances. Each of these areas contributes to a child's quality of life. Learn to Play is one program that specifically aims to increase a child's spontaneous ability to play. As Gray (2011) argued, play that is freely chosen and undertaken for its own sake is vital to a child's mental health and well-being. There is still much research to be done to understand the long-term benefits of a child's knowing how to self-initiate their own play. However, one consistent finding has been that these children become happier in themselves.

REFERENCES

American Psychiatric Association. (2013). *Diagnostic and Statistical Manual of Mental Disorders* (5th ed.). Arlington, VA: Author.

Axline, V. (1974). *Play Therapy*. New York: Ballantine Books.

Ayres, J. (1972). *Sensory integration and learning disorders*. Los Angeles, CA: Western Psychological Services.

Campbell, M., Fitzpatrick, R., Haines, A., Kinmonth, A. L., Sandercock, P., Spiegelhalter, D., & Tyrer, P. (2000). Framework for design and evaluation of complex interventions to improve health. *BMJ*, *321*, 694–696. http://dx.doi.org/10.1136/bmj.321.7262.694

Charman, T., & Baron-Cohen, S. (1997). Brief report: Prompted pretend play in autism. *Journal of Autism and Developmental Disorders*, *27*, 325–332. http://dx.doi.org/10.1023/A:1025806616149

Doidge, N. (2010). *The brain that changes itself*. Melbourne, Australia: Scribe.

Goldingay, S., Stagnitti, K., Sheppard, L., McGillivray, J., McLean, B., & Pepin, G. (2015). An intervention to improve social participation for adolescents with autism spectrum disorder: Pilot study. *Developmental Neurorehabilitation*, *18*, 122–130. http://dx.doi.org/10.3109/17518423.2013.855275

Gray, P. (2011). The decline of play and rise of psychopathology in children and adolescents. *American Journal of Play*, *3*, 443–463.

Henderson, R., & Rheault, W. (2004). Appraising and incorporating qualitative research in evidence-based practice. *Journal, Physical Therapy Education*, *18*(3), 35–40.

Hughes, C., & Leekam, S. (2004). What are the links between theory of mind and social links? Review, reflections, and new directions for studies of typical and atypical development. *Social Development*, *13*, 590–619.

Lawson, W. (2008). *Concepts of normality*. London, England: Kingsley.

Naber, F. B. A., Bakermans-Kranenburg, M. J., van IJzendoorn, M. H., Swinkels, S. H. N., Buitelaar, J. K., Dietz, C., . . . van Engeland, H. (2008). Play behavior and attachment in toddlers with autism. *Journal of Autism and Developmental Disorders*, *38*, 857–866. http://dx.doi.org/10.1007/s10803-007-0454-5

National Health and Medical Research Council. (1998). *A guide to the development, implementation, and evaluation of clinical practice guidelines*. Retrieved from http://www.nhmrc.gov.au/_files_nhmrc/publications/attachments/cp30.pdf

National Health and Medical Research Council. (2007). *NHMRC additional levels of evidence and grades or recommendations for developers of guidelines: Pilot Program 2005–2007*. Retrieved from http://www.nhmrc.gov.au/_files_nhmrc/file/guidelines/levels_grades05.pdf

O'Connor, C., & Stagnitti, K. (2011). Play, behavior, language and social skills: The comparison of a play and a non-play intervention within a specialist school setting. *Research in Developmental Disabilities*, *32*, 1205–1211. http://dx.doi.org/10.1016/j.ridd.2010.12.037

Pierce-Jordan, S., & Lifter, K. (2005). Interaction of social and play behaviors in preschoolers with and without pervasive developmental disorders. *Topics in Early Childhood Special Education*, *25*(1), 34–47.

Sherratt, D. (2002). Developing pretend play in children with autism: A case study. *Autism*, 6, 169–179. http://dx.doi.org/10.1177/1362361302006002004

Stagnitti, K. (in press). Play, narrative, and children with Autism. In S. Douglas, L. Stirling, & A. Goncu (Eds.), *Children's play, pretence, and story: Studies in culture, context, and ASD*. Melbourne, Australia: Taylor & Francis.

Stagnitti, K. (1998). *Learn to Play. A practical program to develop a child's imaginative play*. Melbourne, Australia: Coordinates.

Stagnitti, K. (2004). Occupational performance in pretend play; implications for practice. In M. Mollineux (Ed.), *Occupation for occupational therapists* (pp. 103–121). Oxford, England: Blackwell.

Stagnitti, K. (2007). *The Child-Initiated Pretend Play Assessment manual and kit*. Melbourne, Australia: Coordinates.

Stagnitti, K. (2009). Play intervention: The Learn to Play program. In K. Stagnitti & R. Cooper (Eds.), *Play as therapy: Assessment and therapeutic interventions* (pp. 176–186). London: Kingsley.

Stagnitti, K. (2014). The Parent Learn to Play program: Building relationships through play. In E. Prendiville and J. Howard (Eds.), *Play therapy today. Contemporary practice with individuals, groups, and carers* (pp. 149–162). Oxon, England: Routledge.

Stagnitti, K., & Casey, S. (2011). Il programma *Learn to Play* con bambini con autismo: Considerazioni pratiche e evidenze [The program *Learn to Play* with children with Autism: Evidence and practical considerations]. *Autismo Oggi*, *20*, 8–13.

Stagnitti, K., O'Connor, C., & Sheppard, L. (2012). Impact of the Learn to Play program on play, social competence, and language for children aged 5–8 years who attend a specialist school. *Australian Occupational Therapy Journal, 59*, 302–311. http://dx.doi.org/10.1111/j.1440-1630.2012.01018.x

Sunderland, M. (2007). *What every parent needs to know*. London, England: DK Books.

Turygin, N. C., Matson, J. L., Adams, H., & Belva, B. (2013). The effect of *DSM–5* criteria on externalizing, internalizing, behavioral, and adaptive symptoms in children diagnosed with autism. *Developmental Neurorehabilitation, 16*, 277–282. http://dx.doi.org/10.3109/17518423.2013.769281

Turygin, N. C., Matson, J. L., Beighley, J., & Adams, H. (2013). The effect of *DSM–5* criteria on the developmental quotient in toddlers diagnosed with autism spectrum disorder. *Developmental Neurorehabilitation, 16*, 38–43. http://dx.doi.org/10.3109/17518423.2012.712065

Volkmar, F., Klin, A., & McPartland, J. (2014). Asperger syndrome: An overview. In J. McPartland, A. Klin, & F. Volkmar (Eds.), *Asperger syndrome: Assessing and treating high-functioning autism spectrum disorders* (pp. 1–42). New York, NY: Guilford Press.

Vygotsky, L. (1976). Play and its role in the mental development of a child. In J. Bruner, A. Jolly, & K. Sylva (Eds.), *Play, its role in development and evolution* (pp. 537–554). Middlesex, England: Penguin.

Vygotsky, L. (2004). Imagination and creativity in childhood. *Journal of Russian & East European Psychology, 42*(1), 4–84.

World Health Organization. (2015). Chapter V. Mental and behavioral disorders (F00–F99). In *International Classification of Diseases and Related Health Problems 10th revision (ICD–10)* WHO Version. Retrieved from http://apps.who.int/classifications/icd10/browse/2015/en#/F.84.0

Yasenik, L., & Gardner, K. (2012). *Play therapy dimensions model*. London, England: Kingsley.

13

CHILD-CENTERED PLAY THERAPY FOR CHILDREN WITH AUTISM SPECTRUM DISORDER

MAUREEN C. KENNY, LAURA H. DINEHART, AND CHARLES B. WINICK

By definition, children with autism Spectrum Disorder (ASD) experience deficits in social communication, relationships, and display behaviors that are restricted or repetitive (American Psychiatric Association, 2013). While children must meet certain criteria to receive this diagnosis, the manifestation of ASD in children may vary greatly depending on the severity of the condition, the developmental level, and the chronological age (American Psychiatric Association, 2013). ASD is also believed to be a lifelong, permanent disability, usually first diagnosed in childhood, for which "there is neither a clear explanation nor a universally accepted course of treatment" (Simpson, 2005, p. 141). Children who are brought for psychological treatment are usually experiencing difficulties that are common among this diagnostic group, including peer rejection and parental concerns (Lee, Harrington, Louie, & Newschaffer, 2008). Along with treatment aimed at improving the child's social functioning and increasing his or her range of interests, parents of children with ASD may need support and guidance on how best to help their children achieve their

http://dx.doi.org/10.1037/14776-014
Play Therapy in Middle Childhood, A. A. Drewes and C. E. Schaefer (Editors)

maximum potential. An integrative approach to treatment that utilizes the rapport-building component and relationship aspects of child-centered play therapy (CCPT; Landreth, 1991) along with behavioral techniques and parent training may be optimal. In this approach, CCPT is used to improve the child's social skills and parent education and training are aimed at improving their child's functioning and targeting maladaptive behavior.

This chapter describes an extensive course of therapy with a 10-year-old boy diagnosed with ASD. The rationale for using an integrative approach to this child's treatment was based on the variety of symptoms he displayed, as well as consideration for his developmental level. The treatment integrated CCPT and parent training. During the course of treatment, the child experienced increases in social behavior attributed to the CCPT. In working with the parent, the therapist was able to provide strategies for managing the child's behavior at home that resulted in less disruptive behavior, more appropriate boundaries, and greater compliance with requests at home and in school. The boy's progression in treatment and specific interventions are examined so that others may duplicate efforts with similar children with ASD.

BASIC RATIONALE AND THEORY

Mastrangelo (2009) asserted that much of the treatment for children with ASD often comprises strict medical and therapeutic interventions targeted at deficits and skill development. Behaviorally based interventions (e.g., applied behavior analysis) are the most commonly used approaches. The goal is often to encourage appropriate behaviors through reinforcement and ignore behaviors that limit the independence of the child. Skills are frequently broken down into small steps, and each step is rewarded sequentially (Dionne & Martini, 2011). While this approach has its merits, it may target only certain functional behaviors, taught within very specific contexts that may not generalize to unfamiliar settings or situations (Hadwin, Baron-Cohen, Howlin, & Hill, 1997). Given the breadth of characteristics of children with ASD, other innovative treatments are needed.

Because there is no single recommended treatment for ASD, parents and professionals are willing to consider various treatment approaches that may help improve a child's functioning (Simpson, 2005). In the search for other treatment modalities that may assist with symptoms of ASD, play therapy has made an appearance in the literature. Simpson (2005), in his review of the current treatments for ASD, stated that play-oriented strategies are a "promising practice" for improving interpersonal relationships with children with ASD. While many approaches with ASD children use play as a reward, Preissler (2006) suggested that "play skills are taught so that children with ASD can be busy independently, rather than slipping into a self-created world of isolation" (p. 241). Child-centered approaches to play therapy that are developmentally based have been used successfully in supporting children with ASD in peer play (Yang, Wolfberg, Wu & Hwu, 2003).

In 1947, Virginia Axline pioneered nondirective play therapy, now commonly referred to as child-centered play therapy (CCPT). She fashioned her therapeutic approach with children after the nondirective, humanistic style of Carl Rogers (Landreth, 1991). As Ray, Sullivan, and Carlson (2012) so succinctly stated, "[Virginia Axline] presented the first structure of CCPT by operationalizing the philosophy of person-centered therapy, so aptly described for adults, into a coherent working model for children" (p. 160). Further refined in its approach by play therapy expert Gary Landreth (1991), CCPT is presently suggested as an appropriate means to address some of the impairments that accompany ASD. This approach emphasizes the child's innate ability to strive toward growth and a belief in the child's ability to be constructive and self-directive (Landreth, 1991).

The goals of CCPT are accomplished through the application of the eight basic principles of Axline's (1969) play therapy, which are essential to the success of the treatment (see the Procedures section in this chapter for more details on these eight principles). One such goal is self-acceptance, in which children learn to be themselves and feel accepted through understanding, warmth, and a sense of security from the therapist. Axline's approach emphasizes empathy and building a relationship with the child, wherein the child sets the direction for the play. The child is responsible for the progress of the sessions; the therapist does not force progress (Axline, 1969). In the playroom, children are allowed to make all decisions; no one criticizes them or tells them what to do. This is often an unfamiliar experience for children who are frequently told what to do, as is so often the case with children with ASD. The therapist's role is to facilitate growth in children by allowing them to act out their feelings. Axline (1969) described this as "an opportunity that is offered to the child to experience growth under the most favorable conditions" (p. 16). The therapist should be attuned to the feelings communicated through the child's play and reflect these back to the child. For the child with ASD, who may have difficulty communicating feelings, CCPT may facilitate such emotional expression.

Ray, Sullivan, and Carlson (2012) described CCPT as a natural choice of treatment for children with ASD since it is a way of working with children that emphasizes communication and relationships. They asserted that the very philosophy of CCPT is in line to address the salient characteristics of a child with ASD. CCPT recognizes the relationship between the child and therapist as the mechanism primarily responsible for change in the child (Ray et al., 2012). Through the use of play therapy, the therapist seeks to form a relationship with the child in which the child will be accepted unconditionally. The therapist provides an environment that allows the child to move toward self-enhancing ways of being. With CCPT, the focus is on the whole child and not on the problem. Too often, the treatment of ASD focuses on the problem behavior (e.g., poor eye contact, low verbalizations, repetitive behavior) and does not examine the child as a whole.

The involvement of parents in treatment of children with ASD is also important and necessary for the generalization of learned skills (Dionne & Martini, 2011). Thus, CCPT was designed to include the child's parents so as to assist them in working with the child outside of the treatment office. This extension of the therapeutic approach to the child's other environments enhances the treatment effects. In this chapter's case study, the parents were provided parent training to support them in addressing behavioral concerns at home.

LIMITATIONS

Play therapy may not be helpful for all children with ASD. For those who engage in repetitive, stereotypic play with toys or have accompanying severe intellectual impairment (American Psychiatric Association, 2013), CCPT may not be the treatment of choice. It takes a long time and is ongoing, requiring a certain level of commitment from the parents and adequate resources. Despite these limitations, it seems that some high-functioning autistic children can benefit from CCPT. As Simpson (2005) stated, parents and professionals must ultimately decide whether a particular strategy or method is suitable for an individual child with ASD.

DEVELOPMENTAL ISSUES

ASD is a neurodevelopmental disability with manifest deficits observed in social communication and behaviors; repetitive and restricted behaviors are also characteristic (American Psychiatric Association, 2013). Children with ASD can display a range of behaviors, including failure to engage in normal back-and-forth conversations, abnormalities in body language, and deficits in relationships. One of the most visible signs of ASD is the inability to relate to others (Exkorn, 2005; Mastrangelo, 2009). These children struggle with understanding subtle emotional cues and facial expressions, lack emotional reciprocity, and experience difficulty making and maintaining eye contact. Repetitive or stereotyped behaviors (e.g., echolalia, simple motor stereotypes) are common, as are insistence on sameness and highly restricted interests (e.g., difficulties with transitions, need to eat same food every day; American Psychiatric Association, 2013). This rigidity further contributes to the difficulty children with ASD have with the spontaneous interaction that is required in socialization. The relationship established in CCPT may help to mitigate these challenges for the child with ASD by creating a relationship that is built on unconditional positive regard and allowing the child to move at his own pace.

The current prevalence of ASD is reported to occur in one in 88 children, with higher rates among boys (one in 54; Centers for Disease Control and Prevention, 2013). Apart from any potential reason for an increase in prevalence, there are clearly many children experiencing this disability who require proper education, care, and intervention. Parents of children with ASD have many concerns about their children, including their achievement, learning problems, self-esteem, and their potential of bullying; parents must also deal with their own stress arising from the burden of caring for such children (Lee et al., 2008).

For all children, play provides a disguised opportunity for learning (Preissler, 2006). In this modality, and particularly for children with ASD, play offers opportunities for children to increase their joint-attention skills—the visual coordination between two individuals and an object/event (e.g., engaging in play with someone). Joint attention is typically thought to provide a foundation for theory of mind, which includes awareness of personal thoughts and mental state, as well as awareness of others' intentions (Preissler, 2006). Mastrangelo (2009) confirmed this: "With extensive opportunities for play, the child's awareness of other people's mental states and intentions may be enhanced" (p. 14).

When implementing play therapy with children with ASD there are several developmental considerations. The *International Classification of Diseases* (10th ed.; *ICD–10*), which uses the term *childhood autism*, includes criteria related to deficits in spoken and reciprocal language (World Health Organization, 2011). However, language impairment may not impede the treatment, as much of play is nonverbal and symbolic. Perhaps because *ICD–10* criteria can include an impairment in functional or symbolic play such as the lack of spontaneous make-believe play or social-imitative play, there has been a belief that children with ASD would not benefit from play therapy. However, these criteria are part of a larger set and may not be present in all children with ASD.

Play therapy has been deemed a developmentally appropriate form of counseling (Landreth, 1991). It allows children with developmental disabilities to discover the physical and emotional strengths they have in relation to their deficits (Carmichael, 1993). Thus, given the developmental deficits in ASD, this approach works with children at their stage of development. Further, the playroom and materials used in CCPT serve as a developmentally appropriate form of communication for the child. Employing CCPT for children with ASD seems to be a natural fit as these children experience challenges in their relationships including poor social acceptance, companionship, and less reciprocity in their socialization (Chamberlain, Kasari, & Rotheram-Fuller, 2007; Rotheram-Fuller, Kasari, Chamberlain, & Locke, 2010). In the relationship with the child-centered play therapist, the child has the opportunity to experience a unique relationship of acceptance and positive regard.

PLAY INTERVENTION PROCEDURES AND SETTINGS

The primary play therapy interventions used were taken from Landreth's (1991) description of the basic philosophy of CCPT as

> an encompassing philosophy for living one's life in relationships with children—not a cloak of techniques to put on upon entering the playroom, but a way of being based on a deep commitment to certain beliefs about children and their innate capacity for growth. (p. 55)

Thus, rather than rely on a set of techniques, the therapist displays a warm, caring acceptance and sensitive understanding of the child. His or her role with the child with ASD is unlike any other professional in the child's life. The therapist is there to accept the child as he or she is and not to work toward some behavioral goal on which a condition will be set. To this end, the therapeutic relationship can aid in the development of a social relationship that can assist the child in forming relationships once the treatment ends (Landreth, 1991).

Furthermore, the basic relationship between the psychologist and the child is predicated on Axline's (1969) eight basic principles of play therapy. These principles are explored further in the context of the treatment (see Axline, 1969, for a full description of the principles), but an overarching theme is to be permissive with the child so that the child feels free to express his or her feelings completely, and over time the clinician recognizes these feelings and helps the child gain insight into his or her behavior. There is a deep respect for the child, such that the child is viewed as being able to solve his or her own problems and is given the opportunity to do so. Therapy is viewed as a gradual process that is neither hurried nor directed by the clinician. Limits are few and only those necessary.

The toys and methods employed can be used in a school or agency setting with sufficient access to play materials.

EMPIRICAL SUPPORT

In recent years, there have been several attempts to implement various forms of play therapy techniques with children with ASD to reduce symptoms and improve functioning. It has been applied to individuals as well as groups and in both private practices and schools. Play approaches often target one of the social symptoms of ASD, such as the deficits in social–emotional reciprocity or difficulty developing or maintaining relationships. Despite some documented successful implementations of play therapy with children with ASD, many therapists have been reluctant to use conventional forms of psychotherapy with such children. The repetitive and supposedly non-creative play of children with ASD may hinder the use of play therapy.

Most of the empirical support for play therapy for children with ASD comes in the form of case studies or small samples. Given the wide variability of the symptoms of children with ASD, single-subject approaches may be the most feasible start. Many researchers design a treatment and then recommend replication of the approach with other children with similar characteristics or extended treatment using teachers or parents as the facilitators.

Simeone-Russell (2011) reviewed the use of "theraplay" with children with ASD. Theraplay utilizes the basic elements of play therapy to help children form better attachment relationships with others. Notable successes in the past include children increasing their socialization, social skill development, reduced echolalia, and initiation of interaction with peers, and developing language and interaction skills (see Simeone-Russell, 2011). Theraplay is predicated on the belief that the child will attach to the nonjudgmental, caring, and encouraging therapist during the treatment. From this, the social skills gained are generalized to others when the treatment ends.

Dionne and Martini (2011) described floor time play (FTP) with children with ASD. FTP is a therapeutic approach aimed at moving the child through developmental milestones by following the child's lead during play and building on what the child does to encourage more reciprocal interaction. Essentially, the parent and therapist play with the child on the floor, encouraging him or her to interact in reciprocal fashion. In their 2011 study, Dionne and Martini utilized FTP (with a therapist and at home with the mother) with a young boy with ASD (28 sessions over 7 weeks, with approximately four 45-minute sessions a week). They found his reciprocal communication increased and his mother reported less distress and more spontaneous communication. Utilizing a case-study approach, Hess (2006) describes the treatment of a 10-year-old boy with ASD with guided story and role-play which enhanced his pretend play abilities and understanding of social roles. He was found to increase his use of pretend play and to have more spontaneous, appropriate social exchanges and responses to questions when the treatment was complete.

In a similar single-case study design, Josefi and Ryan (2004) described a nondirective play therapy approach taken with a 6-year-old boy with severe autism. The authors argued that a nondirective approach focuses on positive regard that accepts the child's current functioning and allows the therapist to "enter children's unique inner world" (Josefi & Ryan, 2004, p. 534). The therapy included 16 individualized play sessions, targeted to improve five categories of behavior, including (a) child-initiated physical contact with therapist, (b) child-initiated play activities, (c) time spent by child on play activities, (d) child-initiated interactions with the therapist, and (e) time spent on ritualistic behaviors. On the basis of both qualitative and quantitative analyses, the authors reported significant improvements in the child's development of independence and initiative, as well as empathy. Although less notable improvements were observed with the child's ritualistic behaviors, twice-weekly sessions seemed to result in marked differences compared to sessions offered once a week. Previously, Kenny and Winick (2000) used nondirective play therapy with a girl with ASD in an outpatient setting. Over the course of 11 weekly sessions, she improved her social behavior, was less irritable, and the parental report included increased compliance at home.

Since children with ASD often lack creative, flexible, and innovative play, Lu, Petersen, Lacroix, and Rousseau (2010) used sandplay to stimulate creative play in these children. Using sandplay in a group setting, they found that over time, the children were more at ease communicating with one another, listening to one another, and narrating their sandtrays to the group. The authors concluded that sandplay adapted to children with ASD supported the developmental skills of communication, socialization, and symbolic elaboration.

Yang, Wolfberg, Wu, and Hwu (2003) devised integrated play groups to support children with ASD in mutually enjoyed play experiences with typical peers and siblings. They found that each child made notable gains in both social and symbolic/pretend play and also increased their social engagement. This was an incredible improvement for children with ASD, as they are often described as difficult to engage in pretend play because they view it as a meaningless activity (Hess, 2006).

In an effort to include parents as a source for play therapy, Vismara, Colombi, and Rogers (2009) targeted the attention, communication, imitation, and play skills of young children with ASD. In their primary model, parents were trained to deliver the Early Start Denver Model (ESDM), a method that employs naturalistic interactions as activities and opportunities for learning. The researchers examined (a) whether parents were able to implement the treatment and (b) whether changes in social behaviors were evident in the children as a result of the treatment. Eight parents were trained over a 12-week period for 1 hour a week while engaging in interactions with their children. All of the children ($n = 8$) with ASD were toddlers between 10 and 36 months of age demonstrating varying levels of severity. Overall, the authors report that parents were able to acquire intervention strategies approximately halfway through the intervention, while children demonstrated sustained growth in social communicative behaviors.

It is important to note that the ESDM model implemented by Vismara et al. (2009) utilizes, in part, pivotal response training, which is based on principles of applied behavior analysis (ABA). Given the wealth of research on the effects of ABA on modifying behavior in children with ASD, Bernard-Opitz, Ing, and Kong (2004) designed a study to compare the effects of behavioral therapy versus natural play intervention on the behavior of children with ASD. Eight children with ASD were included in a counterbalanced procedure such that four children with ASD received a behavioral approach to therapy first, followed by a play condition. Four more children with ASD received the play condition first, followed by the behavioral condition. Results indicated differential effects of the two approaches. Although children demonstrated better attention and compliance in the behavioral approach, all children in the study demonstrated improvements in play and communication with their parents (Bernard-Opitz et al., 2004).

In a novel approach to play therapy, François, Powell, and Dautenhahn (2009) utilized robot-assisted play therapy with five children between 7 and 10 years of age. Robots, the authors suggested, elicit various behaviors in children with ASD. Within a school-based setting, participating children engaged with a therapist in a nondirective play session that included the robotic toy for a time of their choosing (no longer than 40 minutes) over a variable number of sessions. The robot was programmed to demonstrate a variety of simple behaviors that became progressively more complex as the child's ability progressed. Children who continued in solitary play were more engaged in increased imitative play with the experimenter, while children who proactively played experienced higher levels of play and more advanced reasoning, as measured by the researchers.

In sum, play therapy has been successfully implemented with children with ASD to address many of the common social and behavioral problems. (For more detailed reading on various play approaches to ASD, readers are referred to Gallo-Lopez & Rubin, 2012.)

CASE ILLUSTRATION WITH CAREGIVER/PARENT INVOLVEMENT

Daniel (pseudonym) is a 9-year-old boy with ASD who was brought to treatment by his mother, Jane (age 32). Her concerns centered on his diagnosis of autism. Specifically, she was concerned about some of his behavior at school. Apparently, he had not been completing assignments at school, was not following directions, and was disrupting his peers. Jane was worried that Daniel was impulsive, aggressive, and had a poor attention span at times. She described him as argumentative, stubborn, having temper tantrums, and talking to inanimate objects.

Daniel's history been compiled from intake forms, case history, and medical and psychotherapy documents provided by the parents and from direct report from the mother. The child's life was characterized by a stable home environment with two parents and two siblings. However, due to the nature of the father's work, they moved multiple times in his childhood. Daniel had been living at his current location for a few months at the time treatment commenced.

Early medical history revealed that Jane's pregnancy with Daniel was somewhat complicated as she developed high blood pressure and a rupture of the placenta forced an early delivery (35 weeks). Despite these complications, Daniel's delivery was without incident and he met his physical developmental milestones within normal time limits. His language was developing well until around 2 years, when he began to lose the language skills he had gained. Daniel received early intervention services, including occupational and speech therapy from approximately 2 years of age and at the age of 3 began school where he received both occupational and speech therapy services. However, he was still evidencing feeding problems at age 3 (e.g., unable to feed himself) and some fine-motor difficulties. During his preschool years, Daniel displayed a multitude of sensory issues. He reacted to loud noises and bright lights and had issues with certain textures. His medical evaluations have consistently found no medical difficulties and his family history is negative for ASD.

His family relocated to another state when Daniel was 5 years old, at which time he attended a preschool program for children with disabilities for a half day and spent the other half in kindergarten. It was at this time also that Daniel began to receive approximately 8 to 12 hours a week of ABA. This treatment also included a social skills group to help him improve his relationships with others. Daniel experienced a move again at age 7. While in first grade, he began experiencing problems at school and was seen by a psychiatrist. At that time he was prescribed Abilify (described as an "add on" antidepressant) to address his aggressive behavior. This problem has greatly improved and he has shown no aggression at school toward peers, although he continues to be aggressive at home with his siblings. When he was in second grade, he had an individualized-education plan at school that included resource time and he also continued his psychiatric care. He was then prescribed Intuniv, and Benadryl for his pacing (an apparent side effect of the Intuniv). This combination of medications was reported by his mother to be the result of a lengthy search for the correct set. The pacing has improved, and Daniel appears to be aware of others' reactions to it and avoids pacing in front of others. However, at times in the classroom he begins to pace as he gets up from his desk and forgets what he is supposed to be doing.

With regard to his social functioning, Daniel has difficulty with topic maintenance and is more likely to recite facts than carry on a mutually participatory conversation. He appears to prefer to talk to adults than children, as they appear more tolerant of listening to his interests. He has difficulty making and keeping friends, as he demonstrates poor social reciprocity. With typically developing children, he will talk about his topic of interest until they avoid him. He makes no apparent attempt to gain information about others' thoughts or feelings. He has been taught "stranger rules," so he will often ask an unknown adult his or her name so that he can talk to them.

Daniel has immediate and delayed echolalia. He has a very literal and concrete understanding of language. He is rule governed and does well if reminded of the rules in a classroom setting. He performs best one-on-one and is able to achieve good grades with academic support. Presently, he continues to have sensory issues, despite years of occupational therapy to address these sensitivities. His food choices are very limited, preferring mostly starches. In terms of progress, he no longer has texture issues or startle responses to loud noises or bright lights.

Daniel has undergone extensive psychological testing, which revealed a full-scale IQ within the average range (Wechsler IQ = 92). In addition, his scores on the Woodcock Johnson Test of Achievement (Schrank, McGrew, Mather, & Woodcock, 2014) showed that he was also performing in the average range at the level expected for him given his age and grade. Daniel's diagnosis is ASD without accompanying intellectual impairment and without accompanying language impairment.

Due to these obvious strengths (i.e., average intellect and no language impairment), play therapy was deemed to be a suitable form of treatment to address Daniel's social issues. In conjunction with weekly play therapy sessions, the psychologist worked with Jane on behavioral issues she brought up that were occurring at home or school. These were largely concerns regarding his inappropriate peer behavior. In addition, Daniel had begun to touch his penis through his pants at school and home. Daniel was seen once a week for 50-minute psychotherapy sessions with conjoint work accomplished with his parents, primarily his mother. Behavioral interventions were incorporated to specifically address Jane's concerns about the child's problems at school with regard to his academics as well as his behavior.

Child Treatment

Although Daniel is still in treatment, at present, this chapter discusses the first 12 months of his therapy, current improvements, and ongoing needs.

The rationale for using a flexible, integrative approach is based on the multiplicity of difficulties displayed by this child as well as his developmental level and past treatments.

The treatment takes place in an outpatient private psychotherapy office. The office is located in a large suburban city in the southeast United States. The town is primarily middle- to upper-middle class, but the office serves a variety of clients from surrounding areas and representing diverse economic and social backgrounds. The office is approximately 10 × 12 feet and consists of two couches, a desk for the counselor, and a variety of toys and play materials. Based on Landreth's (1991) suggestion, the available toys include play food, building blocks, small cars and other vehicles, plastic animals, dolls, doll clothing, two dollhouses, army men figures, plastic dishes, puppets and art supplies (e.g., crayons, paper, colored pencils, glue, scissors).

For the most part, Axline's (1969) eight principles of nondirective play therapy were diligently applied during the course of Daniel's psychotherapy. It was hypothesized that Daniel would respond positively to the essentially unrestricted nature of the play sessions. The following is an exploration of some of these principles within the context of Daniel's psychological treatment. Attention to establishing and maintaining a warm and friendly relationship with Daniel is a priority in every session. The psychologist greets Daniel in an enthusiastic manner and always demonstrates interest in him. Furthermore, in each session, when Daniel brings up issues occurring in his life or issues of interest, the psychologist communicates support in a warm, friendly manner. Daniel is always accepted as he is.

Daniel recognizes that he has permission to express his feelings to the psychologist. Because talking about feelings is difficult for him, and Daniel is aware that the psychologist attempts to facilitate his discussion of feelings, he frequently engages in behaviors geared toward avoiding self-expression. For example, Daniel often brings a stuffed animal into the session, and wants to spend the session talking to the psychologist about the stuffed animal. When the psychologist points out to Daniel his avoidance of expressing his feelings, Daniel is (usually) eventually able to set aside the stuffed animal and engage in both direct and indirect activities that lead to expressing feelings. The psychologist deviates from being nondirective here in order to get Daniel to engage in the treatment. This has resulted in Daniel being responsive to puppet play, therapeutic stories, and art interventions over the course of treatment.

The psychologist is always alert to the feelings Daniel expresses. For example, Daniel's tone of voice sometimes becomes irritated and he seems angry when this psychologist sets an undesired limit, such as reminding Daniel about personal boundaries. The psychologist processes with Daniel how his behavior comes across to other people and offers to process with him the reasons for his anger. As Daniel has difficulty both understanding the effects of his behavior on other people as well as his own emotions, these discussions are often prolonged. The psychologist often comments on how it can be frustrating for Daniel to struggle to understand the material being discussed. Daniel seems to relax when provided this support, and continues to engage in the discussion.

The psychologist always approaches Daniel with respect for his ability to solve his own problems. However, given Daniel's severe limitations in coping skills and social skills, the psychologist often proposes possible problem-solving approaches, but always with respect for Daniel's ability to make choices. Thus, the psychologist deviates from CCPT, but in the interest of helping Daniel, generates potential ways to solve his problem. For example, Daniel was having an issue at school where he was running around the classroom. After multiple discussions with Daniel, it became clear that Daniel was sometimes restless and bored with his work. He was provided with possible alternative behavioral approaches at school, and the psychologist expressed confidence that Daniel could make a choice. This was a prolonged discussion, as Daniel had many questions about the various steps in implementing possible problem-solving plans. However, at no time during the discussion did the psychologist dictate to Daniel what he should do. When Daniel struggles with problem solving and requires repeated explanations and processing, the psychologist does not become frustrated or disappointed. Sometimes, related to Daniel's difficulty understanding social nuances, an entire session is spent helping him with one relatively minor issue. For example, in one recent session Daniel discussed a girl in his class that he liked and expressed a belief that she should move into his family home so that they could spend more time together. The psychologist patiently addressed the various social issues related to this move (e.g., this girl has her own family, boys and girls his age don't live together, just because he likes her does not mean that she likes him).

Although the psychologist does not attempt to direct Daniel's actions or topics of conversation, Daniel sometimes engages in socially inappropriate behaviors and discussions. At these times, the psychologist provides frequent feedback about how his actions or conversation topics may be perceived by others. For example, on one occasion, Daniel began to act out a play scenario by throwing Lego pieces around the office. It was explained to Daniel why throwing Legos in an office would be perceived negatively by other people. This is also in line with the therapeutic limit setting Landreth (1991) described, which focuses on self-control. In addition, Daniel was assisted in finding a more socially appropriate manner in which he could express his thoughts and feelings during the play therapy. On another occasion, Daniel asked to use the bathroom. Upon his return, he began to describe in detail several aspects of his bathroom behavior. The psychologist explained that other people may perceive discussion of this topic in a negative manner.

The psychologist never becomes frustrated with Daniel's extreme difficulty grasping and utilizing appropriate social skills (a manifestation of his ASD). Although the psychologist often refers to previous interactions with Daniel, there is never an implication that Daniel should have already learned this material. Since Daniel's ASD will likely always require ongoing support from caring others, the psychologist instead continues to foster a therapeutic relationship in which Daniel does not feel insecure about receiving ongoing support in utilizing appropriate social/coping skills. Limitations imposed upon Daniel during the psychotherapy session always relate to demonstrating realistic, responsible social interaction. For example, on occasion Daniel becomes so immersed in individual play with the puppet that he appears oblivious to the presence of the psychologist. The psychologist explores this behavior within the context of the mutual responsibility of interpersonal interaction. Daniel is usually able to reengage in the interpersonal interaction with the psychologist. Not unlike other children with ASD, Daniel has a proclivity to be in his own mind and block out others; however, he also values the ongoing relationship with the psychologist. To this extent, he is responsive to feedback from the psychologist as to how his withdrawal from interpersonal interaction is straining the therapeutic relationship.

Parent Education/Training

From the beginning of Daniel's treatment, the psychologist made time to work alone with Jane, typically for the last 10 to 15 minutes of each session. The psychologist encouraged parental patience with the therapeutic process and to look for slow, steady progress. An educational approach was used to help Jane understand Daniel's limitations where the psychologist educated her on common difficulties encountered by children with autism. As do many parents of children with ASD, Jane was feeling high levels of stress and concern for her child (Lee et al., 2008). Jane spoke about Daniel's behavioral problems in school, and the psychologist helped her to understand these behaviors within the context of Daniel's ASD and provided support for the stress she was experiencing. One area addressed was Daniel's boundary issues. For example, when Daniel got in trouble for continually trying to talk to a classmate, this psychologist explained Daniel's behavior as a consequence of having difficulty understanding social nuances, but the psychologist also helped Jane with behavioral planning to shape Daniel's behavior. These boundary problems were also apparent at home in Daniel's interactions with his brother. The psychologist helped Jane to educate Daniel on these issues. Another area targeted in the parent training was how Jane could educate Daniel about self-care needs (e.g., brushing his teeth, bathing, behaving appropriately in public places). In general, the theme with Jane was to help her get Daniel to connect the specific instance to the larger social rule; to help him generalize to apply information learned to new social situations. Children with ASD have difficulty applying experience from one situation to another similar situation, and Jane had to work on this repeatedly with Daniel. Finally, while Jane had been educated previously on ASD, information on Daniel's current functioning and prognosis was provided.

CONCLUSION AND FUTURE DIRECTIONS

This case presented an integrative play therapy approach for a 10-year-old boy with ASD who was experiencing emotional and behavioral difficulties. The goal of the treatment was to combine the use of CCPT with parent training in order to promote communication, socialization, and decrease disruptive behaviors. Based on changes in the child's behavior and reports from the mother, the integration of CCPT and parent education was successful in improved awareness of social nuances, decreased behavioral disruptions (including self-touching), increased ability to connect with others in a positive manner, and improved functioning at home with family members. The treatment focused on a relationship-oriented intervention that allowed Daniel to play nondirectively with the toys while establishing a relationship with the therapist. Later, more directive techniques were focused on deficit behaviors in discussions with the mother. Daniel clearly responded positively to the CCPT, and his emotional progress and behavioral changes can be attributed to such. The child-centered play therapist provides the core conditions of empathy, warmth, and genuine respect for the child (Landreth, 1991). While this experience, if conducted properly, should be beneficial for any child, for the child with ASD who has likely experienced social rejection, this experience can be particularly healing. CCPT allows the child to feel competent and begin to establish a greater sense of self-esteem, something that many children with ASD may be lacking given their frequent reliance on others for assistance with daily tasks. Daniel's affect improved during the course of the therapy, and his play repertoire increased.

Given the variability of the presentation of ASD, there are no universally accepted treatments. Each individual is likely to respond differently to treatment, according to his or her symptomology. There is a need to begin to understand which characteristics of the child respond to which specific play approaches (Mastrangelo, 2009). Further investigation with a range of children with ASD and different approaches to play therapy (e.g., CCPT, directive, filial) will help determine which techniques work best for different children.

In selecting a treatment for children with ASD, Simpson (2005) recommended considering a few basic questions: What are the potential risks associated with the practice? What is the efficacy and anticipated outcomes of a particular practice, and are they in line with the needs of the child? If we respond to these questions based on the present treatment, we yield positive results. There are no anticipated risks or reported risks with the use of CCPT therapy with children with ASD, and the goals are founded in social and emotional growth.

REFERENCES

American Psychiatric Association. (2013). *Diagnostic and statistical manual of mental disorders* (5th ed.). Washington, DC: Author.

Axline, V. (1969). *Play therapy*. New York, NY: Ballantine Books.

Bernard-Opitz, V., Ing, S., & Kong, T. Y. (2004). Comparison of behavioral and natural play interventions for young children with autism. *Autism*, 8, 319–333. http://dx.doi.org/10.1177/1362361304045212

Carmichael, K. D. (1993). Play therapy and children with disabilities. *Issues in Comprehensive Pediatric Nursing, 16*, 165–173. http://dx.doi.org/10.3109/01460869309078273

Centers for Disease Control and Prevention. (2013, May 29). *New data on autism spectrum disorders*. Retrieved from http://www.cdc.gov/Features/CountingAutism/

Chamberlain, B., Kasari, C., & Rotheram-Fuller, E. (2007). Involvement or isolation? The social networks of children with autism in regular classrooms. *Journal of Autism and Developmental Disorders, 37*, 230–242. http://dx.doi.org/10.1007/s10803-006-0164-4

Dionne, M., & Martini, R. (2011). Floor time play with a child with autism: A single-subject study. *Canadian Journal of Occupational Therapy, 78*, 196–203. http://dx.doi.org/10.2182/cjot.2011.78.3.8

Exkorn, K. S. (2005). *The autism sourcebook: Everything you need to know about diagnosis, treatment, coping, and healing*. New York, NY: HarperCollins.

François, D., Powell, S., & Dautenhahn, K. (2009). A long-term study of children with autism playing with a robotic pet. Taking inspirations from non-directive play therapy to encourage children's proactivity and initiative taking. *Interaction Studies: Social Behaviour and Communication in Biological and Artificial Systems, 10*, 324–373. http://dx.doi.org/10.1075/is.10.3.04fra

Gallo-Lopez, L., & Rubin, L. (2012). *Play-based interventions for children and adolescents with autism spectrum disorder*. New York, NY: Routledge.

Hadwin, J., Baron-Cohen, S., Howlin, P., & Hill, K. (1997). Does teaching theory of mind have an effect on the ability to develop conversation in children with autism? *Journal of Autism and Developmental Disorders, 27*, 519–537. http://dx.doi.org/10.1023/A:1025826009731

Hess, L. (2006). I would like to play but I don't know how: A case study of pretend play in autism. *Child Language Teaching and Therapy, 22*(1), 97–116. http://dx.doi.org/10.1191/0265659006ct299oa

Josefi, O., & Ryan, V. (2004). Nondirective play therapy for young children with autism: A case study. *Clinical Child Psychology and Psychiatry, 9*, 533–551. http://dx.doi.org/10.1177/1359104504046158

Kenny, M. C., & Winick, C. B. (2000). An integrative approach to play therapy with an autistic girl. *International Journal of Play Therapy, 9*(1), 11–33. http://dx.doi.org/10.1037/h0089438

Landreth, G. (1991). *Play therapy: The art of the relationship*. Muncie, IN: Accelerated Development.

Lee, L. C., Harrington, R. A., Louie, B. B., & Newschaffer, C. J. (2008). Children with autism: Quality of life and parental concerns. *Journal of Autism and Developmental Disorders, 38*, 1147–1160. http://dx.doi.org/10.1007/s10803-007-0491-0

Lu, L., Petersen, F., Lacroix, L., & Rousseau, C. (2010). Stimulating creative play in children with autism through sandplay. *The Arts in Psychotherapy, 37*(1), 56–64. http://dx.doi.org/10.1016/j.aip.2009.09.003

Mastrangelo, S. (2009). Play and the child with autism spectrum disorder: From possibilities to practice. *International Journal of Play Therapy, 18*(1), 13–30. http://dx.doi.org/10.1037/a0013810

Preissler, M. A. (2006). Play and autism: Facilitating symbolic understanding. In D. G. Singer, R. M. Golinkoff, & K. Hirsch-Pasek (Eds.), Play = *learning: How play motivates and enhances children's cognitive and social–emotional growth* (pp. 231–250). Oxford, England: Oxford University Press.

Ray, D., Sullivan, J., & Carlson, S. (2012). Relational intervention: Child-centered play therapy with children on the autism spectrum. In L. Gallo-Lopez & L. Rubin (Eds.), *Play-based interventions for children and adolescents with autism spectrum disorder* (pp. 139–175). New York, NY: Routledge.

Rotheram-Fuller, E., Kasari, C., Chamberlain, B., & Locke, J. (2010). Social involvement of children with autism spectrum disorders in elementary school classrooms. *Journal of Child Psychology and Psychiatry, 51*, 1227–1234. http://dx.doi.org/10.1111/j.1469-7610.2010.02289.x

Schrank, F. A., McGrew, K. S., Mather, N., & Woodcock, R. W. (2014). *Woodcock–Johnson IV: Tests of Achievement and Tests of Cognitive Ability*. Rolling Meadows, IL: Riverside.

Simeone-Russell, R. (2011). A practical approach to implementing theraplay for children with autism spectrum disorder. *International Journal of Play Therapy, 20*, 224–235. http://dx.doi.org/10.1037/a0024823

Simpson, R. L. (2005). Evidence-based practices and students with autism spectrum disorders. *Focus on Autism and Other Developmental Disabilities*, *20*, 140–149. http://dx.doi.org/10.1177/10883576050200030201

Vismara, L. A., Colombi, C., & Rogers, S. J. (2009). Can one hour per week of therapy lead to lasting changes in young children with autism? *Autism*, *13*, 93–115. http://dx.doi.org/10.1177/1362361307098516

World Health Organization. (2011). *International statistical classification of diseases and health-related problems, 10th revision*. Geneva, Switzerland: Author.

Yang, T. R., Wolfberg, P. J., Wu, S. C., & Hwu, P. Y. (2003). Supporting children on the autism spectrum in peer play at home and school: Piloting the integrated play groups model in Taiwan. *Autism*, *7*, 437–453. http://dx.doi.org/10.1177/1362361303007004009

14

REPLAYS: A THERAPEUTIC APPROACH FOR CHILDREN WITH AUTISM SPECTRUM DISORDER

KAREN LEVINE

Replays (Levine & Chedd, 2007) is a play therapy approach for treating emotional dysregulation in children with autism spectrum disorder (ASD) or other developmental disabilities. While percentages vary across studies, about 75% or more children with ASD also have significant difficulties with anxiety and emotion regulation (Guy, Souders, Bradstreet, DeLussey, & Herrington, 2014; Mayes, Calhoun, Murray, Ahuja, & Smith, 2011; Mazefsky et al., 2013). Replays is a treatment especially tailored to help children with dysregulation caused by anxiety and specific phobias, obsessive–compulsive disorder behaviors, as well as specific distress triggers (e.g., child has intense distress or anger over having to wear boots, or do school work). Replays can be used as a component of a more comprehensive anxiety treatment process (Levine, 2013; Levine & Chedd, in press), or as a stand-alone treatment. It can also be used with other approaches to treat emotional regulation, such as positive behavioral supports, social stories, sensory integration/occupational therapy, and/or psychotropic medication.

http://dx.doi.org/10.1037/14776-015
Play Therapy in Middle Childhood, A. A. Drewes and C. E. Schaefer (Editors)

In brief, to do Replays, the adult engages the child in pleasurable interactive symbolic play about a trigger event. The adult acts out, or pretends to be a figure acting out, a representation of the child's distress response using playful alteration or exaggeration so the child understands the play is representational. The adult's initiation and cessation of pretend distress are controlled by the child, who in turn plays the role of causing the trigger event to occur. For example, a child who is afraid of a dental exam pretends to give the adult a dental exam, and the adult playfully moves away, making overt playfully exaggerated signals of pretend fear. The child, motivated by having fun control over the adult, and being in charge of what has historically been a scary, overwhelming experience, is motivated to engage with the adult to repeat this scenario, and the adult responds accordingly. Based on the child's affective response, the adult tinkers with the play throughout the process, working to maximize child interest, pleasure, and participation, without causing actual distress. The adult experiments with varying intensity of their expression of pretend distress, their use of humor, and the degree of pretend vs. reality needed for the child to simultaneously understand what is being played out while not becoming truly distressed by the props or the play. Once this fun play routine has been established, the adult incorporates increasingly realistic props (e.g., real medical equipment, real food) into the happy play, hence incorporating gradual exposure.

Children often are able to develop decreasing intensity in emotional response to the trigger experience following Replays. In addition to the primary purpose of using Replays, namely to increase emotional regulation capacities, children also often develop increasingly engaged, interactive symbolic play experiences and the beginnings of empathy experiences, both of which are areas of impairment in children with ASD. Throughout Replays the adult is re-creating a symbolic reenactment of an emotional experience with which the child is very familiar. The child responds to this pretend emotional experience of another person, as it is an emotional experience they themselves know so well. Hence this process results in a situation in which the child empathizes, in the truest sense of the word, with the experience of the "other," who is representing themselves.

BASIC RATIONALE AND THEORY

Replays is based in four different but interrelated bodies of research and theory: (a) development of emotional regulation in typically developing children, (b) development of emotional regulation in children with ASD, (c) treatment of dysregulation in typically developing children and children with ASD, and (d) abreaction as an "agent of change" common to many forms of play therapy (Schaefer & Drewes, 2013)

Development of Emotional Regulation in Typically Developing Children

Typically developing infants are easily and frequently dysregulated. They engage in both self-regulating (e.g., finger sucking) as well as coregulating activity, such as being soothed by a caregiver, both through physical means (e.g., rocking, holding, bouncing) and social means (e.g., reading caregiver's calming tone of voice, calming facial expression). Typically developing infants use this social affective interactive set of "channels" to continually read and respond to caregiver's information and express their own distress feelings in what Tronick and Beeghly (2011) and others referred to as a "'biopsychosocial process' involving the interplay of multiple systems at multiple levels of organization acting in a causally circular manner" (Tronick & Beeghly, 2011, p. 5). These socioaffective and communication channels of coregulation (e.g., nonverbal cue reading) are, diagnostically, channels that are limited in children with ASD. Infants who are not able to read these social cues well have less capacity to engage in the complex adult–infant nonverbal social affective attunement dance.

As infants develop into toddlers, they develop more self-regulating and coregulating tools including pretend play, to play out their intense day-to-day life experiences alone and together with peers and with adults. Toddlers and preschoolers repeatedly play out distressing experiences of separation, doctor visits, and soon "bad guys" and monsters and the like, alone and together, decreasing their anxiety and increasing their tolerance of these issues (Barnett & Storm, 1981; Phillips, 2010). This spontaneous insertion of emotion-laden themes from daily life into pretend play is not typically done by children with ASD (Hobson, Hobson, Cheung, & Caló, 2014).

There is a large body of research and clinical writing regarding the emotionally restorative role of children's play, both their spontaneous pretend play and their pretend play guided through play therapy, following trauma (Gil & Terr, 2013). There are many studies of interactive pretend reenactment protocols following natural disasters. Children who engaged in these protocols have fared better in anxiety than those who did not (Chemtob, Nakashima, & Hamada, 2002). Research and theoretical models of this process identify that through pretend re-enactment the child is able to experience components of the event without the effect of intense distress, and with a large measure of control. O'Connor (1994) pointed out that "as if" qualities of pretend allow the child to experience sufficient emotional intactness as they process and master the traumatic experiences.

Typically developing toddlers, preschoolers, and school-age children increasingly use conversational language, chatting with adults and peers, while still using social nonverbal cue reading, role-play and pretend play, to work through issues of distress. However, the social use of language to help make sense of and master internal emotional experiences is much more limited or absent in children with ASD.

Development of Emotional Regulation in Children With ASD

The cause of the strong association between ASD and emotional dysregulation is likely multifactorial and based in developmental biopsychosocial processes. That is, infants with ASD initially may be at greater risk for more emotional dysregulation due to a host of biological factors, and then dysregulation continues in a "cascading deficit" process due to impairments in the very psychosocial processes (e.g., nonverbal cue reading, communication, pretend play) that foster increased emotional regulation in typically developing children.

In Replays, the adult's role is to engage the child in an affectively rich interactive state. This requires continual monitoring and adjusting on the adult's part to compensate for the child's difficulties in verbal, affective, and nonverbal cue reading. The adult scaffolds the interaction including their use of affect, verbal and nonverbal cues, and props, such that the child is an actively, affectively engaged participant throughout.

Children with ASD also have delayed and atypical pretend play, more impaired than would be expected based on their cognitive level in both early emergence in young children, (Charman et al., 1997) and older children (Baron-Cohen, 1987). While school-age children with ASD often demonstrate the ability to understand symbols, doing so on command and/or through modeling (Charman & Baron-Cohen, 1997), they do not tend to create novel pretend play schemas independently, with repetitive and restricted play a topic of research (Honey, Leekam, Turner, & McConachie, 2006).

Hobson, Hobson, Malik, Bargiota, and Caló, (2013) developed a scale of "playfulness" to capture a child's emotional investment in pretend play (e.g., clear signs of having fun as they pretended, incorporating novelty and emotional meaning into the pretend), and it is this composite of components that is diminished in children with ASD even when matched with peers with developmental disabilities with the same level of pretend play ability (Hobson et al., 2013). To use pretend play effectively to effect emotional change, in the way typically developing children do, not only must a child have symbolic understanding, but she or he must also be emotionally engaged in the play as a personally meaningful activity, the factors identified by Hobson et al.'s playfulness rating system as particularly lacking in the natural pretend play of children with ASD.

The therapist scaffolds the play so that the child understands the symbolic component, made easier by the use of pretend themes of personalized, highly emotionally meaningful and frequently repeated experiences of the child. This is in contrast to, for example, video modeling strategies (MacDonald, Sacramone, Mansfield, Wiltz, & Ahearn, 2009) as a way of teaching children with ASD to engage in pretend play by having them copy symbolic sequences shown in a video. When doing Replays with a child with ASD, the therapist strives not just to have the child observe or produce symbolic acts related to the dysregulating experiences, but to reach a state of strong affective engagement and playful fun, akin to the components identified in the playfulness rating system, while observing and participating in pretend with the therapist, a state of engagement in social play that is not readily achievable to children with ASD without this level of adult scaffolding (Hobson et al., 2013). With this adult scaffolding, the child is able to sustain emotional regulation even as adult and child play out scenarios that are typical dysregulating.

Treatment of Dysregulation in Typically Developing Children and in Children With ASD

Treatment of phobias in typically developing children is generally carried out through variations of cognitive behavior therapy (CBT; Wagner, 2005). This treatment involves a collaborative process between child, parents, and therapist. The child is actively involved in learning antianxiety strategies such as self-talk and relaxation, in creating "fear ladders" of gradual exposure the child feels that he or she will be able to tolerate, and in monitoring and giving feedback to the therapist and parents (e.g., rating their distress level). The child engages in experiences of gradual exposure combined with using their anti-anxiety strategies, and hence with diminished anxious responding. This approach has been found to be highly successful for treating phobias in typically developing children (Seligman & Ollendick, 2011), but it is reliant on a level of pragmatic language, executive functioning, and engagement not generally accessible to children with ASD. There have been several adaptations of CBT developed for children at the mild/high end of the autism spectrum with findings of positive effect (Sukhodolsky, Bloch, Panza, & Reichow, 2013); however, even these adaptations involve a high level of social and communication capacities, and the adaptations are hence limited to children on the mild end of the spectrum.

Another model for treatment of emotional dysregulation that has substantial research support is collaborative problem solving (CPS; Greene & Ablon, 2005). This approach is also based in a series of highly collaborative processes between child, parent, teacher, and therapist. While some children mildly impacted by ASD can access adapted versions of this approach, it too is predicated on a level of language and social pragmatics beyond the capabilities of many children with ASD.

The typical treatment paradigm for treating phobias in children with ASD who are not able to access CBT involves gradual exposure combined with, or rewarded by, a tangible preferred item (Jennett & Hagopian, 2008). Unlike in CBT or CPS, the process is done *by* the adult *to* the child. A child afraid of needle injection is for instance given favorite snacks or toys while tolerating closer proximity to a needle. Some paradigms incorporate "escape prevention" where the child is prevented from stopping earlier than the hierarchy dictates regardless of distress, while others stop exposure when the child moves away from exposure, and restart it again later. This paradigm is generally successful over time in the child tolerating the trigger.

This well-studied and common treatment paradigm has many problematic features. Because the treatment is done to the child rather than collaboratively with the child, it is likely experienced as coercive. When escape prevention is part of the paradigm, distress is often induced in the process of gradual exposure. This approach does not involve components that help to expand the child's understanding of their own affective experience. Additionally, this process does not have an affectively strong interactive component, and so is not helping the child develop coregulation capacities.

Replays, like CBT and like the typical gradual exposure paradigm used with children with ASD, also involves gradual exposure to experiencing trigger events incorporating techniques to lower child stress. However, with Replays, the adult and child work collaboratively, incorporating the child's unique emotional experiences through symbolic and emotional engagement, without requiring advanced communication or social pragmatic capacity (Levine, 2013).

Abreaction as an "Agent of Change" Common to Many Forms of Play Therapy

Replays makes the child's distress trigger manageable in part through creating a more manageable representational version of it that the child has control over, much as when typically developing children naturally play through the big and small traumas of their everyday experiences. The child also has control over inducing the pretend representation of distress that the adult acts out.

DEVELOPMENTAL ISSUES

Those who do play therapy with school-age children are often asked whether it is infantilizing to use childish toys and pretend with older children. I am of the opinion that we use the term "age appropriate" as a shortcut for "developmentally appropriate" because most children are typically developing, and hence their age matches their developmental level. If we substitute the term "developmentally appropriate" for "age appropriate," then engaging in pretend play and use of characters that hold interest for a child with developmental delays in play and interaction becomes fitting. Many children with ASD become entranced by specific characters from children's television shows, movies, or electronic games for longer than their age-matched peers (e.g., Sesame Street, Thomas the Tank Engine). Incorporating characters the child can relate to greatly increases the likelihood that she or he will want to engage in the play.

However, one must be mindful of the perceptions of others and the potential impact this may have on the child. For instance, if the child spends time within a culture of peers who might tease them for playing with "childish" characters, or adults who might view this as childish, the therapist can help him or her build a repertoire that includes characters that are not age dependent (e.g., currently the birds from Angry Birds) or are popular within their age cohort (e.g., *Star Wars*) or from current popular movies or electronic games.

Some children find it too childish to engage in pretend play, although many are happy to have the opportunity to do so. It is important to be mindful of this and adapt the approach accordingly. Replays can be done using role-play and age-defying terms such as *drama* instead of *play* as effectively and in the same fashion as pretend play, with older or more advanced children and in a school context. Costumes and props can be incorporated just as they are in drama and theater classes, across ages.

At the other end of the developmental spectrum, some children with ASD—across all ages—don't yet have sufficient symbolic skills to engage in the pretend or role-play aspect of Replays. When that is the case the child wouldn't recognize the relationship between pretend and their own experience. Sometimes simply reflecting back the child's affect in a playful exaggerated way can be beneficial as a presymbolic way to engage in Replays. I was working with a nonverbal presymbolic 7-year-old with sensory reactivity who shrank from touching water in a sink, bath, or pool. I put a basin of water in front of me, reached for it, then pulled my hand away saying, "Ew! Ew!" a few times. This captured his interest, so I then placed the basin closer to him. He reached to touch it, looked up to me, and I said "ew" again and he laughed. Then he reached to touch it again, this time actually touching the water as I repeated "ew!" We did this a few more times, with him getting his hands further into the water and eventually also saying "ew," looking to me and smiling. Parents and school staff quickly learned the "ew" game. Over the next weeks with increasing use of real sink/tub in the Replays, he was increasingly happily participating in hand washing and bathing.

Many children with ASD who do not spontaneously engage in pretend play are able to understand and participate in the adult-scaffolded pretend in Replays. This is likely because the theme and sequence are based on experiences that are of intense emotional salience to the child. Therefore, trying out Replays even with children who are otherwise presymbolic often reveals surprising understanding by the child.

PLAY INTERVENTION PROCEDURES AND BEST SETTINGS TO BE USED IN

Replays can be done in multiple settings (e.g., home, school, therapist's office) by people with diverse training (e.g., mental health clinicians, occupational therapists, speech therapists, parents), individually, or in a team approach. Doing Replays for some children and some issues is quite straightforward, but for those children with more complex challenges, figuring out how to do Replays can be more challenging. For children with more complex profiles, who become more easily dysregulated, and for children with triggers that are multifactorial, more mental health support will be needed. Replays lends itself readily to use in schools for children who already see speech or occupational therapists or mental health counselors. It is especially powerful to work on specific issues with the adults who are involved in the trigger situations, and within the setting in which the dysregulation occurs. That is, for a child who melts down when their assistant places math worksheets in front of him, having that assistant do Replays with the child before math class can be especially powerful. However, this isn't always feasible depending on the child's school set-up and staff involved. It is still often very powerful to work on triggers outside of the context in which they occur and with other adults. To do this, gathering detailed-enough information about what occurs before, during, and after the distress is key for whoever will be doing the Replays, such that specifics can be incorporated into the re-enactment play.

To start the process of using Replays, one first has to determine which issues related to emotional dysregulation are most likely amenable to Replays. In general, it is easiest to start working on distress triggers that are concrete, can be brought into the office or school, and occur frequently. Once those involved have experienced success with this approach, learning how to tinker with the play for this particular child, then the child's more challenging triggers can be worked on. For instance, for a child who is afraid to enter public bathrooms because of fear of the automatic hand dryer and toilet-flushing noises, has sleeping difficulties, won't enter the cafeteria, and is terrified of dogs, selecting working on the fear of sounds in public bathrooms is likely to be the trigger that one can most quickly have the most impact in treating when the key adults and the child are first learning the approach. While it is tempting and makes good clinical sense in some ways to begin with the most interfering challenge, which for the child above may be sleep difficulties, I recommend starting with an issue that is likely to be the easiest to treat. Because using Replays can be initially challenging to learn, due to the highly individualized nature of it, starting with an issue like sleeping problems, which is likely to be multifactorial in causes (and treatments) and which is not possible to work on as directly by adults other than the parents, is less likely to bring initial success.

Once a specific trigger is selected, the therapist learns from the parent or teacher as many specifics of what actually happens when the child is triggered. For the child afraid of bathroom sounds, the therapist would want to know how long-standing this has been, whether there was a specific initial triggering event (which often there is not that parents are aware of), and how the child responds to avoid this trigger and/or if he is accidentally exposed to this sound (e.g., the child will stand outside the bathroom covering his ears but not go in, or if he is in the bathroom and a flusher goes off he will scream and try to run out the door). The therapist also inquires about what is the closest experience to this the child is able to tolerate (e.g., nonautomatic toilet flushes are or are not fine for the child).

The therapist also learns from parents, and from initially playing with the child, what sorts of play the child enjoys, what level of symbolic understanding the child has, and what is calming for the child and what sorts of things the child thinks are funny.

Once one has built some rapport with the child and can effectively engage and play with the child, the adult then incorporates the child's trigger issues in some way, often though pretend. For the child afraid of automatic bathroom sounds, the therapist can use a toy toilet or block to represent a pretend hand dryer, pretend to make the sound, make a pretend flushing or whooshing sound, cover her ears and say "Stop that sound! Too loud!" and then make the sound again as she pretends to flush the toilet or activate the hand dryer, then "scold" the offending toilet again. The adult tinkers with the pacing, the intensity of their display of pretend distress, of playfulness, voice volume, facial expression, the reality of the pretend props, and so on to reach a way of playing that captures the child's interest but does not distress the child. If the child is riveted with attention, smiling and increasingly participating or asking for the adult to do it again verbally or nonverbally, the adult has reached an effective way to play with the child around this trigger issue.

For many children, having the adult act out playfully exaggerated distress responses that the child experiences is clearly hilarious. For example, the child pretends to give adults "*hard* homework" and the adult pretends to protest. For children who do not have symbolic skills to understand this, adults can play with exaggerated responses nonsymbolically. An example of this would be many children who become distressed when offered all but their few favorite foods will likely find it funny when the adult pretends to be grossed out when pretending to eat foods, giving an exaggerated "disgusting" face and expression, playfully pretending to spit food out or throw the food down, while smiling. Children tend to want to see these playful distress displays many times and often especially enjoy that they are the ones in control, causing the pretend distress by giving the adult the offending food items or homework page.

The therapist then gradually changes the specifics of the play to ensure that the child is understanding the experience in a more general way and to help the child gradually and ultimately generalize to the real trigger experience, while also helping the child increasingly understand the feelings involved in becoming overwhelmed, generalizing the affective components specific to the experience of becoming overwhelmed while the concrete components vary. Variation also prevents the repetition from becoming "stuck" or perseverative as can happen especially with children with ASD. This can be done by introducing things such as more pretend characters who have the same response, by having the therapist and parents and other adults join the play and also have this intense playful reaction, by adding more pretend props, or by making different kinds of sound effect.

Once the child is happily engaging in Replays play, the therapist gradually introduces increasingly realistic elements that are components that would typically cause the intense reaction into the play. In this way the child experiences gradual exposure to the real trigger, still in the context of pleasurable interactive play in which the child and therapist are together playing through the fear element.

For instance, with a child who has meltdowns when he has to wear a hat, sunscreen, or glasses, once the therapist and child have played through a sequence of playful distress with props in various ways, the therapist incorporates the child's actual hat, glasses, or sunscreen into the play. Or for a child who becomes distressed in response to a range of foods, the therapist incorporates pieces of real food substituting for pretend. For children afraid of specific sounds, the therapist can either make recordings of the real sounds that can be readily played on a smartphone or a computer, or find the sound on one of the many sound websites. The website Soundsnap (see http://www.soundsnap.com/) has samples of most environmental sounds (e.g., audience clapping, a baby crying, whistles, buzzers, automatic toilet flush) of which children tend to be fearful. The therapist can then incorporate playing with these actual sounds on very low volume, with exaggerated fear, herself and/or with pretend characters, scolding the sound itself, or pretending the sound is coming from the pretend source.

EMPIRICAL SUPPORT

Empirical support for the multiple agents of change involved in Replays has been reviewed above as part of the discussion of the rationale and theory behind this approach. Replays is based in the well-established principles of gradual exposure paired with anxiety-reducing elements, the principles that form the basis of CBT, and exposure with response prevention (ERP).

As with all treatment, it is important to monitor the impact on the child as one proceeds, gathering practice-based evidence. Because Replays is used to target a child's intense responding to specific triggers, it is easy for parents or therapists to collect child-specific practice-based evidence to determine the impact of Replays. This can be done more formally by collecting frequency, intensity, and duration data over multiple observations before and during the time period in which Replays is being used, or informally writing down and discussing what typically occurs and then over time meeting to discuss changes.

It is also useful to collect information by those engaging in Replays (e.g., therapist, parent, teacher) about the child's enjoyment and engagement in the process. Sometimes Replays completely resolves dysregulation in response to the targeted trigger, while other times it reduces the intensity, frequency, or duration of the dysregulation. Sometimes it has little impact on the child's behavior during the situation (e.g., the child still panics during thunderstorms) but reduces anticipatory dysregulation (e.g., the child no longer shows distress on hearing the weather report or seeing a cloudy sky). Sometimes it has no impact on the child's dysregulation but the child is able to become engaged in the process and shows a greater level of social, emotional, and symbolic involvement than was previously seen. This may be helpful for the child's overall development even without treating the targeted distress triggers.

If no benefit is found, it may be that altering components of the process will help make it more accessible and enjoyable for the child, or it may be that adding additional treatment approaches (e.g., positive behavioral supports) will result in benefit, or it may be that this approach is not going to be beneficial for this child's challenges at this point in time and other approaches should be explored.

While there has not yet been systematic study of the effects of Replays, a research grant has recently been awarded by the Williams Syndrome Association for the "Treatment Development Study of Replays" (Klein-Tasman, 2014), to manualize Replays and conduct case studies for its use in treating phobias in children with Williams syndrome, a genetic disorder associated with cognitive, social, and language delays, emotional dysregulation, and phobias.

CASE ILLUSTRATION INCLUDING CAREGIVER/PARENT INVOLVEMENT

Mike is a 12-year-old fifth-grader with ASD. He has several behavioral challenges that have resulted in his referral for treatment. Many of these issues are related to his underlying anxiety for which he is on medication, which has helped somewhat although problems persist. Parents and school staff compiled a list of behavioral triggers they wanted help with including the following: angry responses and refusals when his work was corrected/errors were pointed out to him, or if the work was something he was unfamiliar with; distress in response to unexpected changes in his schedule; and fear of the cafeteria. Various behavioral programs were set up as incentives to help him stay calm through these situations and this had helped somewhat, but the challenges continued. The therapist asked for more details around his response to the school work issues and learned that Mike would often uses phrases such as "I'm outta here!" or "This isn't *fair*," and when more distressed would dive under his desk and refuse to come out. Mike's parents reported similar patterns in response to doing homework that involved new kinds of work or being corrected.

The therapist decided that working on the issues around hard new schoolwork would be the easiest with which to begin. This issue could concretely be brought into the office, and was a difficulty for Mike at home and at school, so the therapist would be able to work collaboratively with Mike's parents as well as his special education teacher at home and at school. Starting with easier issues or "low-hanging fruit" helped the therapist establish that the play was going to be fun and nonthreatening, and allowed the therapist to experiment as she was getting to know the child with what sort of play and humor were going to be most compelling for Mike. Further, having an impact early in treatment would be likely to help everyone feel an increased sense of hope. As the therapist was not part of the school, but someone Mike's parents brought him to privately see, they decided to first have Mike and his parents work together through Replays. Then, once they had developed a way to use Replays effectively with Mike, to teach this to the special education teacher.

The therapist learned from Mike's parents that he delighted in humor around the absurd and that he especially liked Batman. After playing with Mike during the first session, she set up a figure of Batman at the table with a paper in front of it and sternly told Batman that it was time for "hard new math." She then had Batman say, "I'm outta here," one of Mike's own phrases for such situations, and playfully "fly away" under the table to add humor, but also to see if Mike could tolerate that level of similarity to his own experiences without becoming upset. As Mike was already finding it hilarious, she then had Batman come back and pretended to tell him a few more times that he really "Had to get to work on his *very* hard math." She then wrote a very easy math problem and said, "This is your *really* hard new math." Mike laughed, said, "That's easy!" and wrote the answer. She then gave Batman a clearly ridiculous and difficult math problem (987,654,322 ÷ 123,456,789) and again had Batman protest: "That's way too hard. That's not fair!" This is also something Mike often said, and the therapist again made Batman fly under the table. Mike was laughing hard by now and the therapist said, "You write a problem for Batman." She gave him the pencil, and Mike wrote a silly hard problem and then another, saying, "Batman, do this now!" in a very stern tone although he was giggling at the same time. "No way, too hard!" the therapist had Batman say, making him again dive under the table, and then causing his head to peek out now and then to make more negative comments about how hard the work was. At each comment Mike laughed harder, likely with relief, with empathy with Batman's feelings, and with the joy of being in control in the scenario in which he was usually the victim.

After several rounds of this with Mike making more difficult problems, he wrote an easier problem and said to Batman, "Here, I'll help you do this one." Mike then patiently "taught" Batman to do the problem step-by-step while the therapist continued to have Batman pretend it was too hard, alternating with having him try it, saying it might be okay, then saying "I'm outta here" and diving under the table now and then, which kept Mike laughing throughout even as he patiently continued his math explanation to Batman. It was apparent Mike had made a shift in his response from initially enjoying repeated pretend play about it being too hard to ultimately also showing great empathy and nurturing support toward Batman.

With permissions in place, the therapist filmed part of a session to show Mike's school team and parents. Mike's parents did some of this play at home before homework. Mike's teacher was then able to do this at school, and in fact, used it with all of the children, who all could relate to the frustration of hard work even though they didn't all become as dysregulated as Mike did. Mike's tolerance for being tasked with hard work improved markedly both at home and at school.

CONCLUSION AND FUTURE DIRECTIONS

Replays can be a useful approach for treating emotional dysregulation in school-aged children with ASD. Additionally, Replays—intrinsic to its design—is based in pleasurable social engagement. Children as well as parents and therapists are more likely to want to engage in treatments that are experienced as mutually pleasurable. Many approaches for treating intense responding in children with ASD are based in forced gradual exposure and can be experienced as unpleasant.

Replays is based in the same agents of changes as CBT and ERP, of gradual exposure combined with means to decrease child distress, embedded in a collaborative adult-guided play therapy model. The manualization of Replays, training videos for parents and therapists, as well as case studies, are currently being developed through an ongoing grant from the Williams Syndrome Association (Klein-Tasman, 2014). More research is needed to establish and replicate the efficacy of Replays, to continue to refine methods, to study its use in combination with other treatments (e.g., social stories, positive behavioral supports, psychotropic medication), and across the range of children with ASD.

It is my hope that through the use of Replays we are working to improve emotional regulation through fostering development of emotional growth and understanding of self and others, which ultimately results in increased behavior regulation. While in traditional behavioral treatment of children with ASD, which is currently in the US a common treatment paradigm, there is a focus on measuring and treating observable behaviors rather than treating underlying emotions, approaches such as Replays that are based in direct interactive work around the emotional experiences of children can be highly effective. Other autism treatments also emphasizing social-affective work include the DIRFloortime approach (Greenspan & Wieder, 2007), relationship development intervention (Gutstein, 2000), and pivotal response training (Koegel, 2011), all of which are developing increasing bodies of research support and growing in use. Replays is in this growing family of interactive affect-based treatment approaches to support the emotional development of children with special needs.

REFERENCES

Barnett, L. A., & Storm, B. (1981). Play, pleasure, and pain: The reduction of anxiety through play. *Leisure Sciences*, *4*, 161–175. http://dx.doi.org/10.1080/01490408109512958

Baron-Cohen, S. (1987). Autism and symbolic play. *British Journal of Developmental Psychology*, *5*, 139–148. http://dx.doi.org/10.1111/j.2044-835X.1987.tb01049.x

Charman, T., & Baron-Cohen, S. (1997). Brief report: Prompted pretend play in autism. *Journal of Autism and Developmental Disorders*, *27*, 325–332. http://dx.doi.org/10.1023/A:1025806616149

Charman, T., Swettenham, J., Baron-Cohen, S., Cox, A., Baird, G., & Drew, A. (1997). Infants with autism: An investigation of empathy, pretend play, joint attention, and imitation. *Developmental Psychology*, *33*, 781–789. http://dx.doi.org/10.1037/0012-1649.33.5.781

Chemtob, C. M., Nakashima, J. P., & Hamada, R. S. (2002). Psychosocial intervention for postdisaster trauma symptoms in elementary school children: A controlled community field study. *Archives of Pediatrics & Adolescent Medicine, 156*, 211–216. http://dx.doi.org/10.1001/archpedi.156.3.211

Gil, E., & Terr, L. C. (2013). *Working with children to heal interpersonal trauma: The power of play*. New York City, NY: Guilford Press.

Greene, R., & Ablon, S. (2005). *Treating explosive kids*. New York, NY: Guilford Press.

Greenspan, S., & Wieder, S. (2007). *Engaging autism: Using the floortime approach to help children relate, communicate, and think*. Boston, MA: Da Capo Press.

Gutstein, S. E. (2000). *Autism Asperger's: Solving the relationship puzzle—A new developmental program that opens the door to lifelong social and emotional growth*. Future Horizons, Arlington, TX.

Guy, L., Souders, M., Bradstreet, L., DeLussey, C., & Herrington, J. D. (2014). Brief report: Emotion regulation and respiratory sinus arrhythmia in autism spectrum disorder. *Journal of Autism and Developmental Disorders, 44*, 2614–2620. http://dx.doi.org/10.1007/s10803-014-2124-8

Hobson, J. A., Hobson, R. P., Cheung, Y., & Caló, S. (2014). Symbolizing as interpersonally grounded shifts in meaning: Social play in children with and without autism. *Journal of Autism and Developmental Disorders, 45*, 42–52. http://dx.doi.org/10.1007/s10803-014-2122-x

Hobson, J. A., Hobson, R. P., Malik, S., Bargiota, K., & Caló, S. (2013). The relation between social engagement and pretend play in autism. *British Journal of Developmental Psychology, 31*, 114–127. http://dx.doi.org/10.1111/j.2044-835X.2012.02083.x

Honey, E., Leekam, S., Turner, M., & McConachie, H. (2006). Repetitive behavior and play in typically developing children and children with autism spectrum disorders. *Journal of Autism and Developmental Disorders, 37*, 1107–1115. http://dx.doi.org/10.1007/s10803-006-0253-4

Jennett, H. K., & Hagopian, L. P. (2008). Identifying empirically supported treatments for phobic avoidance in individuals with intellectual disabilities. *Behavior Therapy, 39*, 151–161. http://dx.doi.org/10.1016/j.beth.2007.06.003

Klein-Tasman, B. (2014). *Treatment development study of replays*. Current grant funded by the Williams Syndrome Association.

Koegel, L. K. (2011). *Pivotal response treatment: Using motivation as a pivotal response*. Santa Barbara: University of California.

Levine, K. (2013, May 28). Treating the child under the behavior: Affect & relationship in children with autism [Web log post]. Retrieved from http://behavior.net/2013/05/treating-the-child-under-the-behavior-affect-and-relationship-in-mental-health-treatments-for-children-with-autism/

Levine, K., & Chedd, N. (in press). *Attacking anxiety: Treating anxiety in children with autism spectrum* [Working title]. London, England: Kingsley.

Levine, K., & Chedd, N. (2007). *Replays: Using play to enhance emotional and behavioral development for children with autism spectrum disorders*. London, England: Kingsley.

MacDonald, R., Sacramone, S., Mansfield, R., Wiltz, K., & Ahearn, W. H. (2009). Using video modeling to teach reciprocal pretend play to children with autism. *Journal of Applied Behavior Analysis, 42*, 43–55. http://dx.doi.org/10.1901/jaba.2009.42-43

Mayes, S. D., Calhoun, S. L., Murray, M. J., Ahuja, M., & Smith, L. (2011). Anxiety, depression, and irritability in children with autism relative to other neuropsychiatric disorders and typical development. *Research in Autism Spectrum Disorders*, 5, 474–485. http://dx.doi.org/10.1016/j.rasd.2010.06.012

Mazefsky, C. A., Herrington, J., Siegel, M., Scarpa, A., Maddox, B. B., Scahill, L., & White, S. W. (2013). The role of emotion regulation in autism spectrum disorder. *Journal of the American Academy of Child & Adolescent Psychiatry, 52*, 679–688. http://dx.doi.org/10.1016/j.jaac.2013.05.006

O'Connor, K. J. (Ed.). (1994). Play therapy for psychic trauma in children. In C. E. Schaefer (Ed.), *Handbook of play therapy: Vol. 2. Advances and innovations* (pp. 297–318). Oxford, England: John Wiley & Sons.

Phillips, R. D. (2010). How firm is our foundation? Current play therapy research. *International Journal of Play Therapy, 19*, 13–25. http://dx.doi.org/10.1037/a0017340

Schaefer, C. E., & Drewes, A. (2013). *The therapeutic powers of play: 20 core agents of change*. Hoboken, NJ: Wiley.

Seligman, L. D., & Ollendick, T. H. (2011). Cognitive–behavioral therapy for anxiety disorders in youth. *Child and Adolescent Psychiatric Clinics of North America, 20*, 217–238. http://dx.doi.org/10.1016/j.chc.2011.01.003

Sukhodolsky, D. G., Bloch, M. H., Panza, K. E., & Reichow, B. (2013). Cognitive–behavioral therapy for anxiety in children with high-functioning autism: A meta-analysis. *Pediatrics, 132*, e1341–e1350. http://dx.doi.org/10.1542/peds.2013-1193

Tronick, E., & Beeghly, M. (2011). Infants' meaning-making and the development of mental health problems. *American Psychologist*, 66, 107–119. http://dx.doi.org/10.1037/a0021631

Wagner, A. (2005). *Worried no more: Help and hope for anxious children*. Apex, NC: Lighthouse Press.

INDEX

ABOUT THE EDITORS

Athena A. Drewes, PsyD, MA, RPT-S, is director of clinical training and of the APA-accredited predoctoral internship program at Astor Services for Children & Families, where she also serves as a clinician specializing in complex trauma with foster care children. Dr. Drewes is a licensed psychologist, certified school psychologist, and registered play therapist supervisor. She is past director of the Association for Play Therapy, founder and past president of the New York branch of the Association for Play Therapy, and renowned national and international speaker and presenter. She is author, editor, and coeditor of 10 play therapy books, as well as numerous journal and magazine articles and presentations. She is currently adjunct professor, Western Connecticut State University, Danbury.

Charles E. Schaefer, PhD, RPT-S, is professor emeritus of psychology, Fairleigh Dickinson University, Hackensack, NJ. He is cofounder and director emeritus of the Association for Play Therapy. Dr. Schaefer is a renowned author and editor of more than 60 books and 100 research articles. Among his recent play therapy books are *The Therapeutic Powers of Play* (2nd ed.),

Foundations of Play Therapy (2nd ed.), *Empirically Based Play Interventions for Children* (2nd ed.), and *Play Therapy for Preschool Children*. Dr. Schaefer is founder of the International Play Therapy Study Group, which meets regularly in Wroxton, England. He maintains a private practice for children at Fairleigh Dickinson University in Hackensack, New Jersey.